BASEBALL VACATIONS

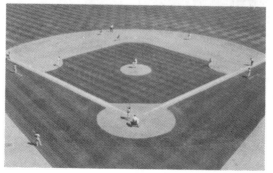

On the cover

Front: Arlington Stadium, courtesy Texas
        Rangers.
Back upper: Astrodome, courtesy Houston
        Astros.
Back center: Royals Stadium, permission
        granted by the Kansas City Royals.
Back lower: Yankee Stadium, courtesy Yankees
        Magazine.

BASEBALL VACATIONS

A Guide To Big League
Teams, Towns & Tickets

Daniel P. George

From the **American Travel Themes** series

BON A TIRER
publishing

Baseball Vacations
A Guide To Big League
Teams, Towns & Tickets

Copyright © 1991 Daniel P. George

Supplementary material and photographs
Copyright © 1991 Bon A Tirer Publishing
unless otherwise indicated

ISBN: 1-878446-02-9

Catalog number BBV-1
CM-JE-SA

Printed in the U.S.A.
Printed on acid-free paper

First Edition
10 9 8 7 6 5 4 3 2 1

From the **American Travel Themes** series

Publisher: Joseph E. Zanatta

Technical Assistance:
BarbarAnn Production Studio
John Del Debbio
Film Graphics
Graphics Four Inc.
Roy Hurwitz
Tony Johnson
Carla Melton, Color Art Inc.
Morrow Typesetting
Conrad Persson
Dave Rhoads, D&A Studios

BON A TIRER
publishing

PO Box 3480
Shawnee, KS 66203
913-236-4828

Distributed to the book trade by:
Login Publishers Consortium/Chicago

Table of Contents

Acknowledgements

Although a writer sometimes feels as isolated as an Atlanta Braves fan, nobody produces a book all by himself, and this is no exception.

The author wishes to express his sincere thanks to everyone who helped in the shaping of *Baseball Vacations*, whether it was through information, editorial guidance or just good old-fashioned support.

Special appreciation is due Glen B. Ruh, editor of Redefinition, Inc., whose fine *World of Baseball* series may well become the definitive popular history of the game.

Likewise, the author is grateful to Linda R. Verigan and Marlene Korim of *Sports Illustrated* and Steven P. Gietschier of *The Sporting News* for their particular cooperation in the use of numerous articles from those publications.

Thanks also to Tom Heitz, head of the National Baseball Library, and his excellent staff for providing photos and other materials essential to the book.

No book like *Baseball Vacations* would have been possible without the cooperation of the teams themselves. All furnished photos, as well as stadium, ticket and other important information. Thanks to: Rick Vaughn, Baltimore Orioles; Dick Bresciani, Boston Red Sox; Tom Mead, California Angels; Chuck Adams and Doug Abel, Chicago White Sox; John Maroon, Cleveland Indians; Dan Ewald, Detroit Tigers; Dean Vogelaar, Kansas City Royals; Tom Skibosh, Milwaukee Brewers; Tom Mee, Minnesota Twins; Arthur Richman and Jeff Idelson, New York Yankees; Jay Alves, Oakland Athletics; Dave Aust, Seattle Mariners; John Blake, Texas Rangers; Howie Starkman, Toronto Blue Jays; Jim Schultz, Atlanta Braves; Ned Colletti and Sharon Pannozzo, Chicago Cubs; Jon Braude, Cincinnati Reds; Rob Matwick, Houston Astros; Mike Williams and Jay Lucas, Los Angeles Dodgers; Richard Griffin, Montreal Expos; Jay Horwitz, New York Mets; Larry Shenk, Philadelphia Phillies; Jim Lachimia, Pittsburgh Pirates; Jeff Wehling, St. Louis Cardinals; Mike Swanson and Jim Ferguson, San Diego Padres; and Matt Fischer, San Francisco Giants.

Thanks also to Joe Zanatta, head of Bon A Tirer Publishing, who saw a rare gap in the burgeoning market of baseball books and was confident *Baseball Vacations* would fill it. He and Mike Morlan also provided expert editing, giving focus to the themes, smoothing the text and questioning facts. Any errors that remain are purely my own, and I welcome all corrections.

Can you accomplish anything without acknowledging a debt to your family? I don't think so. My parents, Chris and Neva George, have always been there for me, comforting, advising, supporting — and somehow finding the time to do the same for my six brothers and five sisters. If there was a Parents Hall of Fame, they'd be there. Thanks also to my myriad siblings, especially that incurable nurturer, Cathy Fritz.

Writing *Baseball Vacations* often meant abbreviated "quality time" with my children, Jeff and Jennie, but they were tireless in their understanding. No one could ask for a finer son or daughter. This book is dedicated especially to them.

And finally, to Janni Benson, not only my deepest appreciation but also my unending love. Her patience is boundless, her encouragement unceasing. My only hope is that she will bless me with those qualities for the rest of our lives. If that sounds like something more than an acknowledgement, it most certainly is ...

Introduction

Every year more than 50 million baseball fans make the trek to a major league baseball stadium. Many see more than one game, and some of the faithful even take baseball tours, making pilgrimages to several ballparks across the country. *Baseball Vacations: A Guide To Big League Teams, Towns & Tickets* is a travel guide for the baseball pilgrim.

You won't find any exotic statistics in this book, no whizbang algebraic formulas that prove once and for all how well Mickey Mantle stacked up against Willie Mays. There's nothing here calculating how many runs Barry Bonds creates, how often Roger Clemens gets ahead of the batter or how much playing on grass helps Ryne Sandberg's fielding.

Numbers are baseball's lifeblood. No one who's ever pored over a box score can deny that, even if some of today's elaborate statistical categories seem to have been created primarily to boost the stock of Texas Instruments. (That's not to say there are no statistics in this book. There are. You'll find out which slugger just missed hitting 72 homers one year, which Hall of Fame pitcher went 36-40 in his first six seasons and which ballclub finished last despite a .315 team batting average.)

Baseball Vacations doesn't pretend to be a scholarly study or a definitive baseball history. Those books generally don't trifle with such curiosities as the heckler who was so good that he was hired by an opposing team, the minor league ballpark that had a tree in center field or the broadcaster who became a manager.

So what is *Baseball Vacations?* This book has two goals. One is to present a casual perspective on all 26 major league teams through a mix of facts, anecdotes and opinions. The other is to provide helpful nuts-and-bolts information for fans who want to see those teams play.

In other words, we want to show you the easiest way to get to the ballpark, then help you enjoy the game by telling you a little about the teams you're watching.

Each chapter focuses on one team and town and contains a variety of information. You will find ticket information (prices, how to purchase them in person, by phone, mail or even FAX, which ones are toughest to get, discounts and promotions), stadium directions and parking availability. There's also a stadium diagram, which should help the out-of-town fan, and facts about the playing surface and field dimensions. We've also included other useful information, like the team's main radio and television broadcast outlets, game times and interesting stadium features.

Another section details the area's major tourist attractions, including those with a baseball connection, such as the Babe Ruth Birthplace, the Canadian Baseball Hall of Fame and the Field of Dreams. There are also phone numbers and addresses for the city and state tourism bureaus, which are more than happy to give you brochures, maps and other free information about attractions, camping, lodging and restaurants.

In this sense, *Baseball Vacations* is a travel guide. You can use it to order tickets, see a ballgame and visit other sights in the city. With this book and schedules that are available directly from the teams and in numerous baseball publications, it's even possible to map out a multi-city tour of ballparks.

But we've also tried to make the book something more, an informal yet informative guide to the 14 American League and 12 National League teams themselves.

The core of each chapter is a team essay that's filled with a little history, some trivia, famous and not-so-famous baseball tales and, yes, even conjecture.

You'll learn which team originated Ladies Day, why Boston Red Sox fans are famous for their fatalism, which radio station owner went to the winter baseball meetings in search of a broadcasting contract and ended up buying a team. There's an argument that cantankerous Charlie Finley should be in the Hall of Fame, a lament on the demise of Yankee-hating and a tongue-in-cheek explanation of what's happened to the Milwaukee Brewers.

Each team essay is accompanied by a feature spotlighting a key player in the franchise's history, ranging from Hall of Famers like Babe Ruth to current stars like Ruben Sierra. Some of the chapters also contain features on major league teams of the past. The New York Mets chapter, for instance, includes brief accounts about both the Brooklyn Dodgers and the New York Giants.

There's also a final chapter covering the Baseball Hall of Fame and Museum in Cooperstown. *Baseball Vacations* would not be complete without a tour of this baseball mecca.

And you'll find at least one photo of every stadium. We felt this was a must, since a ballpark is often as much a part of a town's baseball heritage as its team and players. But for that matter, there are plenty of player photos, too.

There's a multitude of vacation manuals, baseball sourcebooks and team histories available today, but we believe you'll find *Baseball Vacations* an entertaining, one-stop guide that's unlike any other book.

If you're a casual fan, you'll enjoy hearing stories like the time a midget pinch-hit for the St. Louis Browns. Even if you're more serious, you may be surprised by offbeat tidbits like the fact that no pitcher who spent the bulk of his career with the Pittsburgh Pirates is in the Hall of Fame.

And we're confident that all of you, casual fan or baseball junkie, will find this book helpful when you decide to take a trip to the ballpark — or even a journey that covers a little more territory.

So go to it. It's time to play ball!

"Whoever would understand the heart and mind of America had better learn baseball."

— Jacques Barzun, author

"You can observe a lot just by watching."

— Yogi Berra, player

Cleveland Municipal Stadium

Yankee Stadium

AMERICAN LEAGUE EAST

Baltimore Orioles
Boston Red Sox
Cleveland Indians
Detroit Tigers
Milwaukee Brewers
New York Yankees
Toronto Blue Jays

Memorial Stadium, due to be re-placed by the Orioles' new Camden Yards in 1992, has witnessed six American League pennants and three World Series championships since 1954.

Nobody's ever gushed over it in the same breath with Fenway Park or Wrigley Field, and it doesn't boast the genealogy of Tiger Stadium or Yankee Stadium.

Even this summer, it probably won't draw the belated hosannas and sentimental pilgrimages that accompanied Comiskey Park's final season in 1990.

But time is running out on Baltimore's Memorial Stadium, so maybe it's time to say thanks to the unheralded home of one of baseball's classiest teams.

The Baltimore Orioles, after 38 years in Memorial Stadium, are moving to a new $105.4 million ballpark in the city's revitalized Inner Harbor area in 1992.

Designers promise the new stadium, in Camden Yards, will be a blend of the old and new, a classic brick-and-steel, grass-field park with up-to-the-minute amenities.

It will be only two blocks from the Babe Ruth Birthplace/Orioles Museum. Ironically, center field in the new park will be on the spot where Ruth's father once operated a tavern.

Camden Yards will have to go some, however, to match the surprising history and charm that Memorial Stadium has packed into its relatively short life.

The ballpark at 33rd and Ellerslie has witnessed six American League pennants and three World Series championships since the Orioles moved to town in 1954.

Despite their recent struggles, the O's are still baseball's winningest team over the past three decades. They've won 55 percent of their games since 1960, finishing first or second 17 times in that span.

Baltimore's 18 straight winning sea-

Baltimore Orioles

Often overlooked and soon to be gone, Memorial Stadium has been a fitting home for one of baseball's classiest teams.

sons from 1968 to 1985 are second only to the New York Yankees' 1926-1964 streak. And since divisional play began in 1969, no team has won more games than the Orioles' 1,929.

The O's have had their share of hitters. Frank Robinson, for instance, won the Triple Crown in leading them to their first world championship in 1966. But the key to their success has almost always been pitching.

Baltimore pitchers own six Cy Young awards, including three by Hall of Fame right-hander Jim Palmer. Since 1963, the Orioles have had an amazing twenty-three 20-game winners. In 1971 alone, they had four: Palmer, Dave McNally, Mike Cuellar and Pat Dobson.

For that reason — and perhaps also because of the five no-hitters that have been pitched there — Memorial Stadium has usually been regarded as a pitcher's park.

It's true that the Baltimore ballpark, built in 1950 as a 20,000-seat, minor league facility but expanded to 47,700 seats four years later, was once a cavernous place. In 1954, the center-field wall was 450 feet from home plate, and only 42 homers were hit in the park all season.

Still, there have been plenty of notable batting feats at Memorial Stadium. Rocky Colavito belted four homers in one game there in 1959, McNally hit a grand slam in a 1970 World Series game and Ken Singleton had 10 consecutive hits during a three-day stretch in 1981.

Now it's a much friendlier park for hitters, measuring 309 feet down the foul lines and 405 to center field. And even though capacity has swelled to 53,371, that coziness extends to Memorial Stadium's unique ambiance.

There's food. You can get hot dogs in any park, but only in the place the locals call Birdland can you get genuine Bal'mer crab cakes. There's audience participation. It's a Baltimore tradition for the crowd to kick off the final verse of *The Star-Spangled Banner*, which was written in Baltimore by Francis Scott Key in 1814, by shouting "Oh!" in unison.

Tradition runs heavy in Baltimore, despite projects like the National Aquarium that have given a much-needed boost to the harbor and business areas in recent years. The busy port and industrial center is home to historic sites ranging from Fort McHenry to the Pimlico racetrack to the Basilica of the Assumption, the oldest Roman Catholic cathedral in the country.

The city's baseball history is just as proud, stretching back to 1872, when the Lord Baltimores joined the first professional league, the National Association.

Baltimore's first great team, the original Orioles, played only 18 seasons — 1882 to 1899 — but left an indelible mark on baseball with their scrappy, innovative style. The 1894 team that won the first of three straight National League pennants for Baltimore included six Hall of Famers: John McGraw, Wee Willie Keeler, Wilbert Robinson, Hughie Jennings, Joe Kelley and Dan Brouthers.

Some called the Orioles dirty. And, indeed, they weren't averse to stunts like tripping or grabbing an enemy baserunner, skipping a base if the umpires weren't looking, or hiding extra baseballs in the high outfield grass.

But McGraw, later manager of the

New York Giants, and the dimunitive Keeler, who liked to ''hit 'em where they ain't,'' are also credited with devising such famous hitting strategies as the squeeze play, the hit-and-run and the Baltimore chop.

The Orioles folded when the National League cut back to eight teams in 1900. For two seasons, Baltimore had a team — also called the Orioles — in the fledgling American League, but in 1903 it was moved to New York and renamed the Highlanders. Now it's known as the Yankees.

Baltimore was without a major league team for the next five decades, but that doesn't mean it didn't have any major league players. The Orioles played in the International League during most of that time, but under Jack Dunn's ownership from 1907 to 1928, they were often the equal of many American and National League squads.

Baseball's most famous hitter and possibly its best pitcher each played for Dunn's Orioles. Baltimore native Babe Ruth pitched for his hometown team before being sold to the Boston Red Sox in 1914, while Lefty Grove was the star of what many have called the greatest minor league team of all time. Grove is in the Hall of Fame because of his 303-144 career record with the Philadelphia A's and Boston Red Sox. But before he even got to the majors, he was 108-36 with the Orioles from 1920 to 1924.

Baltimore won seven straight pennants from 1919 to 1925, an organized baseball record, not to mention at least 100 games each of those seasons.

The first hint of Baltimore's possible return to the majors came in October 1944, when 52,833 fans jammed into old Municipal Stadium to see the Orioles host the Louisville Colonels in the Little World Series. The same day, only 32,630 showed up at St. Louis' Sportsman's Park to see the final game of the World Series between the Cardinals and Browns.

Nine years later, it happened. Browns owner Bill Veeck, unable to get American League approval to move the team himself, sold the team to a group of Baltimore investors in September 1953, and the Orioles were back in the big leagues.

In their early seasons, the O's weren't any better than the sorry Browns had been. But young stars Brooks Robinson and Jim Gentile led Baltimore to a second-place finish in 1960, and after several other near-misses, the Orioles broke through for their first American League title in 1966.

The key to the pennant was slugger Frank Robinson, who after being acquired from the Cincinnati Reds in an off-season trade for pitcher Milt Pappas became the first player to win a Most Valuable Player Award in both leagues.

Robinson also hit a pair of homers in the World Series. But his performance paled against that of Baltimore's pitchers, who shut out the favored Los Angeles Dodgers three times during a four-game sweep and allowed just two runs overall.

Midway through the 1968 season, the Orioles replaced Manager Hank Bauer with Earl Weaver, who led Baltimore to six A.L. East titles, four pennants and one World Series championship in 17 seasons.

The feisty 5-foot-8 Weaver was renowned as much for his histrionics as for his success, which he admitted

15

Memorial Stadium

came mostly from good pitching and waiting for three-run homers.

He fought with his players, notably Jim Palmer, whom he suspected of being a hypochondriac. Once, when a policeman stopped him for driving while intoxicated and asked if he had any physical infirmities, Weaver said, ''Yeah, Jim Palmer.'' Another time, Pat Kelly, a born-again Christian asked him, ''Aren't you happy I walk with the Lord, Earl?'' Weaver's reply: ''I'd rather you walked with the bases loaded.''

Umpires were another favorite target, and probably no other manager has been thrown out of as many games. Said umpire Marty Springstead of the snappish Weaver: ''The way to test a Timex watch would be to strap it to his tongue.''

Weaver's best team may have been the 1969 club, which won a team-record 109 regular-season games before falling prey to the upstart New York Mets in the World Series.

But the O's bounced back in 1970, whipping Cincinnati in five World Series games as Brooks Robinson hit .429 and stole at least four hits from the Reds with acrobatic defense at third.

Baltimore, behind eight 20-victory seasons from Palmer, dominated the A.L. East over the next decade, finishing lower than second just twice. But

despite stars like Boog Powell, Don Baylor, Bobby Grich, Eddie Murray and Mike Flanagan, the O's were less successful in the post-season, losing league playoffs to the Oakland A's in 1973 and 1974, and the World Series to the Pittsburgh Pirates in 1971 and 1979.

In 1983, however, they caught fire again under new Manager Joe Altobelli and MVP shortstop Cal Ripken, taking the division by six games, beating the Chicago White Sox in the playoffs and rolling past the Philadelphia Phillies to win their third World Series.

Recent seasons haven't been kind to the Orioles — from 1986 to 1988, they had the league's worst record — but a replenished farm system is again turning out prospects.

When the '89 Orioles surprised everyone by finishing a close second to Toronto, the main reason was American League Rookie of the Year Gregg Olson, who had 27 saves. And even the disappointing 1990 season — a fifth-place 76-85 record — produced another apparent star in starter Ben McDonald. The outlook got even brighter when an off-season trade brought former Houston Astro slugger Glenn Davis to Baltimore.

Can you blame the O's and Manager Frank Robinson if they see their last season in Memorial Stadium as the first chapter in a new Baltimore dynasty?

Brooks Robinson

They love Jim Palmer in Baltimore. They admire and respect Cal Ripken Jr. And they'll be forever grateful to Frank Robinson for the 1966 World Series.

There's nobody, though, who occupies a more special place in the hearts of Oriole fans than the man they called "The Human Vacuum Cleaner," Brooks Robinson.

Robinson was the best-fielding third baseman ever to play the game, a hot corner virtuoso with the moves of a gymnast and the hands of a magician.

"Brooks Robinson is not a fast man," sportscaster Curt Gowdy once observed. "But his arms and legs move very quickly."

Brooks Robinson

In 23 seasons with Baltimore, Robinson led American League third basemen in fielding 11 times and in putouts and double plays eight times each.

He won Gold Gloves each season from 1960 to 1975. Fourteen years after he retired, Robinson's .971 career fielding percentage is still tops at his position.

Nobody has played more games at third base than Robinson's 2,687 or made more putouts than his 2,697. In 9,165 chances at third base, he committed only 263 errors.

Unlike many glove men, though, Robinson was also a pretty fair hitter, batting .267 lifetime with 268 home runs and 1,357 runs batted in.

His best year was 1964, when he won the American League's Most Valuable Player Award by hitting .317 with 28 homers and a league-leading 118 RBIs, all career highs.

Robinson was at his most dangerous in the post-season. In five A.L. playoffs, he batted .348 with a pair of homers and seven RBIs. In four World Series, it was .263 with three homers and 14 RBIs.

Twice he hit over .500 in the playoffs, but nothing compared to the 1970 World Series, when he batted .429 in the Orioles' five-game triumph over the Cincinnati Reds. He also belted two homers and drove in the winning runs in the first two games.

When people talk about the '70 Series, however, they remember a defensive show that prompted Cincinnati second baseman Tommy Helms to marvel, "He plays like his car has just been repossessed."

18

First, with Game One tied 3-3 in the sixth, he snared Lee May's shot behind third, twisted in the air and threw him out to keep the go-ahead run off base — crucial, because the next two batters walked and singled.

In Game Two, he took apparent hits away from Bobby Tolan and May with acrobatic grabs, turning the latter into a double play. In Game Three, he made another double play out of Tony Perez's two-on, nobody-out rocket in the first, threw out Helms on a barehanded grab of a swinging bunt in the second and picked off Johnny Bench's screamer with a leaping stab in the sixth. Just for good measure, he robbed Bench on another line drive in Game Five.

"I will become a left-handed hitter to keep the ball away from that guy," said Bench, who was voted the National League MVP that year but hit just .211 in the Series.

Even the umpires were amazed. "He plays third base like he was sent down from another league," said ump Ed Hurley.

Brooks Robinson was voted into the Hall of Fame in 1983, but Baltimore didn't wait until then to show its appreciation for the Orioles' greatest player.

On September 18, 1977, a throng of 51,798 people jammed into Memorial Stadium to honor Robinson with Thanks Brooks Day. Never has a larger crowd watched a regular season ballgame in Baltimore.

Babe Ruth Birthplace/Baltimore Orioles Museum (216 Emory St., 301-727-1539). America's second-largest baseball museum. Features exhibits on Ruth, the Baltimore Orioles and the Maryland Baseball Hall of Fame. Open 10-5 daily from April through October (10-4 during the off-season). Admission $4 adult, $2.50 senior citizen, $1.50 under age 16.

Other Attractions
Baltimore Museum of Art (Wyman Park, 301-396-7101), Baltimore Zoo (Druid Hill Park, 301-366-5466), Fort McHenry National Monument (East Fort Ave., 301-962-4290), Maryland Science Center (601 Light St., 301-685-5225), National Aquarium in Baltimore (Pier 3, 301-576-3800).

Near Baltimore
United States Naval Academy (Annapolis, 301-263-6933). Washington D.C.: the Capitol, the Jefferson Memorial, the Lincoln Memorial, the Smithsonian Museums (Art, Air and Space, American History, Natural History), Vietnam Veterans Memorial, the Washington Monument and the White House.

Tourism Information
Baltimore Area Convention and Visitors Association, One E. Pratt St., Baltimore, MD 21202, 301-659-9300 or 301-837-INFO.
Maryland Office of Tourism Development, 217 E. Redwood St., Baltimore, MD 21202, 310-333-6611 or 800-543-1036.
Washington DC Convention and Visitors Bureau, 1212 New York Ave., NW, Washington, D.C. 20005, 202-789-7000.

Memorial Stadium
1000 33rd. St.

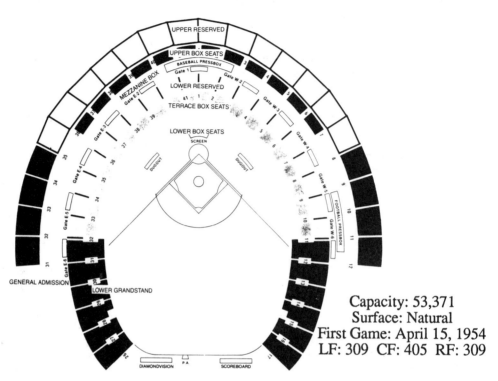

Capacity: 53,371
Surface: Natural
First Game: April 15, 1954
LF: 309 CF: 405 RF: 309

General Information
Baltimore Orioles, Memorial Stadium, Baltimore, MD 21218, 301-243-9800.
Getting Tickets
General Admission tickets held for day of game sales; available 90 minutes before game at Gate E-6.
Stadium ticket window: Gate W2.
By mail: Orioles Ticket Office, Memorial Stadium, Baltimore, MD 21218. Specify game date, number of tickets and price. Check, money order, VISA, Mastercard and American Express accepted. Allow 10 days.
By phone: Ticketron/TicketCenter at 301-481-6000 (In Baltimore), 202-432-0200 (In DC), 301-481-6000 (In Richmond) or 800-448-9009, 10-10 daily. Major credit cards accepted; convenience charge assessed.
Ticket Prices
Lower Box Seats $11, Mezzanine Box $10, Terrace Box $10, Upper Box $8.50, Lower/Upper Reserved $7.50, Lower Reserved Grandstand $6.50, Upper Reserved General Admission $4.75, Lower General Admission $4.75 ($1.50 for 12 and under and senior citizens).

Discounts & Promotions
Promotions scheduled for 12 games. Student Discount Tickets on select dates. (available Gate E-6 90 minutes before game). Bargain Nights (selected Monday and Thursday games with $3.75 Lower/Upper Reserved Seats).
Toughest Tickets To Get
New York and Boston.
Game Times
Sunday 1:35, 2:35 and 8:10. Weekdays 1:35, 6:05 and 7:35. Friday 7:35. Saturday 1:15, 1:35 and 7:35. Eastern time. Gates open 90 minutes before game; 2 hours before game on Sunday.
Broadcasts
WBAL 1090 AM Radio and WMAR-TV (2).
Other Notes
Family section (no alcohol). Stadium tours: 301-243-9800.
Getting To The Stadium
In north-central area of city, just east of intersection of Highway 45 and 33rd St. (east of I-83). Orioles-managed parking facility across the street from the stadium. Accessible by bus (subway does not go to stadium yet).

Washington Senators

It would be a mistake to call the Washington Senators the most hapless franchise in American League history. Remember the St. Louis Browns?

But the Senators were pretty close. And at least nobody zinged the Browns with lines like "Washington: First in war, first in peace and last in the American League."

The Senators were one of the league's charter members, representing the nation's capital from 1901 to 1960, when they left town to become the Minnesota Twins.

During those six decades, they finished last 10 times and next-to-last 14 more. On five unhappy occasions, they subjected their fans to at least 100 losses.

The Senators won just three American League pennants and one World Series. There were only 20 seasons in which they finished higher than fifth.

Maybe it was just tradition. A host of teams, including two different National League clubs also known as the Senators, played in Washington in the late 1800s. None played very well.

Or maybe it was the name. Between 1961 and 1971, an American League expansion team called — yep — the Washington Senators came in last four times and managed just one winning season before moving to Texas.

Actually, in 1905 that first American League team was officially renamed the Nationals in a fan contest. Perhaps they knew something. Too bad everybody still called the team the Senators.

You have to wonder where Washington would have been if the team hadn't possessed one of the best pitchers in the history of baseball, Walter Johnson. From 1907 to 1927, the fastballing right hander they called "The Big Train" won 416 games, second only to Cy Young. Johnson threw a major league-record 110 shutouts, once hurling three in four days. On another occasion, he pitched 56 straight scoreless innings. To top it off, he also was one of the game's best-liked players.

The Senators' most successful period began in 1924, when they won the first of two straight pennants under 27-year-old Manager Bucky Harris and beat the New York Giants in the World Series. The boy manager formula worked again in 1933 as Washington, now guided by 26-year-old Joe Cronin, claimed a third pennant. But just as they had to the Pittsburgh Pirates in 1925, the Senators lost the World Series, this time to the Giants. In their final 25 years, they contended for the pennant just one more time.

A common denominator on all three Washington pennant winners was outfielder Goose Goslin, with a .316 lifetime average and 1,609 runs batted in probably the best hitter in the franchise's history.

Clark Griffith, the team's owner from 1920 until his death in 1955, habitually traded and reacquired some players. Goslin had three tours with the club, as did Harris. But the champ was Bobo Newsom, who played for the Senators five times from 1929 to 1953. A tough, cantankerous pitcher, Newsom was with nine teams all told — four of them more than once.

The Senators played all but a couple of seasons in Griffith Stadium, where William Howard Taft in 1910 launched the presidential ritual of throwing out the first ball on Opening Day. It was a pitchers' park with high, distant fences, but fans still talk about the 565-foot homer Mickey Mantle hit out of the stadium and into a yard behind a building in 1953.

Poor attendance and competition from the nearby Baltimore Orioles prompted the Senators to move to Minneapolis-St. Paul in 1961, but pressure from Congress led the American League to award Washington an expansion team.

The new Senators played one season in the old ballpark before moving into Robert F. Kennedy Memorial Stadium — then called D.C. Stadium — in 1962. But after losing 100 games or more in each of their first four seasons, they didn't draw any better there than the old Senators had in Griffith.

In 1972, owner Bob Short shifted the club to the Dallas-Fort Worth area, where they got a new start as the Texas Rangers. Washington has been without major league baseball ever since.

Fenway Park, once described by author John Updike as "a lyrical little bandbox of a ball park," opened on April 20, 1912, the same day as Detroit's Tiger Stadium.

No fans in all of baseball are more knowledgeable, more rabid or more steadfast than those who follow the fortunes of New England's team, the Boston Red Sox.

Make that "agonize over." Because neither are there any fans anywhere more desperately certain that something will go wrong for their team.

If you grow up in Boston — or Montpelier, Vermont, or Newport, Rhode Island, or Bangor, Maine, for that matter — living and dying with the Red Sox is a way of life.

You scan the Boston dailies with religious fervor, knowing no city's newspapers do a better job on baseball, whether it's fact, rumor or opinion.

You can make the subway trip to Kenmore Square in your sleep, and when you turn on your television set, it automatically flips to Channel 38. You don't worry about missing a game while running an errand, because somebody always has it going on a radio.

You marvel at Wade Boggs' five batting titles but suspect he'd be better off trying to drive in a few more runs. Just like your grandfather railed about Ted Williams' shortcomings in the clutch and your dad was positive Carl Yastrzemski would never fill Williams' spikes.

In Boston, you always hope for the best, but you've lived with disappointment long enough to claim it as a dependent. Your heart's been broken so many times, you're convinced the Tin Man was one lucky fellow.

From April to October in Fenway Park, the healthy skepticism that is New England's trademark makes the leap to something even gloomier: Red Sox fatalism.

Murphy's Law could have been writ-

Boston
Red Sox

It happens every summer. New England's healthy skepticism turns to Red Sox fatalism.

ten expressly for the Red Sox faithful, who take self-flagellating delight in ticking off the reasons why:

1920 — Two years after Boston's fifth World Series title in 19 years, Red Sox owner Harry Frazee sells pitcher/slugger Babe Ruth to the New York Yankees for $100,000 and a $350,000 loan. Ruth leads the Yanks to four world championships from 1923 to 1932. The Red Sox finish last eight times during that span; they are still looking for that sixth world title.

1946 — Boston takes a three game-to-two lead over the St. Louis Cardinals in the World Series, only to lose the final two games, the last after Enos Slaughter scores from first on Harry Walker's two-out liner over short in the eighth. Debate still rages whether shortstop Johnny Pesky hesitated before his relay throw home.

1948 — The Red Sox lose the first playoff game in American League history when the Cleveland Indians pound Boston's surprise starter, 36-year-old journeyman Denny Galehouse, for an 8-3 victory. The loss prevents an all-Boston World Series with the Braves.

1948-50 — Boasting one of the best-hitting teams in history, the Red Sox average 95 victories a year over three seasons but manage only to finish second twice and third once.

1967 — A gutsy Boston club takes St. Louis to seven games in the World Series, but Cardinal ace Bob Gibson pitches a three-hitter and socks a home run to win the finale.

1975 — Carlton Fisk's game-winning, twelfth-inning homer in Game Six against Cincinnati provides one of the great moments in World Series history. It also evens the Series at three wins apiece and seemingly sets the stage for a storybook Boston finish — until the Reds rally from a three-run deficit to win Game Seven by a 4-3 score.

1978 — After blowing a 7 1/2-game lead in late August, the Red Sox win their final eight games to force a one-game playoff with the Yankees, only the second in American League history. Boston takes a 2-0 lead into the eighth, but Bucky Dent's three-run homer propels New York to a 5-4 victory.

1986 — Again, destiny seems to be in Boston's favor after the Red Sox rally from a three-game-to-one deficit to beat the California Angels in the A.L. playoffs. They win three of the first five World Series games against the New York Mets and are leading 5-4 in Game Six with two outs in the tenth and two strikes on Mookie Wilson. But Bob Stanley's wild pitch lets in the tying run, then Wilson's grounder rolls between first baseman Bill Buckner's legs to score Howard Johnson with the winner. In an echo of 1975, Boston leads 3-0 in Game Seven, but the Mets' eventual 8-5 victory seems a *fait accompli*.

1988 — The Red Sox squeak by to win the A.L. East, but the Oakland Athletics blitz them with a four-game sweep in the league playoffs.

1990 — *Deja vu*, anyone? The Red Sox squeak by to win the A.L. East, but the Oakland Athletics blitz them with a four-game sweep in the league playoffs.

Can any other team recite such a litany of heartache? The Boston Red Sox are the undisputed kings of near-miss baseball, the masters of what might have been.

If you're a Red Sox fan, it's frustrating. But, come on. It's not like following the Cleveland Indians or the Seattle Mariners or the Atlanta Braves.

You've got to have hopes before they can be dashed, and over the years the Red Sox have given their followers plenty of reasons to dream of championships.

In addition to its host of pennants and World Series titles, Boston boasts four A.L. East championships. In their 90-year history, the Red Sox have finished in third place or better 40 times.

They also own 21 league batting titles — Williams is one up on Boggs with six — and 17 home run crowns. Red Sox players have won eight Most Valuable Player and three Cy Young awards. In 1986, fireballing right-hander Roger Clemens won both.

The Red Sox are usually in the thick of things. That's one reason the fans, frustrated or not, keep pouring into quaint, jewel-like Fenway Park.

In 1990, for the fifth season in a row, more than 2 1/2 million people turned out to watch the Bosox in the 34,171-seat ballpark that gets a lot of votes as the best in baseball.

Boston, or The Hub as it's called by locals, is one of America's great cities, a financial and banking capital and a major center for research. Think Boston and you think history, a special place that celebrates the nation's beginnings with landmarks like Bunker Hill, the Boston Common, Old North Church and the U.S.S. *Constitution*.

Fenway Park fits right in. Opened in 1912, it joins Detroit's Tiger Stadium as the major leagues' two oldest ballparks, now that old Comiskey Park is gone.

First and foremost, there's the Green Monster, the cozy (315 feet from home plate) but towering (37 feet tall) left-field wall that turns short fly balls into home runs and screaming line drives into ricocheting singles.

Fenway is a fan's park. Even in the bleachers overlooking the crazy angles in center field, you're right on top of the action, you're somehow part of it. It's magical.

As author John Updike once described it: "Everything is painted green and seems in curiously sharp focus, like the inside of an old-fashioned peeping-type Easter egg."

For its first 11 years, though, Boston played in a park called the Huntington Avenue Grounds, winning pennants in the fledgling American League in 1903 and 1904.

That first championship season, Boston also beat the Pittsburgh Pirates of the supposedly superior National League in the first modern World Series. That rankled New York Giant Manager John McGraw so much that he refused to allow his N.L. champions to play Boston the next season, and the 1904 World Series was called off.

They weren't called the Red Sox then. Boston, in fact, may hold the major league record for most nicknames. Until the current name was adopted in 1907, the team answered to Americans, Somersets (after early owner Charles Somers), Puritans, Plymouth Rocks, Speed Boys and, most commonly, Pilgrims.

Cy Young — yes, THE Cy Young — was the star of those early Boston teams, leading the American League in victories its first three seasons and throwing the first perfect game of the modern era, a 3-0 victory over the Philadelphia A's on May 5, 1904.

The only other perfect game in Boston history is prime trivia fodder. On June 23, 1917, against the Washington Senators, Boston's starting pitcher walked the first batter, argued with the umpire and was thrown out of the game. Ernie Shore came on in relief and, after the runner on first was thrown out trying to steal, retired the next 26 hitters in order. The Boston starter whose banishment paved the way for a unique perfect game? Babe Ruth.

The Red Sox's greatest period began in 1912, when they captured their third pennant and finally got a chance to beat McGraw's Giants in the World Series. They did. And they won again in 1915, 1916 and 1918, claiming World Series victories each year.

These were terrific teams, with Hall of Famers Harry Hooper and Tris Speaker, and other standouts like Smoky Joe Wood, Duffy Lewis and Carl Mays. Ruth joined the Red Sox in 1914, winning 89 games in six seasons and twice leading the league in homers before he was sold to the Yankees.

More than a few Boston fans believe the Red Sox are still being punished for dealing away the man who became baseball's greatest player and turned the Yankees into its greatest team — a title the Bosox could claim until 1920.

Factor in seven second-place finishes to New York since 1938, and you begin to understand why Red Sox followers reign supreme among Yankee haters.

Sure, there have been some memorable moments since Harry Frazee sent Ruth packing:

• Lefty Grove winning four ERA titles in a park supposedly anathema to southpaws.

• Ted Williams batting .406 in 1941, still the last hitter to reach that plateau.

• Billy Goodman, the ultimate utility player, winning the 1950 batting title despite not being a regular starter at any one position.

• Carl Yastrzemski winning the Triple Crown in 1967, the year of the Impossible Dream, when the Red Sox win the pennant after finishing ninth the year before.

• Fred Lynn in 1975 becoming the only player to ever win Rookie of the Year and Most Valuable Player honors in the same season.

• Roger Clemens winning Cy Young awards in 1986 and 1987.

That's nice. But if you're a true Boston fan, you won't be happy until the Red Sox finally win that elusive sixth World Series. And when that happens …

Well, when that happens, you'll have to worry about why they won't repeat.

Mike Greenwell in front of the Green Monster

Ted Williams

Theodore Samuel Williams obviously didn't play baseball because of some secret, driving need to be popular.

Moody and private, he feuded with sportswriters he felt treated him unfairly. He made gestures, some of them obscene, at booing fans. He even spit at them.

Ted Williams didn't care that much whether people liked him. He only wanted them to respect what he did in the batter's box.

Ted Williams

"All I want out of life," he once said, "is that when I walk down the street folks will say, 'There goes the greatest hitter who ever lived.'"

Was he? Most people say it's a toss-up between him and Babe Ruth. And Williams might have settled the question for good had he not lost nearly five prime seasons to military service.

Williams was just a tall, skinny, 20-year-old left-handed hitter from San Diego when he joined the Boston Red Sox in 1939.

But he opened eyes from the start, hitting .327 with 31 homers that first year and leading the American League with 145 runs batted in, still a major league record for rookies.

By the time he retired in 1960, there were plenty of impressive numbers, enough to guarantee him a place in the Hall of Fame: a .344 career batting average, 521 home runs, 1,839 RBIs, 1,798 runs scored and a .634 slugging average second only to Ruth's .690.

Williams won six batting titles in 19 seasons, including one when he was 39 and another when he was 40. He led the league four times in homers, four times in RBIs, six times in runs, eight times in walks and nine times in slugging. This despite missing three seasons as a fighter pilot in World War II and nearly two more in the Korean War.

Williams was the American League's Most Valuable Player in 1946 and 1949 and probably should have won the award three more times.

Amazingly, he finished second in MVP voting in 1942 and 1947, even though he won the Triple Crown both years, and in 1941, when voters were more impressed by Joe DiMaggio's 56-game hitting streak than Williams' .406 average (DiMaggio hit .357).

He was famous for his eyesight — the story goes that he could read American League President Will Harridge's signature on a pitched ball — and for a power hitter was amazingly selective.

He walked 2,019 times over his career, again trailing only Ruth, but had just 709 strikeouts. The Bambino struck out nearly twice as often.

Boston equipment manager Johnny Orlando called him "The Kid" because of his boyish enthusiasm, and *The Sporting News* nicknamed him "The Splendid Splinter."

Williams, however, preferred "Teddy Ballgame," a nickname he felt personified his belief that hard work was the biggest difference between himself and other players.

"Ballplayers are not born great," he said. "They're not born great hitters or pitchers or managers, and luck isn't the big factor. No one has come up with a substitute for hard work. I've never met a great player who didn't have to work harder at learning to play ball than anything else he ever did."

He was arrogant and stubborn, refusing to hit to left field when Cleveland Indians Manager Lou Boudreau shifted most of his fielders to the right side after Williams socked three homers and drove in eight runs in one game.

His impatience with reporters and fans, as well as Boston's failure to win more than one pennant during his career, led detractors to claim he was a poor fielder and never hit when it counted. But he played Fenway Park's Green Monster as well as anyone, and his only failure in the clutch was a .200 performance in the 1946 World Series against the St. Louis Cardinals.

What about that marvelous 1941 season? He could have sat out the final day with a .3995 average — which rounds off to .400 — but he didn't. The result? Six for eight with a homer and a double.

Finally, exactly 19 years later to the day, on September 28, 1960, Williams lived a dream of every hitter.

In the last at-bat of his career, after 10,000 screaming Fenway fans gave him a standing ovation for some terrific memories, he gave them one more. He hit a home run.

Boston National Historical Park/Freedom Trail (15 State St., 617-242-5642). Boston Common, Boston Massacre Site, Bunker Hill Monument, Charleston Navy Yard, Old North Church, Old State House, Paul Revere House, State House, U.S.S. *Constitution*.

Other Attractions
Boston Tea Party Ship (Congress St. Bridge, 617-338-1773), Children's Museum (300 Congress St., 617-426-8855), John F. Kennedy Birthplace (83 Beals St., 617-566-7937) and John F. Kennedy Library/Museum (Columbia Point, 617-929-4523), John Hancock Observatory (200 Clarendon St., 617-242-1976), Museum of Fine Arts (465 Huntington Ave., 617-267-9300), Museum of Science (Science Park, 617-742-6088).

Tourism Information
Greater Boston Convention and Visitors Bureau, Prudential Plaza West, Boston, MA 02199, 617-536-4100. Massachusetts 800-447-MASS.

Fenway Park
4 Yawkey Way
Capacity: 34,142
Surface: Natural
First Game: April 20, 1912
LF: 315   CF: 420   RF: 302

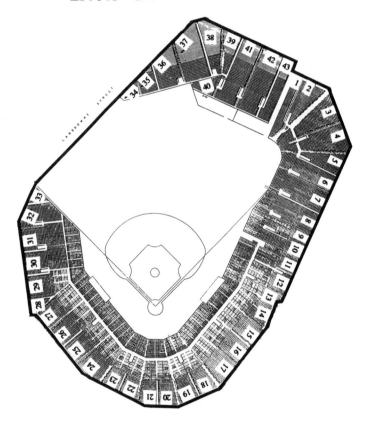

General Information
Boston Red Sox, 4 Yawkey Way, Boston, MA 02215, 617-267-9440.

Getting Tickets
Standing Room Only tickets held for day of game sales (2,800).

By mail: Boston Red Sox Ticket Office, 2 Yawkey Way, Boston, MA 02215. Specify date, number of tickets and ticket price. $2 postage and handling charge. Check, money order, MasterCard or VISA accepted.

By FAX: Ticket Office, 617-236-6640.

By phone: 617-267-1700. MasterCard and VISA accepted.

Ticket Prices
Box Seats $12, Reserved Grandstand $10, Bleachers $6.

Toughest Tickets To Get
New York.

Game Times
Sunday 1:05 and 8:05. Weekdays 1:05, 6:05, 7:35. Friday 7:35. Saturday 1:05, 3:15. Eastern time. Gates open 90 minutes before game time.

Broadcasts
WRKO 680 AM, WSBK TV (38), NESN (cable).

Other Notes
Stadium features non-alcohol section. No stadium tours.

Getting To The Stadium
Near central Boston, west of I-93 on I-90 (near Brookline Ave.). Commercial parking lots available. More accessible by subway.

Boston Braves

Baseball in Boston has meant the Red Sox for so long, it's easy to forget that for nearly 80 years New England also had a National League team.

And those who do remember the Boston Braves most likely have just the vaguest recollection that there were some players named Spahn and Sain and Mathews.

They probably can't tell you that the ancestors of today's Atlanta Braves were baseball's first dominant team, baseball's first true dynasty.

The Braves began playing in 1871, making them the only major league franchise that's fielded a team every year of professional baseball.

As the Boston Red Stockings or Red Caps, they won four pennants in the five-year history of the National Association, including an amazing 71-8 record in 1875.

They moved to the National League the next season and, with Hall of Famers George and Harry Wright, Kid Nichols, John Clarkson, Jimmy Collins and Billy Hamilton, won eight pennants in 22 seasons.

The Braves — also called the Bean Eaters, Doves, Rustlers and Pilgrims until getting their current name in 1912 — were never as successful in the modern era, winning just two more pennants before moving to Milwaukee in 1953.

The high point came in 1914, the year of the Miracle Braves. In last place in mid-July, Manager George Stallings' team won 61 of its last 77 games to beat the second-place New York Giants by 10 1/2 games. With Dick Rudolph (27-10 during the year) and Bill James (26-7) winning two games each, the Braves completed the storybook season by sweeping the favored Philadelphia A's in the World Series.

The next season, they moved into 40,000-seat Braves Field, perhaps the most spacious stadium in major league history. The foul lines were 402 feet away, the center-field wall 550, and it was 10 years before anyone hit a home run out of the park. The fences were eventually moved in, creating Braves Field's most famous feature, a right-field bleacher area so steep it was called the Jury Box.

On May 1, 1920, Braves Field was the site of the major leagues' longest game. Boston's Joe Oeschger and Brooklyn's Leon Cadore locked up in a pitching duel that went 26 innings before it was called because of darkness with score still tied 1-1.

Babe Ruth finished his career with the Braves in 1935, hitting his last three homers in a game at Pittsburgh. In 1944, Boston's Jim Tobin pitched two no-hitters at Braves Field.

But the low points were more frequent. From 1917 to 1945, Boston finished last or next-to-last 11 times, and for a few years in the '30s the team even called itself the Bees in a vain effort to change its luck.

The team owner, Judge Emil Fuchs, tried managing the Braves in 1929, but it didn't work any better for him than it did for Ted Turner decades later. Boston finished last.

During Casey Stengel's tenure as Boston manager from 1938 to 1943, the team never finished higher than fifth, one reason that even with all those pennants with the Yankees, the Old Perfesser's lifetime managing percentage is just .506.

Hall of Fame pitcher Warren Spahn began his career with Boston in 1942 and ended it with the New York Mets in 1965. "I'm probably the only guy who worked for Stengel before and after he was a genius," he said.

Behind the pitching of Spahn and Johnny Sain and the hitting of Bob Elliott and Alvin Dark, the Braves won the National League pennant in 1948, drawing nearly 1 1/2 million fans.

But they lost the World Series to Cleveland, then limped home in fourth the next three seasons. When just 281,000 fans turned out to watch the 1952 team finish seventh, owner Lou Perini moved the team to Milwaukee.

The cold winds blowing in from Lake Erie have helped make cavernous Cleveland Municipal Stadium the most maligned ballpark in the major leagues.

In 1954, Douglass Wallop wrote a whimsical novel about a baseball team that — with a little help from below — upsets the mighty New York Yankees to win the American League pennant.

In Wallop's *The Year the Yankees Lost the Pennant* and its offspring, the smash musical *Damn Yankees*, middle-aged Joe Boyd sells his soul to the devil for a one-season chance to become baseball phenom Joe Hardy and lead his team past the Bronx Bombers.

To complete the underdog fantasy, the author made Hardy's team the Washington Senators, a ballclub that was the very essence of ineptitude. Which means if he were writing the book today, he'd pick the Cleveland Indians.

In the year that Wallop's book came out, the Indians won 111 games and the American League pennant. But in the 36 years since, they have personified mediocrity — at least in their better moments.

That 1954 pennant is still the Tribe's most recent championship. Of the original 16 major league teams of the modern era, only the Chicago Cubs have had a longer drought.

And the Indians remain the only non-expansion team that's never won a division title. Indeed, since the American League was split into divisions in 1969, Cleveland has never finished higher than fourth — its final position in 1990 — and has come in last an unlucky seven times.

Maybe it wouldn't be so bad if on-the-field shortcomings were all the Indians had to worry about. Their problems, though, go way beyond that.

The Senators, at least, never had people also putting the knock on Griffith Stadium and Washington, D.C.

Cleveland
Indians

How far has the team of Hall of Famers Nap Lajoie, Tris Speaker and Bob Feller fallen? The Indians slogan could be "Dare to be Third."

Not only are the Indians much-maligned, but so are their ballpark and city.

Cleveland Municipal Stadium? Most people say it's the worst park in either league, the Mistake on the Lake, a cold, dreary place more suitable for raising bats than swinging them.

And Cleveland — well, you know any city that's still best remembered for a river that caught fire has got some serious public relations work ahead of it.

"The only good thing about playing in Cleveland," former Indian Richie Scheinblum once said, "is that you don't have to make road trips there."

But wait a minute. Municipal Stadium didn't seem like such a bad ballpark in 1948 when the Indians became the first major league team to draw 2 1/2 million fans. And you never hear it blasted as a terrible place for the Browns to play football.

Of course, the Indians won the pennant and a World Series in 1948, and the Browns usually pack in 80,000 people a game on their way to the National Football League playoffs.

Cleveland's bad rep is equally overblown. True, the Ohio city's industrial image is so gray it's become the standard for dullness. Comics, describing a small town's pace, will say: "It's Cleveland without the glitter."

Cleveland is still a major shipping and manufacturing center, but it's getting a grip on its pollution problems and it's also a leader in medical and scientific research. The Mall, with its 708-foot Terminus Tower, is the anchor of a revitalized downtown, and the Cleveland Play House theater, Cleveland Orchestra and Cleveland Museum of Art boast world-class reputations.

Just as winning can cure a lot of ills, losing can exaggerate them. And in baseball, Cleveland's history of losing dates back to the horse-and-buggy days.

The city's first professional baseball team, the Forest Citys, went 16-34 in the old National Association in 1871 and 1872. They're best recalled as the first team to sell season tickets.

The Cleveland Blues, members of the National League from 1879 to 1884, were equally undistinguished but they never slipped as low as their successors, the Cleveland Spiders.

So named because their players were skinny, the Spiders played in the American Association in 1887 and 1888, then spent the next 11 years in the National League, during which they had several winning seasons.

But in 1899, owners Frank and Matthew Robison shipped most of the best Cleveland players, including pitcher Cy Young, to their other team, the St. Louis Browns. The result was a catastrophe. The Spiders played just 42 home games — fans referred to them as the Exiles, the Wanderers and the Forsakens — and finished 84 games out of first with a 20-134 record, still a major league record for incompetence.

That got them kicked out of the National League, opening the door for the young American League to move in. Cleveland's new team had several early names: Blues (or Bluebirds), Bronchos and Naps, the latter after the club's Hall of Fame second baseman, Nap Lajoie.

In 1915, after Lajoie was gone, the team was renamed Indians in memory of Louis "Chief" Sockalexis, a outfielder with the old Spiders who was the first American Indian to play in the majors.

The Indians have won just three pennants, the fewest of any team that's been playing since 1901, and just two World Series. But for their first 68 years, they were a solid team, finishing in the first division 70 percent of the time and bringing up the rear just once.

In 1908, they lost the pennant to Detroit by a half-game when the Tigers refused to make up a rainout, which later forced a rule change requiring such makeup games. Addie Joss threw a perfect game against the Chicago White Sox that year, one of two no-hitters the Hall of Famer posted for Cleveland before dying of tubercular meningitis in 1911 at the age of 31.

Another Hall of Famer, Tris Speaker, was managing the Indians when they won their first championship in 1920. Six of the eight starters hit .300 and three pitchers won 20 games or more. Cleveland beat Brooklyn in the World Series, holding the Robins to six runs in seven games. Elmer Rice's grand slam homer and second baseman Bill Wambsganss' unassisted triple play in Game Five were both World Series firsts.

The triumph was overshadowed, however, by the revelation that eight White Sox players had thrown the 1919 World Series to the Cincinnati Reds. Ironically, one of them, Shoeless Joe Jackson, was a former Indian, hitting a career-high .408 at Cleveland in 1911.

Early on, Cleveland played in League Park, built as a wooden stadium in 1891, then redone in concrete and steel in 1909. Squeezed in among houses and neighborhood taverns, the lopsided park measured 375 feet down the left-field line but only 290 feet to right.

Municipal Stadium was built in 1931, and 76,979 fans watched the Indians' first game there on July 31, 1932. Cleveland played all its home games there in 1933, but the next season moved back to cozier League Park (23,000 capacity) for all but Sunday and holiday games until returning to Municipal Stadium for good in 1947.

That was Bill Veeck's first full season as owner, and the best promoter in baseball history promptly launched the most memorable period in Indian history.

They won. From 1948 to 1956, Cleveland claimed two pennants and finished second five times, third once and fourth once. The Indians drew an amazing 2.6 million people in 1948 — two World Series games packed in more than 80,000 people each — and came back with 2.2 million the next season.

They had fun. Veeck made the grinning cartoon Indian, Chief Wahoo, Cleveland's official mascot. There still may not be a better one in baseball. The rambunctious owner also teased opponents by moving the fences in or out, depending on whom the Indians were playing — a practice now prohibited.

They made history. In 1947, Veeck signed outfielder Larry Doby as the first black player in the American League. (Appropriately, when Frank Robinson became the majors' first black manager in 1975, it also was with the Indians.) The next season, Veeck added black pitching legend Satchel Paige, who as a 42-year-old rookie drew 202,000 fans in his first three home starts.

That year, 1948, the Indians battled the Boston Red Sox all season before winning the pennant in a one-game playoff, then beat the Boston Braves in six games for their second World Series title.

Manager/shortstop Lou Boudreau was the American League's Most Valuable Player, and the Indians led the league in hitting, homers, earned run average, shutouts and saves. Bob Lemon and Gene Bearden won 20 games, Bob Feller 19.

Six years later, under Manager Al Lopez, the Indians were back again, winning a league-record 111 games to beat the Yankees by eight games. Lemon and Early Wynn had 23 victories each, while Bobby Avila hit .341 and Larry Doby clubbed 32 homers with 126 RBIs, all league highs. In one of the most stunning upsets in World Series history, however, the New York Giants swept the Indians in four games.

Those Cleveland teams were blessed with what used to be an Indian trademark: great pitching. Cleveland has had fifty-six 20-game winners; five times they've had three in one season. Lemon won 20 or more seven times, Feller six.

Gaylord Perry won the Cy Young Award at Cleveland in 1972, the only pitcher to do so in both leagues, and Len Barker threw a perfect game for the Indians at Municipal Stadium in 1981.

Herb Score might have been as good as any of them. He was the American League Rookie of the Year in 1955 and went 20-9 the next season. But a line drive off the bat of New York's Gil McDougald struck him in the eye on May 7, 1957, and he won just 17 more games in the next five years. Now he's an Indian broadcaster.

Since then, despite stars like Rocky Colavito, Sam McDowell, Buddy Bell, Brett Butler, Doug Jones and Sandy Alomar Jr., the Indians' memorable moments have been few and often dubious.

There was 10-Cent Beer Night, a 1972 promotion that turned into an on-field riot, and the solid red uniforms that made mammoth first baseman Boog Powell look like, in one observer's words, ''a giant blood clot.'' Mike Hargrove, although a solid hitter, was more dreaded as ''The Human Rain Delay'' because of his time-consuming batting rituals before each pitch.

Finally, there was phenom Joe Charboneau, who blazed onto the scene in 1980, hitting .289 with 23 homers and 87 RBIs to win Rookie of the Year honors. Charboneau was a true character, renowned for stunts like being able to open a beer bottle with his eye socket and setting his oft-broken nose with a pair of pliers. The fans loved him.

But his star fell just as quickly as it had risen. Charboneau's skills suddenly vanished, and by 1983 he was gone from the majors for good.

No one ever explained why Charboneau enjoyed just that one glorious season. But you get the feeling Joe Hardy would have understood.

Bob Feller

Even as a farmboy milking cows and feeding pigs outside the tiny Iowa town of Van Meter, Bob Feller knew what he wanted to be when he grew up. Or at least his father did.

When Feller was eight, his dad warmed him up in the living room, using a pillow as a glove. By the time he was 12, the farm had its own baseball field, complete with lights and a small grandstand.

"I don't think he ever had any doubt in his mind that I would play professional baseball someday," Feller once told baseball historian Donald Honig. "There was no question about it being his ambition for me."

Feller fulfilled that dream, and then some. Walter Johnson and Nolan Ryan notwithstanding, some still say he's the fastest pitcher ever to take the mound.

From 1936 to 1956, the pitcher they called "Rapid Robert" and "Bullet Bob" won 266 games for the Cleveland Indians, struck out 2,581 batters and walked 1,764.

Feller won 20 games or more in six seasons, each time leading the American League in victories, and was the league strikeout king seven times.

Those numbers would be even more impressive if he hadn't spent nearly four years in the Navy during World War II, an absence he figures cost him about 100 victories and 1,000 strikeouts.

It's hard to argue with him. In the three seasons before the war, Feller averaged 25 victories and 256 strikeouts; in the two seasons afterward, his average was 23 victories and 276 strikeouts.

Feller was a 17-year-old right-hander when he joined the Indians after throwing five no-hitters in high school and catching the attention of Cleveland scout Cy Slapnicka.

In his first appearance, a July 1936 exhibition against the St. Louis Cardinals, he struck out eight in three innings. A month later, in his first start, he fanned 15 St. Louis Browns. And in September, he tied the major league record with 17 strikeouts against the Philadelphia A's. Then he went back to Iowa for his senior year in high school.

Bob Feller

37

Feller's career was filled with amazing performances. In 1938, he struck out 18 batters in one game. And when he went 24-9 at the age of 20 in 1939, he was baseball's youngest 20-game winner until Dwight Gooden came along in 1985.

He threw three no-hitters; his first, on April 16, 1940, is still the only Opening Day no-hitter in major league history. He also had 12 one-hitters.

Feller's best season was probably 1946, when he went 26-15, threw 10 shutouts, including a no-hitter, and finished with a 2.18 earned run average and 348 strikeouts, both career bests.

Feller had a nasty curve, but it was the fastball that made enemy hitters sweat — especially early in his career, when he wasn't always sure where it was going.

How fast was he? Washington Senator Manager Bucky Harris advised his team: "Go up and hit what you see. And if you don't see anything, come on back."

Then there's the story about New York Yankee pitcher Lefty Gomez stepping to the plate against Feller as dusk approached and suddenly lighting a match. The umpire said it wouldn't help him see Feller's fastball. "You got it all wrong," Gomez replied. "I just want to make sure he can see me."

A popular newsreel showed Feller throwing his fastball past a speeding motorcycle. A military measuring device once clocked him at 98.6 miles per hour, a record until Nolan Ryan's 100.9 mph in 1974.

Feller, who entered the Hall of Fame in 1962, said Walter Johnson was probably the fastest, simply because he won 416 games without a good curve.

But as Satchel Paige, who had a pretty good heater himself, allowed, "If anybody threw that ball any harder than Rapid Robert, the human eye couldn't follow it."

Pro Football Hall of Fame (one hour south of Cleveland, 2121 George Halas Dr., Canton, 216-456-8207). Open 9-5 daily. Admission $4 adults, $1.50 ages 5-13, free under 5.

Top Attractions
Cleveland Metroparks Zoo (3900 Brookside Park Drive, 216-661-7511), Cleveland Museum of Art (11150 East Blvd., 216-421-7340), Cleveland Museum of Natural History, Lake Erie Nature and Science Center (28728 Wolf Rd., Bay Village, 216-871-2900), Rockefeller Park Greenhouse (750 E 88th St., 216-664-3103), Sea World of Ohio (800-63-SHAMU).

Tourism Information
Convention & Visitors Bureau of Greater Cleveland, 3100 Tower City Center, Cleveland OH 44113, 800-321-1002.

Ohio Division of Travel & Tourism, PO Box 1001, Columbus, OH 43266 (800-BUCKEYE).

Cleveland Stadium
Boudreau Blvd.

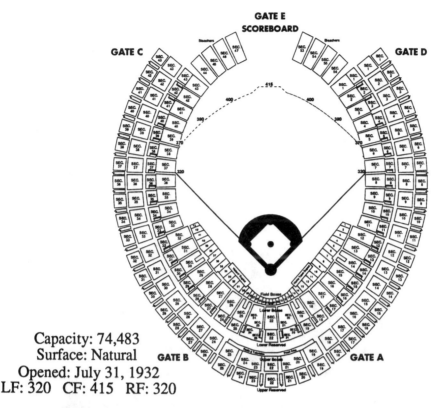

Capacity: 74,483
Surface: Natural
Opened: July 31, 1932
LF: 320 CF: 415 RF: 320

General Information
Cleveland Indians, Cleveland Stadium, Cleveland, OH 44114, 216-861-1200.
Tribe Hotline (game reports, interviews and promotions): 216-861-4755.
Getting Tickets
General Admission tickets sold day of game only.
Stadium ticket window: Gate A, Monday-Friday 9-6, Saturday 10-4.
By mail: Cleveland Indians Ticket Office, Cleveland Stadium, Cleveland, OH 44114.
Specify date of game, number of tickets and price. $3 handling charge. Check, money order, VISA and MasterCard accepted. Order must be received at least 2 weeks in advance to be returned by mail.
By phone: TicketMaster at 216-241-5555 or 800-729-6464. VISA and MasterCard accepted.
Monday-Friday 9-9, Saturday 9-7 and Sunday 9-6.
Ticket Prices
Field Box $10.50, Lower Box $10.50, Upper Box $10.50, Lower Reserved $8, Upper Reserved $8, General Admission $4.50 ($3 for 14 and under, 60 and older), Bleachers $3.

Discounts & Promotions
Promotions scheduled for 25 games. Family sections. Autograph/Photo Sessions every Saturday and Sunday home game.
Toughest Tickets To Get
New York, Oakland and Boston.
Game Times
Sunday 1:35, 8:05. Weeknights 7:35. Friday 5:05, 7:35. Saturday 1:35, 7:05. Eastern time. Gates open 60-90 minutes before game, 2 hours before on Saturday and Sunday.
Broadcasts
3WE 1100 AM Radio and WUAB TV (43).
Other Notes
Stadium tours: contact Community Relations at 216-861-1200. Family Section (Lower Box and Lower Reserved section 12).
Cleveland Indians Gift Shop Catalog at 216-696-4520 or 800-669-2466.
Getting To The Stadium
From I-90, near Lake Erie on Cleveland Memorial Shoreway. Commercial parking lots available. Accessible by bus.

A fixture at Michigan and Trumbull for 79 years, Tiger Stadium has also been known as Navin Field and Briggs Stadium.

When Cecil Fielder returned from a year's exodus in Japan to belt 51 home runs in 1990, he was merely carrying on a couple of time-honored Detroit Tiger traditions.

Not only was Fielder living up to a Tiger hitting heritage that dates back to the days of Ty Cobb, but the 26-year-old first baseman also was making good on a second chance.

Before going to Japan, Fielder hit 31 homers with 84 runs batted in during 506 at-bats for the Toronto Blue Jays, normally pretty respectable numbers.

Trouble was, he did it over four seasons, and when he came back to the States, some people wondered why the Tigers would pay a utility man $1.5 million a year.

Fielder didn't make them wait long for an answer. In late April, he went on a 17-game tear that produced 11 homers, 26 RBIs and a .388 average.

By the time he passed the magical 50 mark with a pair of homers in the season's final game, the Detroit money men looked like a pretty shrewd bunch.

Picked by most observers to bring up the rear in the American League East, the Tigers rode Fielder's power show to a surprising third-place finish.

Only 10 other players have hit 50 homers in a season, and Fielder was the first American Leaguer since Roger Maris belted 61 and Mickey Mantle had 54 for the New York Yankees in 1961. The last National Leaguer was George Foster with 52 in 1977.

Fielder fits right in on a team whose roll call of batting stars includes Hall of Famers Sam Crawford, Harry Heilmann, Mickey Cochrane, Charlie Gehringer, Hank Greenberg, George Kell and Al Kaline.

Crawford's 312 career triples are

Detroit
Tigers

Great hitting and occasionally brilliant pitching are time-honored Tiger traditions. As Cecil Fielder can tell you, so are second chances.

still a major league record, while Heilmann, his successor as the Tigers' right fielder in 1916, led the league in hitting four times.

Cochrane was a career .320 hitter, managed the Tigers to pennants in 1934 and 1935 and is generally considered one of the top two or three catchers of all time. Gehringer, so fluid at second base they called him "The Mechanical Man," hit .300 or better 13 times and had seven seasons with at least 100 RBIs.

Greenberg was Detroit's first great power hitter, a first baseman/outfielder who bashed 331 homers — 58 in 1938 — during a nine-season career shortened by World War II. Kell, a third baseman, won a hitting title at Detroit; so did Kaline, whose .340 at the age of 20 in 1955 made him the youngest batting champ ever.

Plenty of lesser lights have also had their moments. In 1937, Rudy York slugged 18 home runs in a month. In 1952, Walt Dropo had 12 hits in a row. And Cesar Gutierrez had seven straight hits in one game in 1970. All are still major league records.

Then there was Norm Cash, who won the 1961 batting title with a .361 average and also hit 41 homers with 132 RBIs, only to be overshadowed by Roger Maris' 61-homer season. Perhaps that was only justice, since Cash later admitted he did it all with a corked bat.

The Tigers have always hit. There have been 22 batting champions — another major league record — 17 RBI champions and eight home run champions.

A big part of that tradition is venerable Tiger Stadium, a place that Boston Red Sox great Ted Williams once called the best hitter's park in baseball.

Detroit teams have played baseball at the corner of Michigan and Trumbull since 1900, initially in tiny Bennett Park, whose 8,500-seat capacity was the majors' smallest. Tiger Stadium — originally called Navin Field, then Briggs Stadium, in honor of the team's owners — opened on April 20, 1912, the same day as Boston's Fenway Park. With the demise of old Comiskey Park in Chicago, the Detroit and Boston ballparks are the major leagues' oldest.

Double-decked and fully enclosed over the years, Tiger Stadium holds 52,416 people, more than twice its original capacity. At 440 feet, its center field is the deepest in baseball, but the power alleys are an inviting 365 feet in left-center and 370 feet in right-center.

Left-handed hitters love the place. The upper deck overhangs the field in right, cutting 10 feet off the already cozy 325-foot foul line. Twenty of the 22 homers hit over the roof have gone out to right. Ted Williams belted the first in 1939, then returned two years later to win the 1941 All-Star game with a clutch shot into the seats.

With their long lineage of hitters, it's tempting to call the Tigers the American League's version of the Pittsburgh Pirates. Cobb and Honus Wagner, Greenberg and Ralph Kiner, and Kaline and Roberto Clemente seem like mirror images, and neither team has a pitcher in the Hall of Fame.

Detroit's four World Series championships, nine pennants and three A.L. East titles also echo Pittsburgh's totals: five World Series titles, seven pennants and eight N.L. East championships.

But with all their offense, the Tigers have also been blessed with occasionally brilliant pitching. How about 20-game winners? The Tigers have had 43, including the last man to win 30, Denny McLain, whose 31-6 mark in 1968 brought him the first of his two Cy Young awards.

Schoolboy Rowe won 16 consecutive games for Detroit in 1934, tying an American League record. Jim Bunning, one of only three men to throw a no-hitter in each league, was with the Tigers when he tossed the first one in 1958.

As a Detroit rookie, Mark "The Bird" Fidrych won 19 games in 1976 and led the league with a 2.34 earned run average, delighting the country with his curly-headed resemblance to Sesame Street's Big Bird and a comic penchant for talking to the ball.

The Bird wasn't the Tigers' first experience with the unusual. In 1912, be-cause of a player boycott protesting Ty Cobb's suspension for assaulting a fan, the team was forced to use sandlot players in a game with the Philadelphia A's. The result? A not-too-surprising 24-2 shellacking.

And in 1960, the Tigers were involved in two of baseball's oddest trades. First, they shipped the 1959 batting champion, Harvey Kuenn, to the Cleveland Indians for the 1959 home run champ, Rocky Colavito. Four months later, in the only mid-season swap of major league managers, Jimmy Dykes went to Cleveland for Joe Gordon.

The Tigers have always been the pride of Detroit, which despite well-documented racial and crime problems remains one of the nation's great industrial cities. It's home for General Motors, Ford and Chrysler, as well as Motown Records, the country's largest black-owned company. The Detroit Institute of Art has a national reputation,

Tiger Stadium

and the towering Renaissance Center and Belle Isle park are among the city's more successful efforts against urban decline.

Detroit baseball predates all of that, though. The Detroit Wolverines played in the National League from 1881 to 1888, winning one pennant. In 1894, the city joined the Western Association, which evolved into the American League in 1901.

The origin of the Tigers' nickname has often been credited to newspaper editor Philip J. Reid, who noticed in 1901 that their blue-and-orange stockings resembled the colors of Princeton University. Recent research, however, indicates the name was used in a newspaper headline as early as 1895.

The early Tigers, spurred by Cobb's arrival in 1905, captured three straight pennants from 1907 to 1909, but lost all three World Series. Their ace was George Mullin, who won 20 games five times in six years.

The first of Tommy Bridges' three consecutive 20-win campaigns helped the Tigers win their fourth pennant in 1934, and the next year he won two games against the Chicago Cubs to give Detroit its first World Series title.

Bobo Newsom went 21-5 for Detroit in 1940, then won two World Series games in a losing cause against the Cincinnati Reds. Hal Newhouser won 20 games four times, including 1945, when he followed a 25-9 season with two victories in the Tigers' World Series triumph over the Cubs.

Pitching also dominated Detroit's last two trips to the World Series. In 1968, Mickey Lolich won three games against the St. Louis Cardinals, including a 4-1 Game Seven duel against Bob Gibson on two days' rest. And in

1984, Jack Morris won a pair of games and Willie Hernandez, the Most Valuable Player/Cy Young Award winner, saved two in Detroit's romp over the San Diego Padres.

No Detroit pitcher, though, has ever performed more admirably than John Hiller, who was only 27 years old in 1971 when he suffered a heart attack. A year later, after re-signing as a batting practice pitcher, Hiller was back with the Tigers. And in 1973, the left-hander completed his recovery in style, setting an American League record with 38 saves.

But as much as great hitting and timely pitching, second chances are a way of life with the Tigers.

Darrell Evans was 36 when Detroit signed him as a free agent in 1983. Two seasons later, he socked 40 home runs. The Texas Rangers figured Frank Tanana was through when they traded him to Detroit in 1985 for a minor leaguer, but since then the ex-flamethrower has won 70 games.

Gates Brown and Ron LeFlore were even harder cases. Second chance? These guys were in prison before the Tigers signed them. Brown turned into a pinch-hitter deluxe who hit .462 off the bench in Detroit's 1968 world championship season. LeFlore stole 455 bases and hit .278 in nine major league seasons.

And what about Manager Sparky Anderson? Discarded by Cincinnati after guiding the Reds to four National League pennants in nine years, Anderson has won 974 games at Detroit since 1979, not to mention a World Series and two A.L. East championships.

Don't blame Cecil Fielder if he feels very, very much at home with the Detroit Tigers.

Ty Cobb

Lefty O'Doul, who won National League batting titles in 1929 and 1932, was convinced that most old-time ballplayers were generally better than those today.

So it didn't seem to make sense when he told a banquet crowd in 1959 that Ty Cobb, a lifetime .367 hitter, would probably bat only about .340 in the modern game.

Explain yourself, someone demanded.

"Well," replied O'Doul, "you have to take into consideration the man is now 73 years old."

Tyrus Raymond Cobb was the first player inducted into the Hall of Fame in 1936 and there's still plenty of evidence he was the best the game has ever seen.

Pete Rose finally eclipsed Cobb's 4,191 career hits and Rickey Henderson and Lou Brock eventually whizzed past his 892 stolen bases, but "The Georgia Peach" is still very much in the record book.

He won 12 American League batting titles from 1905 to 1928, and his career average is nine points higher than Rogers Hornsby, the only player besides Cobb to hit .400 three times.

Cobb was the king of the deadball hitters, a player whose game was built on chop hits and line drives, but he once socked three home runs in a game and led the league in slugging eight times.

He won the Triple Crown in 1909 and still holds the major league record for most runs scored, 2,245.

He stole 96 bases in 1915, a mark that stood until Maury Wills' 104 in 1962. Six seasons he led the league in

Ty Cobb — and a rare smile

steals, and he stole home a major league record 35 times — six of them after first swiping second and third.

During Cobb's 22 seasons with the Tigers, they won three pennants — although no World Series — and had just six losing records. He also managed Detroit from 1921 to 1926 before playing two final seasons for the Philadelphia A's.

The numbers, though, only hint at what really set Cobb apart from other players: a furious, hell-for-leather style of play that approached the psychopathic.

"I just got to be first — all the time," said Cobb, a Southerner whose early life was as bleak as anything William Faulkner or Flannery O'Connor could have dreamed up.

His domineering father wanted him to be a surgeon and, when young Ty opted for baseball, warned him disapprovingly, "Don't come home a failure." Then in 1905, a month before Cobb joined the Detroit Tigers, his father was shot to death by his mother, who despite suspicious circumstances was cleared of any wrongdoing.

For whatever reason, Cobb was a demon on the diamond, a taunting, snarling, intimidating competitor who did anything he could to gain an edge, even bunting just so he could spike a pitcher who'd brushed him back.

"Every great batter," he blithely theorized, "works on the theory that the pitcher is more afraid of him than he is of the pitcher."

All of which made him admired as a player and detested as a human being. As great as he was, Cobb also may have been the meanest, most vindictive, most paranoid man ever to play the game.

He never forgot a slight, was insanely jealous of Babe Ruth and other stars, and welcomed the chance to settle disputes with his fists after the games.

Once, he beat up umpire Billy Evans under the stands. Another time, he charged into the seats to pummel a crippled heckler, despite cries from bystanders that the man had no hands. "I don't care if he has no feet!" growled Cobb.

After spiking Home Run Baker in a 1909 game, he received death threats the next time he played in Philadelphia, prompting police to escort him to and from the ballpark.

Even his own teammates didn't have much use for him. In 1910, the St. Louis Browns allowed Nap Lajoie to get seven bunt hits on the last day of the season in an effort to help him beat Cobb for the batting title. The next day, before American League President Ban Johnson ruled Cobb the winner, eight Tigers sent a telegram of congratulation — to Lajoie.

Thanks to an early investment in Coca-Cola, Cobb became a wealthy man after his playing days. But he never really mellowed. And when he died lonely and bitter in 1961, just three people attended his funeral.

Top Attractions
Belle Isle Aquarium (313-398-0903), Belle Isle Nature Center (313-267-7157), Belle Isle Zoo (313-267-7160), Boblo Island Amusement Park (4401 Jefferson, 313-843-0700), Detroit Historical Museum (5401 Woodward Ave., 313-833-1805), Detroit Institute of Arts (5200 Woodward Ave., 313-833-7900), Detroit Science Center (5020 John Rd., 313-577-8400), The Motown Museum (2648 W. Grand Blvd., 313-867-0991), Museum of African American History (301 Frederick Douglass, 313-833-9800).

Tourism Information
Metropolitan Detroit Convention & Visitors Bureau (100 Renaissance Center, Suite 1950, Detroit, MI 48243, 313-259-4333).
Michigan Travel Bureau (PO Box 30226, Lansing, MI 48909, 800-5432-YES)
(including Guide To Golf Course and Calendar of Events)

Tiger Stadium
Trumbull and Michigan Aves.

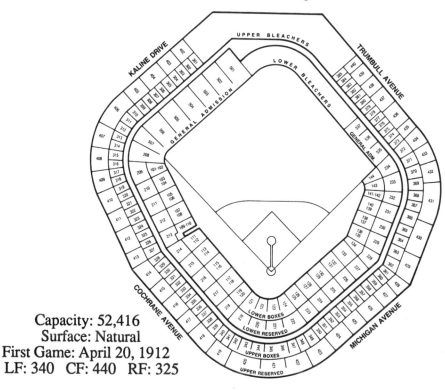

Capacity: 52,416
Surface: Natural
First Game: April 20, 1912
LF: 340   CF: 440   RF: 325

General Information
Detroit Tigers, Tiger Stadium, Detroit, MI 48216, 313-962-4000.
Getting Tickets
Bleacher tickets sold day of game only.
Stadium ticket window: Michigan and Trumbull, 9-6 daily.
By mail: Detroit Baseball Club, Ticket Department, PO Box 77322, Detroit, MI 48277. Specify date, number of tickets and ticket price. $3 handling charge. Check, money order, MasterCard and VISA accepted.
By FAX: 313-962-4600. Specify date, number of tickets and ticket price. MasterCard and VISA accepted. $3 handling fee.
Phone orders: 313-963-7300 or TicketMaster at 313-645-6666, 9-5 daily. MasterCard and VISA accepted.
Ticket Prices
Box Seat $12.50, Reserved $10, Reserved Grandstand $7, Bleacher $4.

Promotions & Discounts
Special events scheduled for 28 games (313-962-4000 for information). Bargain Days (Upper Deck Reserved and Grandstand Reserved $5 on all Saturday afternoon games).
Game Times
Afternoon games 1:35 except Saturdays at 1:15. Night games at 7:35. Twi-light doubleheaders at 5:30. Eastern time. Gates open 2 hours before game.
Broadcasts
WJR 760 AM Radio and WDIV-TV (4).
Other Notes
Catalog of souvenirs: SportService, Inc., 2121 Trumbull Ave., Detroit, MI 48216.
Tiger decals available at no charge: send stamped, addressed return envelope to Public Relations Dept., Tiger Stadium, Detroit, MI 48216.
Getting To The Stadium
Near central Detroit, at the intersection of Lodge and Fisher (I-75) Freeways. Michigan, Trumbull and other surface streets speed access to stadium. Parking commercially operated and plentiful. Accessible by bus.

Tailgate parties are a tradition at County Stadium, which has been home to two major league teams, the Braves from 1953 to 1965 and the Brewers since 1970.

Whatever happened to those swaggering, bruising, homer-happy Milwaukee Brewers?

Just nine years ago, the Brew Crew battered opposing pitchers into submission with 216 homers en route to the team's first American League pennant.

As recently as 1987, the Brewers won 91 games, good enough for third in the A.L. East. But since then: 87 victories in 1988, 81 in 1989 and just 74 in 1990.

Yes, there have been injuries, especially to pitching ace Teddy Higuera and infielders Paul Molitor. And some highly touted prospects, like B.J. Surhoff and Gary Sheffield, are still dogged by the word ''potential.''

But could it be something much simpler than that? In Boston, the Red Sox's failure to win a World Series since Babe Ruth was traded to the New York Yankees in 1920 is called the Curse of the Bambino.

Could this be ... the Curse of Gorman Thomas?

Okay, nobody's ever going to get Thomas confused with Babe Ruth. But Stormin' Gorman was once as much a symbol of the free-swinging Brewers as the Babe was of those great New York Yankee teams. And Milwaukee baseball hasn't been quite the same since the free-spirited, shaggy-haired Thomas was traded to the Cleveland Indians in 1983.

The Brewers have had eight winning seasons since moving to Milwaukee in 1970, five of them during Thomas' reign as the American League's premier home run hitter.

Thomas pounded 175 homers in those years, second only to the Philadelphia Phillies' Mike Schmidt. Twice he led the league in homers; each time, the Brewers won 95 games.

Milwaukee
Brewers

Sure, there have been injuries. And some overrated prospects who haven't panned out. But, heck, maybe the Brewers just miss Stormin' Gorman.

He wasn't a great hitter, not with a .225 lifetime batting average. And he may have been just as celebrated for striking out — once in about every 3 1/2 at-bats — as for hitting home runs.

In 1979, Thomas fanned 175 times, tying a major-league record. And in a 1975 series in Boston, he whiffed eight straight times, then grounded into a double play.

"I got a standing ovation for hitting into the double play," Thomas said. "And when I got out to center field, a dog ran out in front of me and relieved himself, and I got another standing ovation."

Almost as much as his bat, it was the Charleston, South Carolina, native's flaky, slightly wild-eyed spirit that captured the fancy of Milwaukee. He looked like a gunslinger, talked like a longshoreman and played like he couldn't imagine being anywhere else. Brewer fans loved it.

But then, Milwaukee has always loved baseball. Almost, anyway. Historians say the first ballgame in Wisconsin's largest city occurred in 1836, just 18 years after the town was founded on the shores of Lake Michigan.

Today, Milwaukee is a major manufacturer of durable goods like heavy machinery, auto parts and electrical equipment, as well as a growing meat-packing center. Sources of cultural pride include the Milwaukee Museum, one of the country's largest natural history museums, and the annual Summerfest, which has been called the world's biggest music festival.

For most people, though, Milwaukee means beer. Settled largely by Germans, who still make up one-third of the area's 1.5 million people, Milwaukee has been a brewing capital since the 19th century, and Miller, Schlitz and Pabst still call the city home. Despite that, the word "brewers" in Milwaukee has stood for baseball almost as long as it's signified the city's best-known industry.

Milwaukee's first major league team, which played just one season (1878) in the National League, was called the Cream Citys after the color of bricks produced in the city.

But later teams were nicknamed the Brewers, and with the exception of the Braves from 1953 to 1965, that's the name that's stuck. Not surprisingly, playing *Roll Out the Barrel* during the seventh-inning stretch is as hallowed a County Stadium ritual as pre-game tailgating parties.

Actually, the current Brewers are the city's second American League entry. Milwaukee was among the league's eight charter members when it began play in 1901. But after a last-place finish, the franchise moved to St. Louis the next season and became the Browns. Now it's known as the Baltimore Orioles.

From 1902 to 1952, the Brewers played in the American Association, their home ramshackle Borchert Field, which once had a goat grazing on the field between games and was used as an ice skating rink in the winter.

Milwaukee was an ideal place for baseball showman Bill Veeck, who prepared for later stops in Cleveland, St. Louis and Chicago by running the Brewers from 1941 to 1945. Veeck packed in crowds with weird door prizes (everything from a swaybacked horse to a 200-pound cake of ice), morning games for graveyard shift workers and stunts like having a new pitcher jump out of a giant birthday cake on the field. He also put together some fine teams. The Brewers won pennants in his final three years.

In 1950, the city began building County Stadium in hopes of getting another major league team. Three years later, with the $5 million ballpark nearing completion, the effort paid off when the Boston Braves announced plans to come to Milwaukee.

But by 1966, declining attendance had chased the Braves to Atlanta and, except for playing host to a handful of Chicago White Sox games, County Stadium stood idle until 1970.

That's when the expansion Seattle Pilots, after drawing fewer than 700,000 fans in their inaugural year, moved to Milwaukee, where attendance zoomed to more than one million.

Although generally peopled with other teams' castoffs and saddled with losing records in their first six seasons in Milwaukee, the early Brewers were an intriguing lot.

Hank Aaron, a favorite with the Braves, returned to Milwaukee in a 1974 trade and hit his final home run, No. 755, in County Stadium on July 20, 1976.

The Brewers' first 20-game winner was Jim Colborn, who was just as well known for pranks like impersonating groundskeepers, umpires, even mascot Bernie Brewer. Ken Brett made Milwaukee the second stop on what eventually would be a 10-team career. And burly slugger George Scott, asked once to identify the ivory-like pieces dangling from his gold chain, growled, "Second basemen's teeth."

Things began to come together in 1978, when the Brewers celebrated their first winning season in style with a 93-69 record. Free agent acquisition Larry Hisle slugged 34 homers with 115 RBIs; Gorman Thomas, previously a part-timer, blossomed with 32 homers and 86 RBIs.

Grizzled left-hander Mike Caldwell, 22-6 with a 2.36 earned run average, anchored what grew into a solid pitching staff over the next few years.

Relief ace Rollie Fingers won the Cy Young and Most Valuable Player awards in 1981, when he saved 28 games and posted a microscopic 1.04 ERA. A year later, Pete Vuckovich, whose Fu Manchu mustache put him in the scruffiness sweepstakes with Caldwell and Thomas, claimed the Cy Young with an 18-6 mark.

But the Brewer trademark was hitting. Thomas hit a career-high 45 homers and drove in 123 runs in 1979. When Hisle's career ended with a shoulder injury, Ben Oglivie stepped forward, hitting 118 homers in four seasons. Cecil Cooper led the league in RBIs twice and hit .352 in 1980. During one stretch in 1978 and 1979, the Brewers went 212 games without being shut out.

A mid-season strike by the players thwarted Milwaukee's championship hopes in 1981. The Brewers finished with the best record in the A.L. East but lost a division playoff to the New York Yankees under that year's makeshift split-season format.

Finally in 1982, after years of falling just a little short, the Brewers rode one of the finest offensive years in American League history to their only pennant.

"I just told them to go out there and have fun," said Manager Harvey Kuenn, himself a former American

League batting champion, who took over that June and guided the Brewers to 72 of their 95 victories.

Four members of "Harvey's Wallbangers" — Cooper, Oglivie, Thomas and American League Most Valuable Player Robin Yount — hit at least 29 homers and drove in more than 100 runs. The 891 runs scored by the Brewers were the league's most in 32 years, and only five teams have ever hit more than those 216 homers.

They beat the second-place Balti-more Orioles on the last day of the season to win the division by one game, then spotted the California Angels two victories in the best-of-five American League playoffs before rallying in the final three games.

The World Series with the St. Louis Cardinals, dubbed the "Suds Series" because the two cities' beer heritage, was a good one. The Brewers won three of the first five games before getting a little of their own medicine in a 13-1 loss in Game Six, then watched

County Stadium

the Cards rally from a three-run deficit to take the finale 6-3.

That may have been the beginning of the end for Gorman Thomas in Milwaukee. He hit just .115 on three singles in the seven games, ending the Series with, yes, a strikeout against St. Louis reliever Bruce Sutter.

Struggling at .183 with only five homers in June 1983, Thomas was traded to Cleveland. He moved on to Seattle and hit 32 homers one year. But the Mariners cut him midway through the 1986 season, and there wasn't much left when the Brewers re-signed him. He had just six homers in 44 games. At 35, he was through.

And the Brewers? Without Thomas, they limped home in fifth in 1983. A year later, they plunged to seventh and haven't been higher than third since.

Years from now, maybe even decades, when Milwaukee is still trying to figure why that second pennant is so elusive, remember: You heard it here first.

Robin Yount

The list of people with at least 3,000 hits is a short one, just 15 players. It begins with Pete Rose at 4,256 and ends with Roberto Clemente at exactly 3,000.

George Brett should join their ranks before he's through, and there's a good chance Wade Boggs and Tony Gwynn will also wind up in the club. A handful of others are possibilities.

But barring serious injury, the next player to reach 3,000 hits will be a man who broke into the majors because he looked pretty good with a glove.

Robin Yount was a wispy-haired 18-year-old in 1974 when then-Milwaukee Manager Del Crandall watched him pick groundballs one day in spring

Robin Yount

training and decided he was the Brewers' starting shortstop.

Yount's fielding since then has been Gold Glove-caliber, but it's his numbers with the bat that will probably get him into the Hall of Fame.

Harvey Kuenn, then the Brewers' batting coach, compared Yount as a rookie to Al Kaline. Former Milwaukee pitcher Don Sutton said the only better all-around athlete he'd ever seen was Roberto Clemente. Ex-St. Louis Cardinal Manager Whitey Herzog once called Yount one of the top two or three players in baseball.

High praise for a man who, in 17 years with the Brewers, has never led the American League in hitting, home runs or runs batted in. In fact, he's only led in any offensive category just five times.

But even allowing for a disappointing 1990 performance, few have been steadier at the plate. That's why he has 2,747 career hits, including a major league best 1,731 in the 1980s.

Yount is one of only six players who got 1,000 hits before their 25th birthday. Four of them — Ty Cobb, Mel Ott, Al Kaline and Fred Lindstrom — are in the Hall of Fame.

Of those with 3,000 hits, only Cobb and Hank Aaron reached 2,000 at a younger age than Yount, who was 30 when he did it in 1986.

With a respectable but not particularly eye-popping .286 lifetime batting average, the unassuming Yount is quick to attribute his success to longevity.

"It's just that I've stayed healthy

enough," he said after notching his 2,500th hit in 1989.

That's not to say perfectly healthy. Shoulder problems limited him to 122 games in 1985 and eventually prompted his move to the outfield.

Still, he's batted .300 or better in six seasons, had four seasons with at least 20 homers and knocked in more than 100 runs three times.

The pinnacle was 1982, a magic season for all the Brewers, and none more so than Yount, who was named the league's Most Valuable Player. He batted .331 with 29 homers and 114 homers — all career highs — and became the first shortstop to lead the league in slugging and total bases. He also won a Gold Glove.

When the Brewers won the pennant on the final day of the season, Yount's two homers off Baltimore Orioles ace Jim Palmer had a lot to do with the 10-2 victory. He didn't miss a beat in the World Series, hitting .414 against the St. Louis Cardinals and becoming the first player to have a pair of four-hit games in the Series.

In 1989, Yount won his second MVP award, the first American League winner from a team that failed to finish above .500 and the league's first two-time winner since Mickey Mantle in 1962.

His numbers weren't as gaudy as in 1982 — a .318 average, 21 homers and 103 RBIs — but they were good enough for him to join Stan Musial and Hank Greenberg as the only players to win MVP awards at two different positions.

That got Yount a new three-year contract for $9.6 million, which means he should still be in a Milwaukee uniform when he reaches 3,000 hits. Manager Tom Trebelhorn is happy about that.

"He's an exceptional athlete who does things in a day-in and day-out professional manner," said Trebelhorn. "You'd like every player who ever played to do things the same way."

Brewery Tours
Miller Brewing Company (4251 W. State, 414-931-2153), Pabst Brewery (915 W. Juneau, 414-223-3709), Sprecher Brewing Company (730 W. Oregon St., 414-272-BEER), Water Street Brewery (1101 N. Water, 414-272-1195).

Top Attractions
Bradley Center (Fourth & State Sts., 414-227-0400), Discovery World - Museum of Science, Economics & Technology (818-W. Wisconsin Ave., 414-765-9966), Milwaukee Art Museum (750 N. Lincoln Memorial Dr., 414-271-9508), Milwaukee County Zoo (10001 W. Blue Mound Rd., 414-771-3040), Milwaukee Public Museum (800 W. Wells, 414-278-2702).

Tourism Information
Greater Milwaukee Convention & Visitors Bureau, 756 N. Milwaukee St., 414-273-3950 or 800-231-0903 (outside WI).
Wisconsin Tourism Development, PO Box 7606, Madison, WI 53707, 608-266-2162 or 800-372-2737 (In WI and area states).

Milwaukee County Stadium
201 S. 46th St.
Capacity: 53,192
Surface: Natural
Opened: April 14, 1953
LF: 315   CF: 402   RF: 315

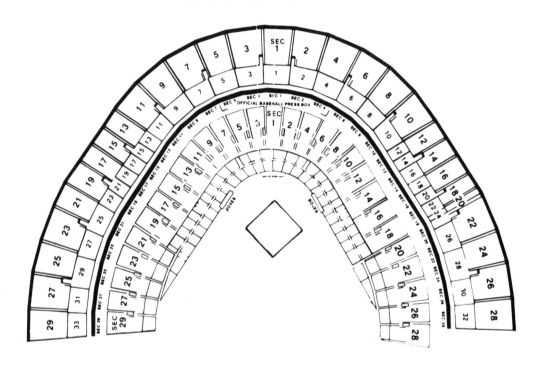

General Information
Milwaukee Brewers Baseball Club, Milwaukee County Stadium, Milwaukee, WI 53214, 414-933-4114.
Ticket Information: 414-933-1818.

Getting Tickets
No tickets held back for day of game sales; bleacher seats (6,000) go on sale at conclusion of the previous day's game.
By mail: Allow one week lead time.
By phone: 414-933-9000 until 3 pm day of game. MasterCard and VISA accepted.

Ticket Prices
Deluxe Mezzanine $14, Mezzanine $13, Lower and Upper Box $12, Lower Grandstand $10, Upper Grandstand $7, Bleacher $4.

Promotions & Discounts
Promotions scheduled for 28 games. Kids and Senior Citizen Days ($3.50 off reserved seats).

Toughest Tickets To Get
Chicago on a weekend, Minnesota and New York.

Game Times
Day games 1:30. Doubleheaders 1:00. Twilight singles 6:00. Night games 7:00, 7:30, Twinight doubleheaders 5:30. Central time. Gates open approximately 90 minutes before game.

Broadcasts
WTMJ 620 AM, WCGZ-TV (24).

Other Notes
Brewers Fan Club, PO Box 614, West Bend, WI 53095, 414-342-5532.

Getting To The Stadium
West of downtown Milwaukee, at intersection of East West Freeway (I-94) and Stadium Freeway (41). Parking plentiful (opens 2 hours before game). Accessible by bus.

Milwaukee Braves

The team that now calls itself the Atlanta Braves has generally had more troubles than triumphs since 1900, losing a whopping 1,040 more games than it has won.

And despite its storied baseball past, Milwaukee's experience with the major leagues has been a mixed bag. Three of its four big league teams have had losing overall records.

But for 13 seasons, from 1953 to 1965, the Braves and Milwaukee got together long enough to form one of the winningest partnerships in baseball history.

In 1953, after watching his Boston Braves lose $1 million in three years, Lou Perini decided to do something that hadn't been done in the major leagues in 50 years: move his team.

He chose Milwaukee, which had lost its previous major league franchise to St. Louis way back in 1902, because the city was already building a new stadium. It was a good choice and even better timing. A meager 281,278 people had turned out in Boston to watch the Braves finish 64-89 in 1952.

But a year later, the Braves went 92-62 — their best record since 1914 — and initiated a fervent, if brief, love affair with Milwaukee by drawing a National League-record 1.8 million fans to County Stadium.

The Milwaukee Braves never had a losing season, something no other modern major league team that's played more than one year in any city can say.

They won a pair of National League pennants, converting one into a World Series championship, and finished second five times.

Their success also showed up at the ticket gate. In 1954, the Braves became the first National League team to draw two million fans. Then they did it again the next three seasons. Their 2.2 million in 1957 remained a Milwaukee record until the Brewers hit nearly 2.4 million in 1982.

From start to finish, the Milwaukee Braves boasted one of the most impressive collection of hitters in either league.

Eddie Mathews, in only his second season when the Braves debuted in Milwaukee, made an immediate impression by hitting .302 with 47 homers and 135 runs batted in. The next year, a rookie named Hank Aaron joined the team; he hit 398 homers and drove in 1,305 runs over the next 12 seasons in Milwaukee.

Joe Adcock, who hit four homers in one game in 1954, Joe Torre, Wes Covington, Lee Maye, Rico Carty and Felipe Alou also added plenty of punch over the years.

Left-hander Warren Spahn was simply the best pitcher the Braves have ever had, no matter which city they've been in. He was 25 years old before he won a major league game in 1946, but by the time he was through 20 years later, the total was 363, tops for any southpaw. He won 20 games 13 times, including nine seasons in Milwaukee.

The Braves rolled to their first pennant in 1957 as Spahn won the Cy Young Award and Aaron was named Most Valuable Player. They led the league in homers and runs scored, but it was Burdette's three victories that lifted them past the New York Yankees in the World Series.

Milwaukee won the pennant easily again in 1958 and took three of the first four games in a World Series rematch with the Yanks, but New York won the last three to avenge its '57 loss.

Maybe it was a case of too much too soon, but the Milwaukee magic began to fade. Attendance dipped below two million in 1958.

A series of so-so finishes didn't help. In 1962, the fifth-place Braves played in front of fewer than 800,000 Milwaukee fans. Three years later, with the team openly courting Atlanta, Milwaukee's apathy turned into rejection. Barely 550,000 people watched the Braves finish fifth again.

On Opening Day 1966, the Braves were playing in brand-new Atlanta-Fulton County Stadium. Milwaukee would have to wait 12 years before it had another winning team.

Numerous major league ballparks are newer or more stylish than Yankee Stadium, but ''The House That Ruth Built'' is still the most famous.

There was a time when many baseball fans, to paraphrase a popular bumper sticker, had two favorite teams: the hometown nine and whoever was playing the New York Yankees.

Oh sure, there were plenty of Yankee fans. New York is a big city, and the country is chock-full of Republicans and other assorted frontrunners.

The Yankees were the best in baseball. They had the strongest hitters, the craftiest pitchers, the most famous stadium. In those pinstripes, they even dressed for success.

It was a hard formula to beat. Sometimes impossible. There's still no other team remotely close to their 33 American League pennants and 22 World Series titles.

Americans love a winner. But they also root for the underdog, and to many baseball fans the Yankees were just too much of a good thing. As sportswriter Red Smith once remarked, "Rooting for the New York Yankees is like rooting for U.S. Steel."

It was easy to dislike the Yankees, especially around World Series time when they were beating up some luckless National League team, usually the Brooklyn Dodgers.

For the most part, Yankee-hating was an honorable but futile vocation, so the occasional upset by the Dodgers or St. Louis Cardinals or Pittsburgh Pirates was something to be cherished. The Yanks were the bully you enjoyed seeing get his comeuppance.

But, alas, judging by the sorry state of affairs in the Bronx, Yankee haters may be going the way of the dodo, Democratic presidents and vinyl records.

What's the fun in hating a team that hasn't won a pennant since 1981 or a

New York Yankees

Yankee-hating was once an honorable profession. Today it's going the way of the dodo, Democratic presidents and vinyl records.

World Series since 1978? The Yanks haven't even been higher than fourth since 1986. That was five managers ago.

And in 1990 — well, let's just say the Yankees have never experienced another quite like it. They finished last for just the fourth time since moving to New York in 1903. Only the Atlanta Braves, much more experienced at this sort of thing, had a worse record than the Yanks, whose 67-95 showing marked their worst season since 1912.

Even when the Yankees excelled, they fouled up. Andy Hawkins became the tenth Yankee to throw a no-hitter and — after the Chicago White Sox turned three eighth-inning errors into a 4-0 victory — only the second player in major league history to lose while doing it.

Some things, to the dismay of Yankee fans, weren't much different than in other recent seasons. The Yankees made their usual mid-season managerial switch, dumping Bucky Dent for Stump Merrill. Which didn't make much difference, since they also made their usual assortment of baffling player moves.

The 1989 International League batting champ, Hal Morris, was traded to Cincinnati for pitcher Tim Leary. Morris hit .340 for the Reds; Leary lost 19 games. The Yanks gave a three-year contract to flaky Pascual Perez, who pitched three games before a season-ending injury. Dave Winfield was traded for retread Claudell Washington, who didn't last the season. And the Yankees kept talking about the potential of bigmouth Deion Sanders right up to the moment they waived him.

But the most bizarre development came when Commissioner Fay Vincent forced George Steinbrenner to resign as principal owner of the Yankees because of Steinbrenner's dealings with gambler Howard Spira.

Save for a previous 15-month suspension, "The Boss" had run the Yankees since 1973, during which time they won four pennants, two World Series and a reputation for fractiousness best typified by their nickname, "The Bronx Zoo."

Initially, the egocentric Steinbrenner was a hero to Yankee fans, but as the team declined in the 1980s, his manager-switching and other headline-hunting antics became more tiresome than entertaining. When Vincent's ban put him in the same category as William Cox, the Philadelphia Phillies' owner who was kicked out of baseball in 1943 for betting on his team, there was cheering at Yankee Stadium.

A sad commentary for a franchise that once stood not only for success, but also for class and pride. Like them or not, the Yankees were special, a fitting representative for the nation's most dynamic city.

The Yanks were the baseball equivalent of a hit musical on Broadway, of a blue-chip stock on Wall Street, of a priceless painting at the Guggenheim Museum. New York has more people (over seven million), more money, more of just about everything than any city in United States. The Yankees typified the Big Apple's need to be the biggest and the best.

No other team boasts a lineup of Hall of Famers to match the Yanks: Babe Ruth, Lou Gehrig, Miller Huggins, Lefty Gomez, Joe DiMaggio, Bill Dickey, Joe McCarthy, Yogi Berra, Mickey Mantle, Whitey Ford and

Casey Stengel. And that's the short list.

They didn't win a pennant until 1921, and their first World Series title didn't come for another two years. But they've captured at least one American League flag in every decade since.

The Yankees' early highlights were the stuff of trivia books. The team began play in 1901 as the Baltimore Orioles — John McGraw was the manager — but moved to New York two years later when a pair of bartenders plunked down $18,000 for the ballclub and renamed it the Highlanders.

That wasn't much fun for headline writers, though, and when one New York sports editor began calling the club the Yankees, other newspapers rushed to follow suit. The name became official in 1913, but only after the papers ignored owner Jacob Ruppert's campaign for Knickerbockers, after a brand of beer he sold.

There's a story that Ruppert put the Yankees in pinstripes so Babe Ruth wouldn't look quite so portly. But the classic uniforms were actually unveiled in 1915, five years before Ruth arrived on the scene. Another Yankee contribution to baseball fashion came in 1929. That's when they became the first team to wear numbers on a regular basis.

By then, however, the Yanks had plenty of other accomplishments, all of which stemmed from the shrewdest acquisition in baseball history: Ruppert's January 3, 1920, purchase of Ruth from the Boston Red Sox for $125,000, plus a $300,000 loan.

From 1920 through 1932, Ruth won 10 home run titles while the Yankees captured seven pennants and four World Series championships.

Ruth's arrival brought record crowds to Yankee games at the Polo Grounds, which embarrassed the landlord New York Giants so much they kicked their tenants out. In 1922, though, the Yankees began building their own mammoth ballpark in the Bronx directly across the Harlem River from the home of the haughty Giants.

And when Ruth slugged the first home run in Yankee Stadium on Opening Day 1923, a crowd of more than 74,000 jammed into the shiny new ballpark to see it. No wonder sportswriters called it "The House That Ruth Built."

"The Bambino" was the heart of the 1927 Yankees, regarded by almost every baseball authority as the best team in the history of the game. They led the American League from start to finish, winning a then-record 110 games, and then swept the Pittsburgh Pirates in the World Series.

Nicknamed "Murderers' Row" by sportswriter Arthur Robinson, the Yanks hit .307 with 158 homers, nearly three times as many as the next best team. Ruth batted .356 with 60 homers and 164 runs batted in. Amazingly, Lou Gehrig bested him in two of those categories with a .373 average, 47 homers and 175 RBIs. New York also boasted the league's top pitching. Nobody had better numbers than Waite Hoyt's 22-7 record and 2.63 earned run average, but five other Yanks won at least 10 games.

These days, winning two or three pennants in a row is enough to make some people start babbling about a dynasty. The Yankees gave real meaning to the word. Beginning in 1949, they won 14 pennants in 16 years. They also took home nine World Series trophies, including five straight from 1949 to 1953. Only one other team has won as many as three in succession.

It would take another book to give full due to all the great players and moments in Yankee history, and more than a few have been written.

But you can't ignore feats like Gehrig's 2,130-game playing streak, Joe DiMaggio's 56-game hitting streak in 1941, Don Larsen's perfect game in the 1956 World Series, Roger Maris' 61 homers in 1961 that broke Ruth's single-season record, Bucky Dent's playoff game-winning homer in 1978 after the Yanks rallied from 14 games back to catch the Red Sox.

The Yankees have captured 20 Most Valuable Player awards; DiMaggio, Berra and Mantle won three apiece. There have been 26 home run champions, 19 RBI leaders and seven batting champions. Pitching? How about fifty-three 20-game winners? The best was Whitey Ford, their great left-hander of the 1950s and '60s, who still holds most of the team pitching records. But you could also make a case for Red Ruffing, Lefty Gomez and the usually forgotten Spud Chandler, who won nearly 72 percent of his games from 1937 to 1947, still a major league best for anyone with at least 100 pitching decisions.

Despite their machine-like precision on the field, the Yankees could be colorful, too. Gomez kept the teams of the '30s loose by stopping in the middle of games to watch airplanes pass overhead and originating lines like "I'd rather be lucky than good."

Yogi Berra banged out 71 hits in 75 games over 14 World Series, all records, while Casey Stengel managed the Yankees to 10 pennants from 1949

to 1960. But both are just as noted for their eccentric way with the English language. There were Yogiisms like "Nobody goes there anymore. It's too crowded," and the legendary "It ain't over till it's over." And Stengelese: "All right, everyone, line up alphabetically, according to your height," and "Good pitching will always stop good hitting, and vice versa."

Some of that wackiness returned with the last great Yankee teams, which won four pennants and two World Series from 1976 to 1981, but it contained a meaner spirit. There was Reggie Jackson and Thurman Munson matching egos, Jackson and Billy Martin scuffling in the dugout, Martin punching out a marshmallow salesman, Steinbrenner claiming to have fended off two assailants in an elevator. And always there was Steinbrenner firing and rehiring managers. As Graig Nettles put it, "When I was a little boy, I wanted to be a baseball player and join the circus. With the Yankees I've accomplished both."

But Munson was killed in a plane crash, Jackson fled to the California Angels and others left or were traded. The sniping remained but the talent evaporated, save for a few stars like Don Mattingly and Dave Righetti. And they were no match for the chaos caused by The Boss' meddlesome ways. The 1980s turned into a lost decade for Yanks, and the '90s didn't start out any better.

Now, though, thanks to the unlikely combination of Howard Spira and Fay Vincent, Steinbrenner is gone, too. That may give new purpose to Yankee fans and Yankee haters alike.

Babe Ruth

Few players could swing a bat or handle a glove like Tris Speaker, but the Hall of Fame outfielder wasn't quite so steady with a crystal ball.

Speaker was managing the Cleveland Indians in 1920 when the New York Yankees bought Babe Ruth from the Boston Red Sox and agreed to let him play the outfield full time.

"Ruth made a grave mistake when he gave up pitching," Speaker warned. "Working once a week, he might have lasted a long time and become a great star."

Speaker didn't realize he was talking about a man who was destined to be not only baseball's best-loved hero but also the most famous athlete on the planet.

Babe Ruth was the greatest home run hitter in baseball history. His 60-homer season in 1927 was bested by Roger Maris' 61 in 1961, and his 714 career homers now trail Hank Aaron's 755. But that hardly diminishes Ruth's stature.

Consider: Ruth led the American League in homers a record 12 seasons. He was the league leader in slugging 13 times, walks 11 times, runs scored eight times, runs batted in six times and batting once.

Ruth averaged 8 1/2 homers for every 100 at-bats; nobody's ever hit them more often. His .690 lifetime slugging percentage is still unsurpassed, and so is his season mark of .847 in 1920. Although not particularly selective at the plate, Ruth batted .342 over 22 seasons, reaching .393 in 1923. He also drew 2,056 walks, including 170 in 1923. Both are still records.

Although 1927 is the year everyone remembers, Ruth's best season was probably 1921. He socked 59 homers, drove in 171 runs, scored 177, hit .378 and had an .846 slugging percentage.

If he'd never moved to the outfield, he might have made the Hall of Fame as a pitcher. In 10 seasons, he was 94-46 with a 2.28 earned run average. Twice he won 20 games or more, and in 1916 he led the American League with a 1.75 ERA and nine shutouts. He was even tougher in the World Series, going 3-0 and throwing 29 2/3 consecutive scoreless innings, a record that stood till Whitey Ford broke it in 1962.

Babe Ruth

But as glittering as those numbers are, the legend of Babe Ruth, the man they called the "Bambino" and the "Sultan of Swat," extended far, far beyond.

A Baltimore bartender's son who spent much of his boyhood in a Catholic boys' home, George Herman Ruth singlehandedly changed baseball. And he probably saved it.

With his mammoth swing and tape-measure results, Ruth rekindled the imagination of fans disenchanted by the 1919 Black Sox Scandal. Until then, baseball was a game of hit-and-runs, bunts and stolen bases. But once baseball's moguls found that fans loved home runs, they made sure everyone could hit them. In 1917, there were 338 homers hit in the majors. By 1922, the number was 1,055. The lively ball was here to stay.

Flamboyant, bigger than life, the Babe could touch the nation's heart by hitting a home run for a hospitalized child, then amuse it with his world-class appetite for food, drink and carousing.

"I don't room with Babe," teammate Ping Bodie said. "I room with his suitcase."

He was idolized, and he enjoyed it without apology. In the early days of the Great Depression, when most ballplayers were happy to make $15,000 a year, Ruth got an astonishing $80,000. When someone noted it was more than President Herbert Hoover's salary, the Babe replied, "I had a better year than he did."

How big was Ruth? During World War II, years after his career was over, Japanese soldiers would bait GIs by hollering, "To hell with Babe Ruth!"

He loved being around children, freely handed out autographs and greeted everyone with a cheerful "Hiyah, keed!" He was also coarse, overbearing, foul-mouthed and petty.

But whether he was calling his shot off Charlie Root in the 1932 World Series or, at age 40, hitting the final three homers of his career in one game, the Babe had style.

Summed up longtime teammate Waite Hoyt: "He was the greatest crowd pleaser of them all."

New York Attractions
See information in New York Mets chapter.

Tourism Information
New York City Convention and Visitors Bureau, Two Columbus Circle, New York, NY 10019, 212-397-8222.

New York State Division of Tourism, One Commerce Plaza, Albany, NY 12245, 518-474-4116 or 800-225-5697

Yankee Stadium
Capacity: 57,545
Surface: Natural
First Game: April 18, 1923
LF: 318   CF: 408   RF: 314

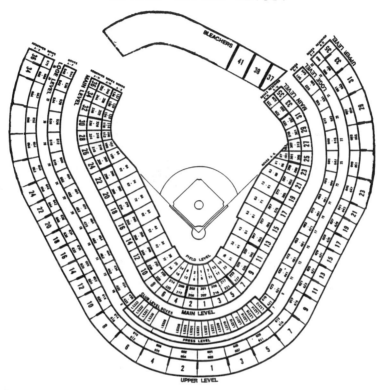

General Information
New York Yankees, Yankee Stadium, Bronx, NY 10451, 212-293-4300.
Ticket information: 212-293-6000.

Getting Tickets
No tickets held back for day of game only sales.
Stadium ticket window: near Gate 4.
By mail: Ticket Department, New York Yankees, Yankee Stadium, Bronx, NY 10451. Specify game date, number of tickets and price. Include $1.75 postage and handling charge. Check, money order or credit card. Orders received less than 7 days prior to game date cannot be mailed and must be picked up at the paid reservation window.
By phone: TicketMaster at 212-307-7171, 914-965-2700, 516-888-9000 or 201-507-8900.

Ticket Prices
Lower and Loge Box Seats $12.50, Tier Box Seats $12, Lower Reserve $10.50, Tier Reserve $8.50, Bleachers $4.50.

Discounts & Promotions
Senior citizen discount games. Family discount games.

Toughest Tickets To Get
Boston, Oakland and Toronto.

Game Times
Day games 1:30. Night games 7:30. Occasionally times vary. Eastern time. Gates open two hours before game on Friday, Saturday and Sunday, 90 minutes before game on weekdays.

Broadcasts
WABC 77 AM, WPIX TV (11).

Other Notes
Monument Park (Section 36/left field, opens 45 minutes prior to the game). Stadium features Fantasy Play-by-Play Booth and The Food Court. Non-alcohol sections available.

Getting To The Stadium
In the Bronx (north of Manhattan), at 155th St. Commercial parking lots. Accessible by subway.

Both the Blue Jays and their new SkyDome are a hit with Toronto fans, who poured through the turnstiles nearly 3.9 million strong in 1990.

Judging by the matchups on television's game of the week, network executives believe all baseball fans root for the New York Yankees, the Los Angeles Dodgers or the Boston Red Sox.

Even if they were right, you'd have to wonder if it was an allegiance spawned by television, a kind of self-fulfilling video prophecy.

Would the Texas Rangers suddenly be in vogue if they popped up on national TV two or three times a month? After all, thanks to cable even the Chicago Cubs and Atlanta Braves have loyal national followings.

When you talk about faithful fans, though, none of TV's fair-haired boys — not even the Dodgers — can compare with the Toronto Blue Jays.

Just 14 seasons after beginning play as a typically bad expansion team, the Blue Jays can call themselves baseball's most popular hometown team.

On the road, the American League's only Canadian ballclub isn't an especially hot ticket. In 1990, the Blue Jays played before barely 25,000 fans a game in opposing parks, lowest in the league.

Put them in Toronto, however, and it's a different matter. There, in a city whose long sports tradition includes the hockey Maple Leafs and the football Argonauts, the Blue Jays are the main event.

Two years ago, 3.375 million fans turned out in Toronto to watch the talented Blue Jays claim their second A.L. East title in five years.

That was just a warmup for 1990, though, when 3.885 million people poured into Toronto's new SkyDome, a remarkable figure that:

• shattered the old major league at-

Toronto
Blue Jays

Forget the Dodgers, Yankees and Red Sox. If SkyDome crowds are any indication, the Blue Jays are baseball's most popular team.

67

tendance record of 3.6 million set by the Dodgers in 1982.

• translated into an amazing average of nearly 48,000 a game.

• was almost one million fans more than the team with the league's second-best attendance, the pennant-winning Oakland Athletics.

No question that a big reason for the Blue Jays' popularity is the dazzling Skydome, the first and possibly most unique entry in baseball's latest wave of new stadiums. If Dodger Stadium and Royals Stadium are classics, the ballpark equivalents of, say, a '57 Chevy, the $578 million Skydome complex is a fully loaded Cadillac.

Everything about it is impressive, if not downright ostentatious. There's the retractable roof, which covers eight acres when closed and is as high as a 31-story building. There's the $17 million scoreboard, featuring the largest video display board in the world. The gadgetry even includes TV monitors in the dugouts so managers can keep an Orwellian eye on the bullpens.

Those are just the basics. The complex also includes a Hard Rock Cafe, a lounge with a 300-foot-long bar overlooking the field, an entertainment center, a health club, a hotel and a McDonald's that boasts some of the world's most expensive Big Macs.

The most eye-popping thing about the SkyDome, in fact, may be the prices. Most of the tickets in 1990 were for $17.50 and $13.50, tops in the American League. Food and drinks are right up there, too.

"What do you say to the family?" outfielder Pat Sheridan wondered after the Blue Jays' palace opened. " 'Hey, kids, what do you want to do — go to a ballgame or go to Europe?' "

Of course, there are some extras you can't get at other ballparks. Cubs broadcaster Harry Caray is a Wrigley Field institution, but his seventh-inning bellowing of *Take Me Out to the Ballgame* can't touch the special show SkyDome fans got last summer when some amorous guests in hotel rooms overlooking the outfield neglected to close their bedroom curtains.

But even in the pre-SkyDome years, the Blue Jays drew well. Except for the strike-shortened 1981 season, Toronto's attendance has never dropped below 1.2 million fans, and the Blue Jays have been over two million every season since 1984.

You can't turn around in Toronto without spying someone in a T-shirt or cap bearing the team's stylized blue jay-baseball-and-maple leaf logo. In the Blue Jays' first season alone, fans snapped up $10 million worth of souvenirs and other paraphernalia.

Maybe they knew something, since after the New York Mets and the Kansas City Royals, Toronto is the majors' most successful expansion team.

The Blue Jays were seven years old before their first winning season in 1983. Since then, though, the Mets are the only team in either league that's won more games.

The Jays have been so successful, it's starting to work against them. Since 1984, they've finished first or second in the A.L. East five times. That's led to high expectations — and disappointment when they've gone unfulfilled. The Blue Jays are still looking for their first trip to the World Series, and when people talk about them, the word "gifted" is often followed by "underachievers."

Still, the fans love them, no big surprise in light of Toronto's long-held affection for baseball. Canada's largest city (3.5 million people) is a commerce and cultural center, a place renowned for its neat, orderly streets, a metropolis whose industries range from brewing to publishing, whose sites include the 1,821-foot CN Tower, the Royal Ontario Museum and the Ontario Place entertainment complex. Toronto has also been a baseball hotbed since its first pro team debuted in 1885.

The Toronto Maple Leafs played in the International League from 1896 to 1967. The early years included games in a ballpark on an island in the Don River, which required fans to take a ferry. That park, called Hanlan's Point, was where Babe Ruth, playing for the Providence Grays on September 5, 1914, swatted his only minor league home run.

Maple Leaf owner Jack Kent Cooke promoted Toronto as a potential major league city as early as 1952, when the team drew 440,000 fans. But repeated efforts to build a new ballpark failed, undermining the Maple Leafs, who folded after attendance plunged to 67,000 in 1967.

Work began in 1974 to convert the Canadian National Exhibition grandstand into a baseball park — Exhibition Stadium — reviving the city's major league aspirations. The San Francisco Giants appeared to be headed for Toronto in January 1976 until a California group made a successful eleventh-hour bid to keep the National League team on the West Coast.

But two months later, Toronto's hopes came true. The American League voted to add two teams, awarding one franchise to a Canadian group that included LaBatt's Breweries. The

name "Blue Jays" was chosen in a contest that included 30,000 entries.

The early seasons may not have been very productive — the Blue Jays averaged 106 losses over their first three years — but they were never dull.

In 1977, Toronto was awarded a 9-0 forfeit win over Baltimore when Oriole Manager Earl Weaver took his team off the field at Exhibition Stadium because the Blue Jays refused to move a tarp in their bullpen. That same year, Toronto starter Jerry Garvin picked off 22 runners — impressive till you realize it means an awful lot of guys must have been reaching base.

Toronto's colorful cast included NBA star Danny Ainge, who spent three seasons with the Blue Jays before deciding it was easier to hit baskets than curveballs. The Blue Jays were a haven for castoffs like John Mayberry, Willie Aikens, Otto Velez and Cliff Johnson. When another, Rico Carty, asked for a three-year contract in 1979, General Manager Pat Gillick noted that Carty was 39 years old. "I don't mind paying a player," Gillick said. "But I don't want to pay for his funeral." Good move. Carty played one more season.

The most widely publicized event of the Blue Jays' fledgling years was also the silliest. Yankee outfielder Dave Winfield was warming up at Exhibition Stadium on August 4, 1983, when one of his throws beaned a scavenging seagull and nearly started an international incident. Not only did the fans take it as a personal affront, booing and throwing debris at Winfield, but after the game he had to post a $500 bond when police cited him for cruelty to animals. Only later, when the charge was dropped, did sanity prevail.

But people stopped laughing at the Blue Jays as their farm system began pumping out stars like Jesse Barfield, Lloyd Moseby, Tony Fernandez, Dave Stieb and Jimmy Key.

Two years after its first winning season, Toronto rolled up 99 victories in 1985 to win the A.L. East by two games over the Yankees. Bobby Cox was manager of the year, Gillick was executive of the year and the Blue Jays were baseball's new success story.

The euphoria was tempered, however, by Toronto's collapse in the American League playoffs against the Kansas City Royals, who rallied from a three games-to-one deficit, and the Blue Jays extended the disappointment in 1986 by skidding to fourth place.

George Bell was the league's Most Valuable Player in 1987, and Tom Henke led the league in saves, but the Blue Jays lost their last seven games to blow a 3 1/2-game lead and finish second behind the Detroit Tigers.

A slow start kept the Blue Jays from climbing any higher than third the next season, but a change of managers from Jimy Williams to Cito Gaston, the move into the SkyDome and the addition of sparkplug Mookie Wilson rallied them from a 10-game deficit in July to their second A.L. East title in 1989. Again, though, they came up short in the playoffs, losing to Oakland in five games.

They went into the 1990 season the favorite in the A.L. East, but a summer-long duel with the Red Sox produced an 86-76 record, another frustrating second-place finish and a change in personnel.

Bell was allowed to sign with the Chicago Cubs as a free agent, and the Blue Jays traded Junior Felix for Devon White, and Tony Fernandez and Fred McGriff for Joe Carter and Roberto Alomar.

It's hard to tell how long fans will continue filling the SkyDome in hopes of seeing the Blue Jays capitalize on their talent and go all the way. Possibly their interest will wane once the techno-stadium loses some of its novelty. Or maybe these tribulations will only make their faith stronger.

There's a showbiz axiom that a performer should always leave the audience wanting more, but only a cynic would suggest that's what would be best for the Blue Jays.

Then again, it's worked for the Red Sox for more than 70 years.

George Bell

George Bell is now playing for the Chicago Cubs. But that doesn't change the fact that he's the best — and most enigmatic — player ever to wear a Toronto Blue Jay uniform.

Some call him hot-headed and thin-skinned, a man so sure he's misunderstood, unappreciated and discriminated against that it approaches paranoia.

Others say he's simply an intense, tough competitor, well-liked by his teammates and nothing less than a hero in his native Dominican Republic.

Just 31 years old, George Bell is the Blue Jays' career leader in home runs (202) and runs batted in (740). And he was zeroing in on Lloyd Moseby's marks for hits and doubles before he joined the Cubs as a free agent after the 1990 season.

In 1987, he put together one of the finest seasons in recent memory to become the only Blue Jay ever to win the American League Most Valuable Player Award.

He batted .308 and led the league with 134 RBIs. His 47 homers were not only a team record but also the most ever by any Latin player.

It was an impressive enough display that Gene Mauch, then manager of the California Angels, called him the most intimidating hitter in the league.

On April 4, 1988, Bell socked three home runs to set an Opening Day record; the next season, he put together a Toronto-record 22-game hitting streak.

Unhappily, the hard-hitting outfielder's accomplishments on the field have often been overshadowed by his reputation as one of baseball's bad boys.

George Bell

Detroit Tiger pitcher Walt Terrell once called him a dirty player and former Boston Red Sox first baseman Bill Buckner branded him a cheap-shot artist. Bell says he merely plays hard.

"I know I have a bad temper," Bell said a few years back. "But I never fight in the street. I never fight in a restaurant. When I'm in uniform, I'm different. I want to win. I think that's how you're supposed to play the game."

Still, Bell charged the mound and karate-kicked Boston pitcher Bruce Kison after being hit by a pitch in 1985. And he's been suspended at least three times for bumping or touching umpires.

He accused Toronto sportswriters of racism when they chose Dave Collins over him as the Blue Jays' player of the year in 1984. The next season, after several calls went against the Blue Jays in the American League playoffs, he called the umpires anti-Dominican and anti-Canadian, then said he'd been misquoted. In 1988, he walked off the field in protest of the Blue Jays' attempt to make him a full-time designated hitter.

If Bell's personality is hard to figure, his talent isn't. A Toronto scout spotted it in 1980 when Bell ripped dozens of balls out of a Dominican Republic stadium one day, and the Blue Jays drafted him from the Philadelphia Phillies for $25,000.

Four years later, Bell became a regular. In nine seasons in Toronto, he led the team five times in RBIs and three times in homers and hits. The 1990 season was his worst since 1984, but he still hit .269 with 21 homers and 86 RBIs.

Other Toronto players insist his swaggering, combative style is a response to some unhappy years in the minors and his first exposure to racial prejudice. Underneath that brusque exterior, they claim, the private George Bell is a popular, good-humored man who revels in clubhouse byplay.

There's another side, too, the side that remembers his roots. Bell still lives in San Pedro de Macoris and regularly helps the needy in the Dominican Republic, raising money and donating food and clothing.In the winter, he coaches and provides sports equipment to youngsters on the baseball-crazy island.

All he's lacking, contends former teammate Jesse Barfield, is a little better PR.

"George is misunderstood," said Barfield. "He's the type of guy you hate to play against but love to play with."

Canadian Baseball Hall of Fame and Museum(Ontario Place islands/complex, Pod 5). Hands-on displays, videos and batting cage. Open daily during the season.
Canada's Sports Hall of Fame (Exhibition Place, Lake Shore Blvd. W.) National sports museum displaying thousands of artifacts. Open daily.
The Hockey Hall of Fame (Exhibition Place, Lake Shore Blvd. W.) Home of the Stanley Cup. Open daily.

Top Attractions
Art Gallery of Ontario (Dundas St. W., 2 blocks west of University Ave.), CN Tower & Observation Deck (301 Front St. W.), McLaughlin Planetarium (100 Queen's Park), Metro Toronto Zoo (Highway 401 on Meadowvale Rd.), Ontario Science Centre (Don Mills Rd. and Eglinton Ave. E.), Royal Ontario Museum (100 Queen's Park).

Tourism Information
Metropolitan Toronto Convention and Visitors Bureau, 207 Queen's Quay West, Suite 509, PO Box 126, Toronto, Ontario, Canada M5J 1A7, 416-965-4008 (English) or 800-ONTARIO.

SkyDome
277 Front St. West
Seating: 50, 516
Surface: Artificial
First Game: June 5, 1989
LF: 328 CF: 400 RF: 328

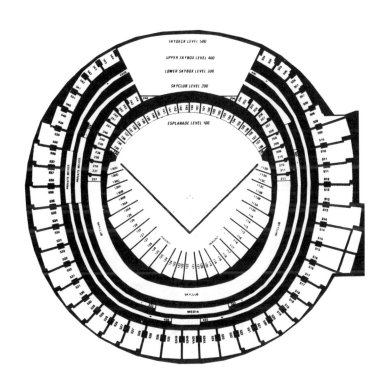

General Information
Toronto Blue Jays, SkyDome, 300 The Esplanade West, Box 3200, Toronto, Ontario, Canada M5V 3B3, 416-341-1000.
Getting Tickets
No tickets held back for day of game only sales. No standing room tickets sold.
By mail: Toronto Blue Jays Ticket Office, 300 Bremner Blvd., Suite 3200, SkyDome, Toronto, Ontario, Canada M5V 3B3. Checks, VISA, MasterCard and American Express accepted.
By phone: 416-341-1111 or 416-341-1234.
Ticket Prices
Esplanade Level 100 $17.50, Skyclub Level 200 $13.50, Upper Skybox Level 400 $10, Skydeck Level 500 $4.

Toughest Tickets To Get
Very difficult to get tickets to most series, particularly Boston.
Game Times
Sunday 1:35, 8:05. Weekdays 12:35, 1:35, 7:35. Fridays 7:35. Saturdays 1:15, 1:35, 3:15. Eastern time. Gates open 90 minutes before game.
Broadcasts
CJCL 1430 AM Radio, CFTO-TV.
Other Notes
Stadium tours: 416-341-2770.
Getting To The Stadium
At the base of the CN Tower, Harbour area, where Highway 11 intersects Highways 5 and 2. City and commercial parking available. Very accessible by subway.

73

Anaheim Stadium before it was en-closed in 1979

Oakland-Alameda County Coliseum

AMERICAN LEAGUE WEST

California Angels
Chicago White Sox
Kansas City Royals
Minnesota Twins
Oakland Athletics
Seattle Mariners
Texas Rangers

Anaheim Stadium is pure Southern California. You can get mixed drinks and oysters on the half shell — and put it all on your credit card.

The curse of the California Angels is that they play in the shadow of a team that's often regarded as the perfect major league baseball franchise.

The Angels are a perfectly fine ballclub. Over the past dozen seasons, they've won three American League West titles and drawn more than two million fans 11 times.

One former Angel, Rod Carew, is in the Hall of Fame and two others, Nolan Ryan and Reggie Jackson, are almost certainly headed there.

The Angels' owner, former singing cowboy Gene Autry, is one of the most respected figures in baseball. And they play in glorious, sunny Southern California.

But admit it. Can you think about the California Angels without also thinking about their neighbors up the highway, the Los Angeles Dodgers? Be honest now.

And don't you know the Angels just hate that? They've had success, but the Dodgers are like that perfect older brother you can never measure up to.

With 21 pennants and six world championships, the Dodgers are one of baseball's storied franchises, a team that in 1990 celebrated its 100th season in the National League. The Angels began play in 1961 as an expansion team. They've never won a pennant, much less a World Series.

The Dodgers have had but two managers since moving to California in 1958. The Angels have had twelve — thirteen if you count Gene Mauch's two terms separately.

Stylish Dodger Stadium is the standard for modern ballparks, and you could make a similar case for the Dodgers' classic blue-trim uniforms. The Angels prefer a cute heavenly motif. They used to sport a silver halo

California
Angels

The Angels often seem overshadowed by their neighbors in Chavez Ravine. But it's nothing a World Series wouldn't cure.

around the crown of their caps, and there's still a big one atop the old A-frame scoreboard outside Anaheim Stadium.

The Dodgers play in Los Angeles, the glamor and entertainment capital of the world. They've pulled in at least three million fans a major league-record eight seasons. The Angels, who've never outdrawn the Dodgers, play in Anaheim, the prototype L.A. suburb. Even today, it's best known as the home of Disneyland and Mickey Mouse.

California's second-class blues, of course, would be cured by a world championship or two. You can't say the Angels haven't tried. Every year, it seems, Autry ventures into the free agent market to add a big-name hitter or pitcher.

Only the New York Yankees have been busier. But whereas former Yankee owner George Steinbrenner got some bang for his bucks — Catfish Hunter, Reggie Jackson, Goose Gossage and others contributed to five A.L. East titles, four pennants and two world championships from 1976 to 1981 — Autry often came out firing blanks.

The Angels signed Bobby Grich, Joe Rudi and Don Baylor before the 1977 season. Grich and Rudi promptly got hurt and Baylor batted just .251, although he hit 25 home runs with 75 runs batted in. The Angels finished fifth.

Baylor and Grich bounced back in 1979 to lead California to its first A.L. West title, and Autry's signing of Reggie Jackson paid off in another division championship in 1982. But there were plenty of high-priced turkeys, like pitcher Geoff Zahn in 1981 and Ellis

Valentine in 1983. The most tragic free agent was Lyman Bostock Jr., who signed a big contract with the Angels in 1978, then was shot to death that season while riding in a car in Gary, Indiana.

If they still feel like poor relations, the Angels must find it all the more frustrating because success once looked like it would be so easy.

When the American League decided to expand for the 1961 season, Los Angeles, then the nation's third-largest city, was a logical choice. The Dodgers were already a big hit, and there seemed to be plenty of room for two teams.

Gene Autry hadn't planned on owning a baseball team. He had a Los Angeles radio station and went to the 1960 winter meetings hoping to get the broadcast rights for the new expansion team. But when Autry learned the league was having difficulty selling the franchise, he decided to buy it.

No expansion team has won sooner than the Angels, who finished a third-place 86-76 in 1962, just their second season. Of course, it would have been even better if the Dodgers hadn't gone 102-63.

In a nod to tradition, the fledgling ballclub was initially called the Los Angeles Angels, after the longtime Pacific Coast League franchise. The 1934 Angels, who won 137 games and lost just 50, are still considered one of the great minor league teams.

The new Angels, in fact, spent their first year in the old Angels' ballpark, tiny Wrigley Field, where they clubbed 126 homers but drew barely 600,000 fans. Attendance improved in 1962 when the Angels began a four-year stay in Dodger Stadium, but it was an uneasy tenancy marked by squabbles with landlord Walter O'Malley, the Dodgers' owner, over who should pay for such things as toilet paper and mowing the grass.

Autry was already eyeing the fast-growing Orange County suburbs south of Los Angeles and in 1966, one year after changing its name to the California Angels, the team moved down the freeway into $24 million Anaheim Stadium.

Although overshadowed by Dodger Stadium, the Big-A boasts one of the finest natural grass fields in baseball and its 64,593 seating capacity is second only to Cleveland's Municipal Stadium.

It's also pure Southern California — kind of the fern bar of ballparks. How many other stadiums offer shrimp cocktail, oysters on the half shell and crab salad, not to mention cocktail lounges and rolling bars stocked with liquor? And how many let you put it all on a credit card? Outside, BMWs, Volvos and Land Rovers dot the parking lot. If they don't remind you where you are, all the other cars cruising the nearby freeways will. There are two million people in Anaheim and surrounding Orange County, and most of them seem to be going somewhere.

When they come to the Big-A, they often see something different, even weird. Granted, the stadium hasn't been quite the same since the trademark Big-A scoreboard was moved to the parking lot several years ago. But people still talk fondly about 1984, when fans sailing tortillas from the upper deck like Frisbees became a seventh-inning ritual. It might still be the rage had not the city enacted a $1,000 fine for throwing food. And

what about 1976, when groundskeepers discovered marijuana plants growing wild in the outfield? Seems The Who had held a rock concert in the Big-A a few weeks earlier, and some of the crowd's leftovers took root amid the legal grass.

Maybe fans figured they needed such diversions to watch the Angels. After that surprising 1962 season, the reality of being an expansion team set in. California went a 71-91 in 1963 and enjoyed just three more winning seasons over the next 14 years.

There were some individual successes. After the Cincinnati Reds traded him to the Angels, surly Alex Johnson grumbled, "I'd rather play in hell than for the Angels." Then he went out and hit .329 in 1970 to become California's only batting champion. Don Baylor was the league's Most Valuable Player in 1979, Reggie Jackson tied for the 1982 home run title with 39 and Rod Carew had five straight .300 seasons from 1979 to 1983.

But most of the Angels' lasting heroics have occurred on the mound, as you might expect of a team that's already logged eight no-hitters in its brief history. The first was thrown in 1962 by a brash left hander named Bo Belinksy, who had an even greater talent for enjoying Hollywood's night life. "Happiness is a first-class pad, good wheels, an understanding manager and a little action," said Belinsky, who romanced B-movie queen Mamie Van Doren and married former Playmate of the Year Jo Collins.

Nolan Ryan, the best pitcher in Angel history, tossed an astonishing four no-hitters in eight seasons with California and led the league in strikeouts seven times. He and lefty Frank Tanana gave California probably the hardest-throwing tandem of the 1970s.

The finest single season by an Angel hurler came in 1964 when 23-year-old Dean Chance pitched 11 shutouts with a 20-9 record for a fifth-place team. Throw in a 1.65 earned run average, and you see why he won the Cy Young Award.

At the other end of the scale, Paul Foytack set a major league record by giving up four straight homers in a 1963 game, the last to a rookie named Larry Brown. "You may not believe this, but I was trying to knock him down with the pitch," Foytack said later. "That shows you what kind of control I had."

Good pitching or not, the Angels' most consistent trait has been disappointment. Despite Ryan and Tanana, California endured seven straight losing seasons from 1971 to 1977. The Angels, in fact, have never had more than two winning years in a row — and that's happened just twice.

Even their most successful seasons have ended in heartache. In 1979, the best-hitting team in California history scored nearly 5 1/2 runs a game to win the A.L. West but was easily eliminated by the Baltimore Orioles in the playoffs.

Three years later, the Angels won a team-record 93 games to give Gene Mauch his first division title in over 20 seasons of managing. Then, thanks to the Milwaukee Brewers' come-from-behind 4-3 victory in Game Five, California became the first team ever to lose a playoff series after winning the first two games.

Mauch took the Angels to a third A.L. West title in 1986, only to experience a nightmarish sense of *deja vu*. California was just one strike away from a playoff-clinching 3-2 victory over the Boston Red Sox in Game Five — until Dave Henderson socked a two-run homer off Angel reliever Donnie Moore. Henderson won the game with a sacrifice fly in the eleventh, also off Moore, and Boston rode that momentum to easy victories in the last two games. In a tragic epilogue, Moore shot himself to death in 1989. Some teammates said he never got over that homer to Henderson.

Since then, despite a farm system that's produced current stars like Chuck Finley, Bryan Harvey and Wally Joyner, the Angels have had just one winning season.

Manager Doug Rader has vowed to revitalize the team through trades and player development, and California did make deals in 1990 for veteran Dave Winfield and promising Junior Felix.

But the Angels also spent $16 million on free agent pitcher Mark Langston, only to watch him go 10-17 in 1990 as they finished a fourth-place 80-82. And after the Dodgers made headlines by adding free agents Darryl Strawberry, Brett Butler and Kevin Gross for the 1991 season, the Angels responded by giving a four-year $11.4 million contract to 32-year-old third baseman Gary Gaetti.

Even when you've been burned a few times, it's hard to break old habits.

Nolan Ryan

If the California Angels had gotten the man they really wanted from the New York Mets in 1971, life would have been a whole lot easier for American League hitters.

But the Mets refused to throw in promising pitcher Gary Gentry with three other players they were offering in trade for veteran California infielder Jim Fregosi.

So the Angels had to settle for another youngster. His name was Nolan Ryan.

"We knew Ryan was wild but had a sensational arm," said Harry Dalton, then the California general manager, "and we decided it was worth a shot."

That's how the Angels pulled off one of the most lopsided trades in baseball history and wound up with the greatest strikeout pitcher the game has ever seen.

Ryan, of course, now plies his trade with the Texas Rangers, and the indestructible right hander also spent nine of his 24 major league seasons with the Houston Astros.

In 1990, at the venerable age of 43, Ryan threw the sixth no-hitter of his amazing career — breaking his own major league record — and he won his 300th game.

If those two accomplishments don't make him a lock for the Hall of Fame, then his 5,308 career strikeouts — over 1,100 more than second-place Steve Carlton — should.

Ryan draws raves these days for his wondrous durability, something that's especially enjoyable because he's also one of baseball's nicest guys. His fastball is still clocked at well over 90 mph, he's led his league in strikeouts the last four years in a row and he's easily the oldest player ever to pitch a no-hitter.

But it was during his eight seasons with the California Angels, from 1972 to 1979, that the flamethrower from Alvin, Texas, posted most of the 40-plus major league records he still holds.

The Angels learned he was something special almost immediately when he went 19-16 with nine shutouts that first season, leading the American

Nolan Ryan

League with 329 strikeouts.

In 1973, everybody else caught on when he threw two no-hitters in two months and struck out a major league-record 383 batters en route to a 21-16 season.

The next season was almost a carbon copy: his third no-hitter, a league-best 367 strikouts and a 22-16 record — all for a team that went 68-94 and finished last in the A.L. West.

No-hitter No. 4 came in 1975, breaking Bob Feller's American League record and tying the major league mark set by Sandy Koufax in 1965.

From the beginning, the key to his success has rested in one word: speed. In 1974, Ryan's fastball was clocked at 100.9 mph. Even for fastball hitters, that's a little much.

"Every hitter likes fastballs, just like everybody likes ice cream," said one of the best, Reggie Jackson. "But you don't like it when somebody's stuffing it to you by the gallon."

While he was with the Angels, Ryan struck out 19 batters four times, 18 once and 17 on three occasions. In those eight seasons, he led the American League in strikeouts seven times. He also threw six one-hitters and 13 two-hitters.

Even now, 12 years after California let him sign with Houston as a free agent, Ryan is still the Angels' career leader in victories, strikeouts, shutouts, complete games and innings pitched.

Control used to be a problem — his 2,614 walks are also a major league record and he's led the league in that category eight times — but no more.

Critics also complain about Ryan's unspectacular .526 winning percentage, but it should be noted that he's pitched for very few good-hitting teams. Over 23 seasons, they've averaged fewer than four runs a game with an 82-80 annual won-loss record.

"My job is to give my team a chance to win," he once said. "I have no control over how many runs they score."

The record shows that Ryan has more than held up his end. Indeed, the most amazing thing about his career may be that he's never won a Cy Young Award.

But then, he's only 44.

Disneyland (1313 Harbor Blvd., 714-999-4565).
Knott's Berry Farm (8039 N. Beach Blvd., Buena Park, 714-220-5200).
Queen Mary and Spruce Goose (Pier J at Harbor Scenic Dr., Long Beach, 213-435-3511).

Tourism Information
Anaheim Area Convention and Visitors Bureau, 800 W. Katella Ave., Anaheim, CA 92802, 714-999-8999.

Discover the Californias, California Tourist Corp., 5757 W. Century Blvd., Los Angeles, CA 90045, 800-862-2543.

Anaheim Stadium
2000 State College Blvd.

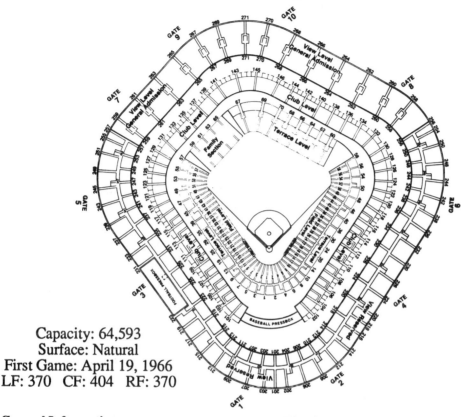

Capacity: 64,593
Surface: Natural
First Game: April 19, 1966
LF: 370 CF: 404 RF: 370

General Information
California Angels, PO Box 2000, Anaheim, CA 92803, 714-937-6700 or 213-625-1123.
Ticket Information: 714-634-2000.

Getting Tickets
General Admission tickets go on sale 90 minutes prior to the game.
Stadium box office: Gate 1, Monday - Saturday 9-5:30.
By mail: California Angels Baseball Club Ticket Office, PO Box 2000, Anaheim, CA 92803. Specify date, number of tickets and price (indicate preference of home, first base or third base). $4 postage and handling charge. Checks, MasterCard and VISA accepted. Orders received 7 days prior to game must be picked up at Paid Will Call window (Gate 1).
By FAX: 714-937-7246
By phone: Ticketron at 213-642-4242 (information) or 714-634-1300, 213-410-1062, 619-268-9686, Monday-Saturday 9-9, Sunday 10-8.

Ticket Prices
Field Box and Club Box $11, Terrace Seat $9, View Seat $7, Family Section (no alcohol) $6, General Admission $4.

Discounts & Promotions
Promotions scheduled for 20 games.

Toughest Tickets To Get
Oakland and New York

Game Times
Night games 7:00, 7:30. Sunday 1:00. Eastern time. Gates open 90 minutes before game.

Broadcasts
KMPC 710 AM, KTLA TV (5).

Other Notes
Original Big-A located in parking lot behind right field.
Stadium tours: 714-937-7333.
Catalog of souvenirs: ARA, PO Box 2000, Anaheim, CA 92803.

Getting To The Stadium
Located at intersection of Katella with Santa Ana (I-5) and Orange (57) Freeways. Parking around stadium (15,000 spaces).

Although new Comiskey Park is up to date in every way, stadium designers have tried to capture some of its predecessor's old-style flair.

It has the same name and it's just about in the same place, but today's Comiskey Park bears little resemblance to the landmark that stood at 35th and Shields for 80 years.

The new home of the Chicago White Sox is a sleek $120 million stadium that seats 43,000 fans, none of whom are likely to miss the view-obstructing metal poles of the old park.

The fences are a little closer, the grass is cut shorter and home plate faces southeast instead of northeast, all of which makes it friendlier to hitters.

And even the pitchers should like new Comiskey's roomy clubhouses and a modern drainage system that makes the old ballpark's treacherous field just an unpleasant memory.

It's a wonderful park, the major leagues' first new baseball-only stadium in nearly 20 years, and a worthy successor to what was once called "The Baseball Palace of the World."

But die-hard White Sox fans and other traditionalists will be happy to know that even though old Comiskey has been demolished, a special part of it lives on.

Shortly after the final game in the ancient ballpark on September 30, 1990, workers dug up the infield dirt, carted it across the street and put it down in the new stadium.

Yes, the White Sox's shiny new residence couldn't be more up to date. But at its heart, the same clay upon which Nellie Fox and Luis Aparicio turned double plays three decades ago provides a comforting link to the past.

Why not? To be sure, old Comiskey was creaky, dark and dreary, chock full of terrible seats, and plagued by a nightmarish combination of cold winds and soggy turf. And at the end, it was crumbling.

Chicago
White Sox

Old Comiskey Park was creaky, dark and dreary. It had bad seats and nightmarish playing conditions. But White Sox fans will be happy to know a special part of it lives on.

But the historic park on the tough South Side also was as much a part of Chicago's burly heritage as rigged elections and gangland wars. Today, Chicago is the country's third-largest city, with a metropolitan area of more than eight million people. It's vibrant, prosperous and sophisticated, a city whose attractions include landmark skycrapers, busy shopping districts and cultural highlights. The John Hancock Building, the Merchandise Mart and the Chicago Symphony are Windy City trademarks.

Old Comiskey Park, however, harkened back to Chicago's blue-collar roots. Wrigley Field is quaint. Comiskey was rugged, a working man's ballpark, just about perfect for the "City of the Big Shoulders." Carl Sandburg must have loved it.

Old Comiskey — to many fans, it'll always be the only Comiskey — also hosted most of the key events in White Sox history, which is as colorful as any in baseball.

The "Black Sox" of 1919, the only team to throw a World Series, played there. Babe Ruth liked the park because he could slip across the street to McCuddy's bar for a cold one between innings. Comiskey was the site of the first All-Star Game, a 4-2 American League victory in 1933. And Larry Doby of the Cleveland Indians became the league's first black player when he pinch hit at Comiskey on July 5, 1947.

There have been marathon games. The longest in American League history lasted two days, going 25 innings before the White Sox beat the Milwaukee Brewers 5-4 on May 10, 1984. And aborted ones. Chicago forfeited a 1925 game to Cleveland when an overflow crowd stormed the field before

the contest was over. The same thing happened in 1979 after rowdy fans tore up the turf during Bill Veeck's Disco Demolition Night stunt between games of a double header.

The raucous "Na-na-na-na, hey-hey-hey" taunt that's now a sports fixture was born in Comiskey in the 1970s. And the park was renowned for both baseball's best food and its top organist, clever Nancy Faust.

Some fine teams have graced the South Side. The White Sox's five pennants include the American League's very first in 1901, when they played in South Side Park. They've also won two World Series.

The 1990 squad, although falling short of those achievements, nevertheless ushered the old ballpark out in style by finishing a surprising second in the A.L. West. Buoyed by Bobby Thigpen's major league-record 57 saves, the White Sox went 94-68, the franchise's second-best record in 25 years.

Playing in a hitter's park will be a dramatic change for the White Sox, whose reliance on pitching, speed and defense has often reached extremes. They were the first American League team to be no-hit for nine innings, by Cleveland's Earl Moore on May 9, 1901, although they won 1-0 on a tenth-inning hit. Curiously, they pulled off the same feat last July 1, 1990, using four unearned runs to beat the New York Yankees' Andy Hawkins 4-0, even though he held them hitless.

The 1906 White Sox were so feeble at the plate they were called "The Hitless Wonders." But despite hitting just seven homers all year, they upset the powerful Chicago Cubs in the World Series in six games. That had to be sweet for owner Charles Comiskey, who had improvised on the Cubs' old name, White Stockings, to gain acceptance in the Chicago.

The first White Sox star was Ed Walsh, the game's first great spitball pitcher. Walsh's career 1.82 earned run average is the lowest in major league history. In 1908, he went 40-16 with a league-record 464 innings.

Appropriately, Chicago also had the American League's last legal spitballer. Red Faber, a Hall of Famer like Walsh, beat the New York Giants three times in the 1917 World Series. But the White Sox's top pitcher that season was Eddie Cicotte, who went 28-12 with a 1.53 ERA. That team, which won 100 games, was probably the franchise's best club. It also was the only one ever to bring a championship to Comiskey Park, which opened in 1910.

But it shouldn't have been. The White Sox, with slugger Joe Jackson leading a rare good-hitting lineup, were heavy favorites over the Cincinnati Reds in the 1919 World Series. But eight players, including Jackson and Cicotte, agreed to throw the series in a deal with gamblers. All eight "Black Sox" were thrown out of baseball when the scandal became public the next year, and it devastated the team. The White Sox spent the next 15 years in the second division; it was four decades until their next pennant.

Yankee Manager Joe McCarthy said Ted Lyons would have won 400 games in New York. Instead, Lyons, a crowd favorite, pitched his entire career for mediocre-to-bad White Sox teams. He still won 260 from 1923 to 1946 and is in the Hall of Fame. So is Luke Appling, a shortstop who hit .388 in 1936

and .328 in 1943 to win the White Sox's only two American League batting titles. Nicknamed "Old Aches and Pains" because of his career-long hypochondria, Appling nevertheless played 20 years, all for Chicago.

The White Sox, also known as the Pale Hose and Chisox, are big on nicknames. After stealing a league-high 99 bases in 1951, they were promptly tagged the "Go-Go Sox."

They also began a string of 17 winning seasons, peaking in 1959 with their fourth pennant. Again, the speedy White Sox were a team that usually scratched. Scrappy second baseman Nellie Fox was the league's Most Valuable Player and 39-year-old Early Wynn, with a 22-10 record, won the Cy Young Award. Wynn threw one of the team's two shutouts against the Los Angeles Dodgers in Chicago's last World Series to date, but the White Sox lost in six games.

Showman Bill Veeck bought the team in 1958 and got everyone's attention by installing an exploding scoreboard and putting players' names on uniforms. Pitching and Luis Aparicio's base stealing kept the White Sox in the hunt through most of the next decade, but they had only two winning teams from 1968 to 1980. Attendance slipped enough that there was talk of moving to Milwaukee, and the White Sox did play some games there in 1968 and 1969.

Veeck, who had sold the club because of poor health in 1961, bought it again in 1975 to save it from being moved to Seattle. Again he left his mark. The previous owners had changed the stadium's name to White Sox Park and installed artificial turf in the infield, but Veeck restored both its original name and its grass. He also put a shower for fans in the bleachers and decked out his players in old-style uniforms with collars. In one 1976 game, they even played in shorts. Harry Caray was broadcasting for the White Sox when Veeck convinced him to first sing *Take Me Out to the Ballgame* to the crowd in 1976.

Still, only one Veeck team, the powerful 1977 club called the "South Side Hitmen," won more games than it

Bill Veeck's exploding scoreboard dominated old Comiskey Park.

lost, and he sold the club once more in 1981, this time for financial reasons.

Two years later, however, the White Sox raced to a 99-63 record, winning the A.L. West by a major league-record 20 games and drawing two million fans for the first time. Four players slugged more than 20 homers and LaMarr Hoyt, one of two Chicago 20-game winners, won the Cy Young Award. But the league's highest-scoring team managed just three runs against the Baltimore Orioles in the American League playoffs and lost in four games.

The current owners, Jerry Reinsdorf and Eddie Einhorn, pumped much-needed money into the White Sox, streamlined the team's image and forced construction of the new stadium. But even their tenure has included flashes of wackiness. How else to explain the muddle-headed hiring of broadcaster Ken Harrelson as general manager in 1985? And Veeck, who died in 1986, had to be smiling somewhere when White Sox infielder Steve Lyons absent-mindedly dropped his pants on national television during the 1990 season.

The modern ballpark marks a new beginning for the White Sox — but thankfully, team officials have not turned their backs on the club's lively past.

New Comiskey also has an exploding scoreboard. And the White Sox's new uniforms bear a heartening resemblance to those worn by the Go-Go Sox of 1959.

Joe Jackson

Baseball fans across the country couldn't believe it, didn't want to believe it. Eight members of the Chicago White Sox had made a deal with gamblers to throw the 1919 World Series.

Knuckleballer Eddie Cicotte was one of the top pitchers in the American League. So was Lefty Williams. And Buck Weaver had become the game's best third baseman.

But now they were heroes-turned-villains, a group derisively called the "Black Sox," banned from baseball for deliberately losing to the Cincinnati Reds.

None of the eight shocked or sad-dened the country more than Shoeless Joe Jackson, the No. 1 player on what had been considered the game's No. 1 team.

A great hitter, outfielder and baserunner, Joe Jackson may have been the most gifted man ever to play the game. He also was one of the dumbest or crookedest.

Joseph Jefferson Jackson batted .356 over 13 seasons, a lifetime average bettered by just two players, Ty Cobb and Rogers Hornsby. He hit .408 in 1911, his first full season, and .370 or better four other times.

He was good enough to be a model for Babe Ruth. "I decided to pick out the greatest hitter to watch," said Ruth, "and Jackson was good enough for me."

Speed? In 1912, Jackson became the first American Leaguer to steal home twice in one game. Defense? He could whip the ball to home plate on the fly and covered so much ground that his glove was called "the place triples go to die." Cobb once called him the best left fielder of all time.

Proud accomplishments for a South Carolina country boy who couldn't read or write. Jackson was playing ball on a semi-pro mill team before he was 14; he got his nickname in the minors after playing one game barefoot because his new spikes gave him blisters.

Two appearances with the Philadelphia Athletics were cut short because of homesickness, but Jackson blossomed after being sold to the Cleveland Indians in 1910. Fans, other players, even some teammates taunted him because of his illiteracy and his southern drawl. He answered at the plate with

Joe Jackson

Black Betsy, his huge 48-ounce bat. At one time or another before the Indians traded him to the White Sox in 1915, he led the league in hits, doubles, triples and slugging.

"I ain't afraid to tell the world that it don't take school stuff to help a fellow play ball," he said.

Then Jackson threw it all away. Approached by others on the team who, like Jackson, were fed up with tightfisted Chicago owner Charles Comiskey, he agreed to help throw the 1919 series.

Whether he actually took part in the fix is open to debate. He told a grand jury that he did, but he later recanted. And no Chicago player had a better series than Jackson, who hit .375 on a series-record 12 hits, drove in six runs, scored five and threw the tying run out at the plate in Game Six.

But certainly he knew about the conspiracy. He asked to be benched before the series began, pleading illness. And he admitted taking $5,000 in fix money from Lefty Williams.

That was enough for Judge Kenesaw Mountain Landis, the tough baseball commissioner who had been hired because of the scandal. Even though Jackson and the other seven players were acquitted in court — largely because several confessions mysteriously disappeared — Landis nevertheless barred them from the game for life.

Although his fans were dismayed, Jackson, 33 at the time, was hardly destroyed by the ban. He won a settlement on $18,000 in back salary, then capitalized on his celebrity by playing in very profitable semi-pro games for several years. He also had a liquor store and a prosperous dry cleaning business.

Still Jackson was a proud man. And when he went to his grave in 1951, it was with the painful knowledge that he was the best player to never make the Hall of Fame.

Field of Dreams (US 136 and US 20, Dyersville, Iowa). From the 1989 movie, light posts, field, farmhouse and corn rows where Kevin Costner watched the Chicago "Black Sox" play. Playing on field allowed. No admission charge. Free maps to the site are available from local businesses or by contacting Dyersville Area Chamber of Commerce, PO Box 187, Dyersville, IA 52040, 319-875-2311.

Chicago Attractions
See information in Chicago Cubs chapter.

Tourism Information
Chicago Convention and Visitors Bureau, McCormick Place, Chicago, IL 60616, 312-567-8500
Illinois Office of Tourism, 310 S. Michigan Ave., Suite 108, Chicago, IL 60604, 312-793-2094 or 800-223-0121.

Comiskey Park
35th and Shields Sts.

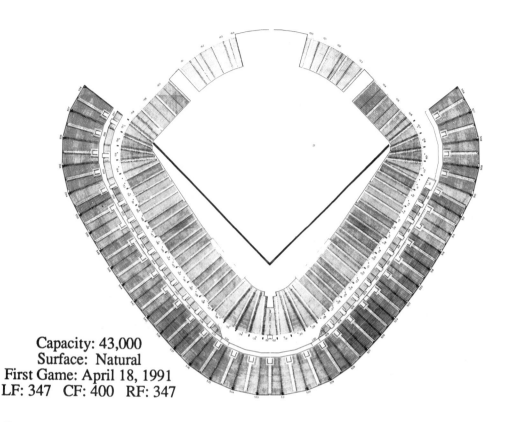

Capacity: 43,000
Surface: Natural
First Game: April 18, 1991
LF: 347   CF: 400   RF: 347

General Information
Chicago White Sox, 333 W. 35th St., Chicago, IL 60616, 312-924-1000.
Getting Tickets
Stadium box office: Weekdays 10-6, weekends 10-4, game days 9-9.
By mail: Chicago White Sox Ticket Office, 333 W. 35th St., Chicago, IL 60616. Specify game date, number of tickets, price and location preference (first base/right field or third base/left field). $3 handling fee.
By phone: Ticketmaster at 312-559-1212.
American Express, MasterCard or Visa accepted. Credit card purchases accepted until 3 hours prior to game time. Tickets mailed or held at Ticketmaster "will call" window. Per ticket convenience charge.
Ticket Prices
Club Level $16, Lower Deck Box $13, Upper Deck Box $11, Lower Deck Reserved $9, Upper Deck Reserved $8, Bleachers $6.
Discounts & Promotions
Promotions scheduled for over half of the games.

Toughest Tickets To Get
Oakland and Boston.
Game Times
Monday-Friday day games 12:05, night games 7:05. Saturday 6:05. Sunday 1:35. Central time. Gates open 2 hours before game.
Broadcasts
WMAQ 67 AM, WGN TV (9).
Other Notes
White Sox Hall of Fame (main concourse behind home plate). "Kids Corner" (play and concession area) in stadium.
Tours start in June.
Souvenirs: Sportservice Corporation, White Sox Park, 324 West 35th St., Chicago, IL 60616. 312-285-3411. Monday - Friday 10-4.
Getting To The Stadium
South of the Loop area. Exit from Dan Ryan Expressway (I-90/94) just south of I-55 intersection. Parking across from stadium (7,000 spaces). Accessible by subway.

Royals Stadium sits side by side with football's Arrowhead Stadium (upper right) as part of the one-of-a-kind Harry S Truman Sports Complex.

A sure way to make someone from Kansas City hot under the collar is to ask just how long the streets in the one-time cowtown have been paved.

Yes, the annual American Royal Livestock Show and Rodeo and the Future Farmers of America Convention proudly carry on the city's home-on-the-range tradition.

But everything really is up to date in this metropolis on the Missouri River, even though it remains a major grain and livestock center.

There's the elegant Country Club Plaza, touted as the nation's first shopping center when it was built in 1920. And the William Rockhill Nelson Gallery of Art. And the myriad water displays that have earned it the name "City of Fountains." Hallmark Cards sends its pleasant greetings from Kansas City, and U.S. Sprint, Russell Stover Candies and Marion Laboratories call it home as well.

However, there are few things Kansas Citians are more proud of than their Royals — the winningest expansion team in major league history — and gleaming Royals Stadium.

Anchored by future Hall of Famer George Brett for most of their existence, the Royals have won one World Series, two American League pennants and six A.L. West titles since their debut in 1969.

A town that still recalls the bumbling Kansas City Athletics can even forgive the Royals for a rare flop like 1990, when they finished 75-86, their worst record in 20 years.

Except for the strike-split 1981 season, the Royals have dropped below fourth just twice. With 1,821 victories and 1,673 losses through 1990, they are the only expansion team with a winning overall record. Indeed, in the

Kansas City
Royals

There are few things that Kansas Citians are more proud of than their Royals, the winningest expansion team in baseball, and gleaming Royals Stadium.

Royals' 22-year history, only the Oakland A's have won more games in the A.L. West.

Throw in Royals Stadium, with its 12-story scoreboard and one-of-a-kind water display, and it's easy to see why the Royals have drawn more than two million fans a year 10 times since 1978. It's a far-flung following, too. Their radio network includes more than 130 stations in 12 states.

But the Royals are just the latest chapter in Kansas City's baseball history, which dates back to the days when cattle really did wander some of its streets. In 1886, the city's first and only National League team — the Cowboys, believe it or not — finished 58 1/2 games out of first, establishing a precedent unhappily followed by a lot of Kansas City ballclubs.

K.C. also fielded distant also-rans with the Blues in the old American Association in 1888-89, the Packers in the short-lived Federal League in 1914-15 and the Athletics in the American League from 1955 to 1967.

There were some winners. Hall of Famers Satchel Paige, Jackie Robinson and Ernie Banks, as well as about two dozen other major leaguers, first played for the Kansas City Monarchs, a powerhouse in the old Negro leagues for four decades. And the 1953 Kansas City Blues, with Bill Skowron, Elston Howard, Vic Power and Bob Cerv, are still considered one of the best-hitting minor league teams of all time.

The Blues were a New York Yankee farm club, and some say things didn't change much after the Athletics moved to town from Philadelphia in 1955 — except that the Blues had won.

After 13 seasons that produced an identical number of losing records, un-derstandably poor attendance prompted the A's to flee west to Oakland before the 1968 season.

Kansas City's baseball hiatus was brief, however. Pressure from U.S. Senator Stuart Symington of Missouri prompted the American League to award an expansion franchise to local pharmaceutical magnate Ewing Kauffman, and the Royals were born.

From the beginning, they were as efficient as the A's had been inept. On April 8, 1969, the Royals won the first game they ever played, 4-3 over the Minnesota Twins in Municipal Stadium, a revamped minor league park that had been built in 1923.

Royals Stadium opened in 1973, and Kansas City, emphasizing speed and pitching to take advantage of the big ballpark, has usually been in contention ever since.

Shrewd trades put Lou Piniella, Amos Otis, Hal McRae, Cookie Rojas, Fred Patek and John Mayberry in Royal uniforms. The farm system spawned George Brett, Willie Wilson, Steve Busby, Paul Splittorff, Dennis Leonard and Dan Quisenberry. And Kauffman's experimental Royals Academy produced Frank White.

Some say the best K.C. team was the 1977 squad that won 102 games and the second of three straight A.L. West titles under Manager Whitey Herzog. There's also some sentiment for the '80 Royals, mostly because they finally beat the hated Yankees in the American League playoffs. After that, losing the World Series to the Philadelphia Phillies was almost anti-climactic.

But no team is dearer to Kansas City fans than the 1985 Royals, classic underdogs who won the division by a game, then surprised the Toronto Blue Jays in the playoffs to set up an all-Missouri World Series with the St. Louis Cardinals.

As against the Blue Jays, the Royals fell behind the Cards three games to one before rallying, this time with the help of one of the most controversial plays in Series history.

In Game Six, St. Louis led 1-0 in the ninth — three outs away from a world championship — when umpire Don Denkinger declared the Royals' Jorge Orta safe at first on a groundball. Television replays showed the call was wrong, and the outraged Cards never recovered. Moments later, first baseman Jack Clark allowed a catchable pop foul to drop safely, then catcher Darrell Porter's passed ball put the winning run in scoring position for Dane Iorg's pinch-hit single that gave K.C. a 2-1 victory. The next night, the Royals put the Cards away 11-0 to claim their only World Series crown.

Think of the Kansas City Royals, and you think of George Brett, a man Whitey Herzog said could climb out of bed on Christmas Day and get a hit. It's almost impossible to imagine the 13-time All-Star in any uniform other than the Royals' blue and white.

But there was also pitcher Steve Busby, who threw two no-hitters before a shoulder injury cut short his career. Relief ace Dan Quisenberry led the American League or tied for the lead in saves five times. Hal McRae was the best designated hitter in baseball for most of a decade, narrowly losing the batting title to Brett in 1976. Willie Wilson won the 1982 batting championship, the only Royal other than Brett to do so. Second baseman Frank White claimed eight

Gold Gloves; center fielder Amos Otis won three.

Such has been their success that even in 1990 the Royals, although playing in one the major leagues' smallest cities, drew 2.2 million fans.

But if you said Royals Stadium is as big an attraction as the team that plays there, you might be right. Some claim it's the best ballpark in baseball.

First, there's the scoreboard, the back of which forms a gigantic Royals crest that looms over traffic on nearby Interstate 70. Its functions are simple compared to the pyrotechnics in other parks — there are no fireworks and the Royals only this season added a $5.5 million color video screen — but that fits the stadium's clean, classic style.

The other thing that catches your eye is the illuminated water spectacular that stretches 322 feet from center field to the Royals' bullpen in right. The waterfall and fountains may not seem traditional — Fred Patek and Cookie Rojas took a very untraditional leap into the water display to celebrate the Royals' 1976 A.L. West title — but they're as distinctive as Wrigley Field's ivy.

Make no mistake, Royals Stadium is a baseball park and only a baseball park. Kansas City fans have been called a bit taciturn, but they showed their enthusiasm in 1967 by approving separate stadiums for the Royals and the Kansas City Chiefs of the National Football League. That's why, in an arrangement like no other in sports, Royals Stadium sits side-by-side with the Chiefs' Arrowhead Stadium in the Harry S Truman Sports Complex.

Royals Stadium has the obligatory luxury suites and a semi-formal restaurant. But its designers made good

Royals Stadium

on the basics, too. Every one of its 40,625 seats is positioned to watch a baseball game, and there's not a poor view in the house.

About the only knock on Royals Stadium comes from purists who claim the artificial turf keeps it from being a perfect ballpark. But when many of your fans come in from Iowa and Nebraska and Oklahoma, you want to be sure they'll see a game. And the turf has helped the Royals average just two rainouts a season since the stadium opened 18 years ago.

For Kansas City fans, of course, the entire 1990 season was a washout. Free agent pitchers Mark Davis and Storm Davis fizzled, and after the Royals' sixth-place finish, General Manager John Schuerholz sought new employment with the Atlanta Braves.

Injuries limited starters Bret Saberhagen and Mark Gubicza, who had combined for 38 victories in 1989, to a mere nine and forced the Royals to use a league-high 23 pitchers. About the only bright spot was veteran George Brett, who rebounded from a dismal start to hit .329 and win his third American League batting title.

But don't be surprised if the Royals, still the only major league team that's never finished last, come back strong.

Saberhagen, who won Cy Young awards in 1985 and 1989, Gubicza, Tom Gordon, Kevin Appier and free agent acquisition Mike Boddicker make up one of baseball's top starting rotations.

The Royals stunned the baseball world when they released Bo Jackson before the 1991 season because of an injury he suffered while playing football for the Los Angeles Raiders. Jackson, who hit homers, stole bases and struck out with equal flair, may have been the most exciting player in either league; with his myriad TV commercials, he was certainly the most visible.

But Bo never led Kansas City to a pennant, and the Royals seem confidant they'll survive his loss. Hal McRae's son, Brian, is a promising newcomer and a solid complement to steady Jim Eisenreich and hard hitting Danny Tartabull in the outfield. And free agent Kirk Gibson should add a competitive spark.

Talent is a hard thing to keep down, especially when it's combined with tradition.

And part of the Royals' history is that they bounce back. It's been 21 years since the pride of Kansas City has had back-to-back losing records. Odds are they'll make it 22.

George Brett

When George Brett hit .125 after the Kansas City Royals called him up from their Omaha farm club in 1973, he hardly looked like a player destined for Cooperstown.

But Brett, just two years out of high school in El Segundo, California, wasn't thinking about that. He was happy just to be in Kansas City.

"I never thought when I first signed my contract out of high school in '71 that I'd make it to the major leagues," Brett said years later.

"I mean, every kid wants to be a major league baseball player, but in reality, can they be? ... I was going to play five years in the minors, and if I didn't make it, I was going to quit."

But the Royals saw something they liked, and after they traded third baseman Paul Schaal to the California Angels in 1974, Brett was in the big leagues to stay.

Now it's difficult to remember when the 13-time American League All-Star with the sweet left-handed swing wasn't in the middle of the Kansas City lineup.

George Brett is the Kansas City Royals. He's been at the core of every significant thing that's happened to them during his 18-year career.

He was the first Kansas City player to win a batting title, bouncing a controversial inside-the-park homer over Minnesota Twins outfielder Steve Brye on the last day of the 1976 season to slip past Royal teammate Hal McRae.

His second batting crown was even more dramatic. After flirting with the .400 mark for most of the 1980 season,

George Brett

Brett finished at .390, the highest average since Ted Williams hit .406 in 1941.

In 1990, he did it the other way, hitting almost .400 over the last three months to overcome a wretched start and finish at .329. That made him, at age 37, the third-oldest player ever to win a batting title and the first to win one in three different decades.

"George Brett could get good wood on an aspirin," said Jim Frye, who managed the Royals in 1980 and 1981.

Brett has always credited Charley

Lau, the Royals' late hitting coach, for his success. But Brett's impeccable sense of timing is something that can't be taught.

In 1978, he slammed three home runs off the New York Yankees' Catfish Hunter in an American League playoff game. Two years later, his three-run shot off Goose Gossage helped the Royals sweep the Yanks for their first pennant.

Injuries have cost the third baseman-turned-first baseman more than 300 games over his career. He's always been there for the big ones, though, hitting .337 with 10 homers and 23 RBIs in 43 playoff and World Series games.

In 1980, when fans feared hemorrhoids would keep him out of the World Series, Brett showed up at the ballpark and said with a grin: "All my problems are behind me."

Even now, a good part of Brett's appeal is his boyish charm. People still chuckle over the night he turned the tables on Morganna, the "Kissing Bandit," by dashing on stage during her act at a Kansas City burlesque house and giving her a kiss.

Still, it's Brett the competitor that fans will remember. Who can forget the crazed look on his face as he charged out of the dugout after the "pine tar" ruling that briefly disallowed his homer against the Yankees in 1983?

The Kansas City veteran has talked about 1991 perhaps being his final season, but don't bet on it. Two more good years, and he'll have 3,000 hits.

Then he'll have a real good reason to think about that trip to Cooperstown.

Negro Leagues Baseball Museum (1601 E. 18th St., 816-221-1920). Photographs, uniforms, other memorabilia. Temporary office; museum under development.

NCAA Visitors Center (6201 College Blvd., Overland Park, 913-339-0000). Permanent and changing photographic displays representing 21 intercollegiate sports. Weekdays 10-7, Saturday 10-6, Sunday 10-5.

Top Attractions
Country Club Plaza (Main and 47th St. area, 816-753-0100), Crown Center (Grand and Pershing, 816-274-8444), Kansas City Museum (3218 Gladstone Blvd., 816-483-8300), Kansas City Zoo (Swope Park, 816-333-7406), Nelson-Atkins Museum of Art (4525 Oak St., 816-561-4000), Thomas Hart Benton Home (3616 Bellview, 816-931-5722), Harry S Truman Library & Museum (24 Highway and Delaware St., Independence, 816-833-1225), Worlds of Fun (816-454-4444) and Oceans of Fun (816-459-WAVE).

Tourism Information
Convention & Visitors Bureau of Greater Kansas City, City Center Square, 1100 Main St., Suite 2550, Kansas City, MO 64105, 816-221-5242 or 800-523-5953 (outside MO).
Missouri Division of Tourism, Truman State Office Building, PO Box 1055, Jefferson City, MO 65102, 314-751-4133.

Royals Stadium
1 Royal Way

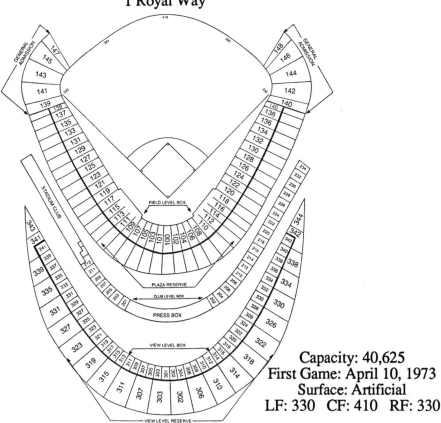

Capacity: 40,625
First Game: April 10, 1973
Surface: Artificial
LF: 330 CF: 410 RF: 330

General Information
Kansas City Royals, PO Box 1969, Kansas City, MO 64141, 816-921-2200.
Ticket information: 816-921-8000.
Fan Information Line: 816-921-8800.

Getting Tickets
General Admission tickets on sale 90 minutes before game at Gates C and D only (5,000 tickets).
By mail: Kansas City Royals, Ticket Office, PO Box 419969, Kansas City, MO 64141. Specify date, number of tickets and preferred location. Check or money order accepted. $2 handling charge.
By phone: 816-921-4400 or 800-422-1969 (outside Kansas City). Monday-Saturday 9-9, Sunday 9-6. Orders accepted 24 hours prior to a game. VISA, MasterCard, American Express and Discover Card accepted. $2 service charge per order.

Ticket Prices
Club box $11, Field box $10, View (upper) Box $8, Plaza Reserved $8, View (upper) Reserved $7, General Admission $4.

Discounts & Promotions
Monday and Thursday games View Level Reserve seats $3.50. Wednesday game autograph sessions 6:15-6:45. Promotions scheduled for 15 games (816-921-8000 for information).

Toughest Tickets To Get
New York, Oakland, Toronto and Boston.

Game Times
Sunday 1:35 , 7:35. Weeknights 7:35. Saturdays 12:15, 1:35, 7:05. Central time. Gates open approximately 90 minutes before game.

Broadcasts
KMBZ 980 AM Radio and WDAF-TV (4).

Other Notes
Royals Hall of Fame display (Plaza Reserve Level behind section 105). Stadium tours: 816-921-8000.

Getting To The Stadium
East of city on I-70 at Blue Ridge Cufoff (east of I-70 and I-435 intersection).
Royals-operated parking surrounding stadium.

Kansas City Athletics

Roger Maris triggered a lot of emotions when he slugged 61 home runs in 1961. Many were thrilled by the feat. Others were angry that he had dared to break Babe Ruth's record.

Followers of the lowly Kansas City Athletics were only wistful. To them, Roger Maris was a sad, perfect symbol of their team's chronic futility.

Two years earlier, Maris had been a dependable if not outstanding player for the A's, hitting 16 homers and with 72 runs batted in. But in late 1959, Kansas City swapped him and two other players to the New York Yankees for Hank Bauer, Norm Siebern, Marv Throneberry and Don Larsen.

Maris promptly won the American League's Most Valuable Player Award in 1960 and 1961, and the Yankees won five straight pennants, not to mention a couple of World Series.

The A's were a different story. During that same period, 1960 to 1964, they finished eighth, ninth, ninth, eighth and tenth. And some of those were among their better teams.

The Athletics spent 13 seasons in Kansas City after moving from Philadelphia in 1955, and did not have a winning record in any of them. They finished last five times and never climbed higher than sixth. Four teams lost 100 games or more.

One reason was curious trades like the one that sent Maris to New York and prompted critics to call the A's a Yankee farm club. Over the years, Kansas City also shipped Clete Boyer, Bobby Shantz, Art Ditmar, Ralph Terry and Hector Lopez to the Yanks.

Flamboyant Charles O. Finley bought the team in 1960, and if the Athletics didn't get any better, they did become more colorful. Finley draped them in green-and-gold uniforms in 1963, starting a gaudy fashion trend that's only recently calmed down. And for reasons never really explained, brightly colored sheep — real dyed-in-the-wool fans — nibbled grass on a hill in old Municipal Stadium just beyond the right-field fence. Behind the plate, a mechanical rabbit named Harvey popped out of the ground to deliver baseballs to the umpire.

With the Pennant Porch and the One-Half Pennant Porch, Finley tried to bring in the right-field fence and duplicate what he called Yankee Stadium's unfairly short 296-foot foul line. They made headlines, but the American League made him take them down.

Some highlights occurred on the field. Hall of Famer Early Wynn was in Municipal Stadium with the Indians in 1963 when he won the 300th — and final — game of his career.

Two years later, A's shortstop Campy Campaneris played all nine positions in one game. In another stunt, Finley brought back Satchel Paige, then 59 (maybe), to pitch against the Boston Red Sox. Paige tossed three shutout innings, perhaps not that surprising for a man who once said, "Age is a question of mind over matter. If you don't mind, it don't matter."

Finley's efforts even went beyond baseball. In September 1964, he pulled off a publicity coup by arranging for the Beatles to perform in Municipal Stadium as part of their first American tour.

Under Finley, the A's future began looking up with the signing of young players like Catfish Hunter, Blue Moon Odom, Rick Monday and Reggie Jackson.

But for years the Athletics' owner had feuded with city officials over the stadium lease, threatening to move the team to Louisville and Dallas, even nearby Peculiar, Missouri.

In 1967, bonds were approved for a new stadium, but it was too late. Both Finley and Kansas City had already had enough of each other.

The A's finished last, the fans stayed away and Finley moved the team west to Oakland. The next season, to no one's surprise, the A's posted their first winning record in 16 years.

Its soft translucent roof and ear-shattering acoustics give the Hubert H. Humphrey Metrodome an atmosphere like no other in baseball.

Baseball fans in Minnesota's Twin Cities have had plenty to cheer about since the old Washington Senators packed up and moved to the North Star State 30 years ago.

Rod Carew bagged seven American League batting titles in Minnesota. Another Hall of Famer, Harmon Killebrew, led or tied for the lead in home runs six times.

In 1969, Carew swiped home seven times, a major league record. Ken Landreaux once hit in 31 consecutive games. Versatile Cesar Tovar played all nine positions in a 1968 game.

But nothing in the history of the Minnesota Twins compares to what happened the night of October 25, 1987, in the clamorous confines of the Hubert H. Humphrey Metrodome.

When reliever Jeff Reardon came in to lock up a 4-2 victory over the St. Louis Cardinals, a long wait for the folks in Minneapolis and St. Paul was over. The Twins, after decades of good teams that just missed and others so bad that fans called them the "Twinkies," had won the World Series.

They were unlikely champions. Sure, they could hit and had upset the Detroit Tigers in the American League playoffs. But their pitching was awful and the lost tribes of Israel had a better road record.

St. Louis had won 95 games, 10 more than Minnesota, and the Cardinals' pitching and speed figured to be too much for the Twins. St. Louis Manager Whitey Herzog thought so. "They'd probably finish fourth in the National League East or the American League East," he said of the Twins.

But Minnesota had a big edge: four games in the Metrodome. And in that funny indoor ballpark with fake turf, a

Minnesota Twins

It will be a long time before fans in Minnesota forget 1987. It was a magic season in which the Twins made up for all the near misses and disappointments of the past.

giant shower curtain for a right-field wall, weird lighting and ear-splitting acoustics, the Twins, at 56-25, were the best team in baseball.

It was "Dome Sweet Dome" and St. Louis quickly found out why. In front of more than 55,000 Homer Hanky-waving fans, the Twins easily won the first two Series games. And after the Cardinals bounced back with three victories in St. Louis, the Dome worked its magic once more in Game Six as Minnesota rallied to an 11-5 victory.

St. Louis led again in the finale, 2-0, but by now the Cards must have realized this year belonged to the Twins. Kirby Puckett tied the game with a fifth-inning double, Greg Gagne's infield hit put Minnesota ahead in the sixth and Reardon set St. Louis down in order in the ninth. The Twins were the baseball champions of the world.

It was a triumph long overdue for Minneapolis and St. Paul, and just about the only one that had eluded them since baseball began in Minnesota more than a century earlier.

Today, the Twin Cities are a clean, bustling metropolis of nearly 2.5 million people, many of them ancestors of the Norwegians, Swedes, Finns and Germans who settled the region in the 1800s.

Minneapolis boasts myriad flour companies and the world's largest cash grain exchange, but it's more than an overgrown farm town. Businesses range from Honeywell to 3M to Northwest Airlines; the IDS Tower is the tallest building between Chicago and San Francisco. Culturally — and culture is a point of civic pride — there's the Walker Art Center and the Tyrone Guthrie Theater. The city's 153 parks include the falls that inspired Henry Wadsworth Longfellow's *The Song of Hiawatha.*

St. Paul, on the other side of the Mississippi River, has a strong New England feel that belies its original name, Pig's Eye. If Minneapolis is progressive, St. Paul reveres its past. The Minnesota state capital is more than a little proud of landmarks like the majestic Cathedral of St. Paul, Indian Mounds Park and nearby Fort Snelling.

Appropriately, St. Paul fielded the area's first major league baseball team. Also its shortest-lived one. The St. Paul White Caps played just eight games in the Union Association in 1884 before the league went broke.

From 1902 until the Twins came to town, the Twin Cities were represented by two very successful minor league ballclubs. The St. Paul Saints won nine American Association pennants, posting 115 victories in 1920. The 1910 Minneapolis Millers won 107 games. Minor league legend Joe Hauser slugged 69 homers for Minneapolis in 1933, and a fella named Willie Mays hit .477 with the Millers in 1951.

By the late 1950s, Minneapolis and St. Paul figured they were ready for major league baseball. Calvin Griffith, owner of the Washington Senators, agreed.

For nearly 60 years in the nation's capital, the Senators had struggled on the field and at the ticket gate, and Griffith was ready to move. He liked the Twin Cities' new Metropolitan Stadium, and he really liked the idea of playing in a virgin market hundreds of miles from other major league teams.

Congress, upset at the prospect of losing its hometown team, threatened to fight the move. But that ended when the American League agreed to replace the Senators with an expansion team, and in 1961 Minneapolis and St. Paul joined the majors.

An immediate question was what to call the new team. "Twins" was obvious, but Griffith didn't decide to incorporate the state's name until after the uniforms had been made. That's why his players took the field on Opening Day wearing caps that still bore the letters "TC" — for his first choice, Twin Cities Twins.

The change of scenery had an almost instant impact on the Twins. They finished second to the New York Yankees in 1962 with a 91-71 record, the franchise's best since 1933. Only twice over the next eight eight years did they finish lower than third.

The Twins always hit — 225 homers in 1963, 221 the next season — and sometimes they also had pitching. Muscular Harmon Killebrew was the heart of the offense, but he got lots of help from Bob Allison, Tony Oliva and Jimmy Hall. On the mound, Jim Kaat, Mudcat Grant, Dean Chance and Dave Boswell each won 20 games or more

once; Camilo Pascual and Jim Perry did it a couple of times.

Many people still say the 1965 Twins were the most talented team in Minnesota history. Grant and Kaat combined for 39 wins, shortstop Zoilo Versalles and Oliva finished one-two in Most Valuable Player voting, and the Twins cruised to their first pennant with a franchise-record 102 victories. Only Sandy Koufax's three-hitter in the seventh game of the World Series, which gave the Los Angeles Dodgers a 2-0 victory over the Twins, stopped it from being a perfect season.

Under new Manager Billy Martin, Minnesota was back four years later, winning the A.L. West as Killebrew bagged MVP honors with 49 homers and 140 RBIs. Jim Perry's 24-12 record in 1970 was good enough to win the Cy Young Award and lead the Twins to their second straight division title. The American League playoffs, however, were also a repeat. For the second straight year, the Baltimore Orioles swept Minnesota in three games.

But as Minnesotan Bob Dylan might

The Metrodome

say, the times they were a-changin'. The Twins slipped to fifth in 1971 and it was 13 years before they again finished higher than third. Attendance also nosedived, dropping to barely 660,000 in 1974.

Griffith wanted to blame Metropolitan Stadium, which had been built in 1956 in suburban Bloomington and could be pretty chilly during Minnesota's spring and fall. But even after the $55 million Metrodome opened in downtown Minneapolis in 1982, the Twins drew just 921,000.

The Metrodome is a strange stadium, and that's giving it the benefit of doubt. Name another ballpark where outfielders have to play flyballs off a huge sheet of plastic in right field and where the tent-like roof once caved because of heavy snow.

It used to be even stranger. The Metrodome's original turf was so spongy that soft line drives ricocheted over players' heads like Superballs. And poor lighting made it almost impossible to spot flyballs against the translucent fabric ceiling. Those shortcomings were corrected, but the Metrodome remains the noisiest stadium in the majors. And its ceiling is still just 180 feet above the field — low enough that Dave Kingman once hit a popup through a hole in it for a ground-rule double.

Still, the Twins' main problem was Griffith's refusal to accept the rising salaries caused by the free agent system. Minnesota standouts Bill Campbell, Larry Hisle, Lyman Bostock, Geoff Zahn and Dave Goltz fled to other teams for more money.

Griffith didn't help matters in 1978 when he told a civic group that he had moved the team to Minnesota "when I found out you only had 15,000 blacks here."

By 1984, the Minnesota owner had given up trying to compete with his free-spending competitors. He sold the team to Minneapolis banker Carl Pohlad. The Twins responded by finishing in a tie for second and drawing nearly 1.6 million fans.

Nobody, though, wore a bigger grin than Calvin Griffth when the Twins surprised everyone by beating the Cardinals in the World Series three years later.

He had drafted Kent Hrbek, Gary Gaetti and Kirby Puckett, and he'd traded for Tom Brunansky. In that magic 1987 season, each had at least 28 homers and 85 RBIs. Left-hander Frank Viola, the Twins' ace at 17-10 with a 2.90 earned run average, was another Griffith product. The old man may not have liked paying for talent, but he could always spot it.

The Twins were rewarded for their world championship the next season when they became the first American League team to draw more than three million fans.

Since then, however, pickings have been slim. The 1989 club slipped to fifth, and subpar years by virtually everybody in the lineup sent 1990's team into the cellar.

Can Minnesota expect to fare much better in the tough A.L. West in 1991? Maybe not. But Hrbek, Puckett and Dan Gladden still remain from that 1987 team, and newly acquired relief ace Steve Bedrosian and starter Jack Morris should bolster the pitching staff.

And it's not like the Twins haven't come back before. The 1986 club, after all, finished sixth.

Harmon Killebrew

Some ballplayers are just naturally colorful. They make clever jokes, date Hollywood starlets, get in nightclub brawls or simply play with a flair that's impossible to ignore.

Then there's Harmon Killebrew.

If they'd paid "The Killer" for personality, he'd have wound up on food stamps. He was quiet and modest, didn't smoke or drink and liked to relax — really — by washing dishes.

Killebrew also never hit for average and was a journeyman on defense. And despite debuting in the major leagues as a pinch-runner, he stole just 19 bases in 22 seasons.

But when Harmon Killebrew stepped into the batter's box, the one thing he did very well gave him all the charisma he needed. Five hundred seventy-three home runs' worth, to be exact.

A throwback to muscular sluggers like Jimmy Foxx and Hack Wilson, the burly, free-swinging Killebrew bashed 393 homers during the 1960s, more than Hank Aaron, Willie Mays or anybody else.

Eight times in a career spent almost entirely with the Washington Senators and the Minnesota Twins, he belted more than 40 homers. On four occasions, he led the American League in homers; in two other years, he shared the honor.

By the time he retired in 1975, Killebrew was the No. 1 right-handed home run hitter in American League history and trailed only Aaron, Babe Ruth, Mays and Frank Robinson on the all-time list.

Killebrew was a 17-year-old second baseman from Payette, Idaho, when the Senators, at the urging of U.S.

Harmon Killebrew

Senator Herman Welker of Idaho, signed him in 1954 for $4,000.

He spent most of his first five seasons on the bench or in the minors, but the Senators started him at third base in 1959 and he responded with 42 homers and 105 runs batted in.

He added 31 homers the next season while dividing his time between third and first, and had no trouble keeping up the barrage once the Senators moved to Minnesota in 1961.

Because of his so-so glove, Killebrew annually rotated from third to first to the outfield to make room for better fielders. Because of his bat, he was an All-Star at all three positions.

There was nothing fancy about his technique at the plate. A big-shouldered 5-feet-11 and 210 pounds, Killebrew simply believed in keeping his head down and taking a big swing.

"You can be an offensive hitter or you can be a defensive hitter," he once said. "When you become a defensive hitter, that's when you get in trouble."

Not surprisingly, The Killer struck out a lot, 1,699 times in all. But he also was patient enough to draw 1,559 walks — just about the only way to stop him when he was hot.

In 1962, he hit 11 homers in the final 11 games of the season. The next year, he socked seven in the last six. In 1964, he had 32 homers in just 10 weeks. All three years, he won the home run crown.

A torn hamstring muscle limited Killebrew in 1968, but he rebounded the next season with his finest performance, hitting 49 homers with 140 RBIs, both career highs, to win the American League's Most Valuable Player Award.

A friendly but private man, Killebrew never quite got used to the attention given to his power displays, even after he was elected to the Hall of Fame in 1984.

His wife, Elaine, once said there was a sure-fire way to tell when he had walloped another home run: "He always comes into the house looking sheepish."

Top Attractions
Foshay Tower (Minneapolis, 821 Marquette Ave., 612-341-2522), Minneapolis Institute of Arts (2400 3rd Ave. S., 612-870-3131), Minnesota Air Guard Museum (Minnesota/St. Paul International Airport, 612-725-5609), Minnesota Museum of Art (St. Paul, 305 St. Peter St., 612-292-4355), Minnesota Zoo (Apple Valley, 12101 Johnny Cake Ridge Rd., 612-432-9000), Science Museum of Minnesota (St. Paul, 30 E. 10th St., 612-221-9456), Stroh Brewery Company (St. Paul, 707 E. Minnehaha, 612-778-3275), Walker Art Center and Minneapolis Sculpture Garden (Vineland Place, 612-375-7600).

Tourism Information
Greater Minneapolis Convention & Visitors Association, 1219 Marquette Ave., Minneapolis, MN 55403, 612-348-4313 or 800-445-7412.

St. Paul Convention & Visitors Bureau, 600 North Central Tower, 445 Minnesota St., St. Paul, MN 55101, 612-297-6985 or 800-328-8322.

Minnesota Office of Tourism, 375 Jackson St., St. Paul, MN 55101, 612-296-5029 or 800-657-3700.

Hubert H. Humphrey Metrodome

900 S. 5th St., Minneapolis
Capacity: 55,883
Surface: Artificial
First Game: April 6, 1982
LF: 343   CF: 408   RF: 327

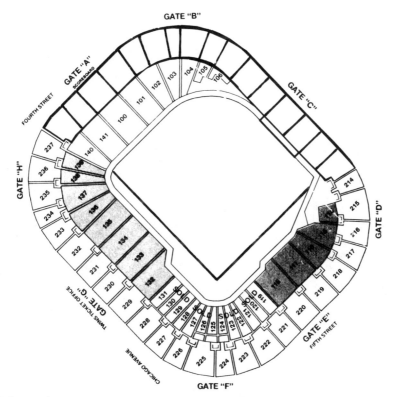

General Information
Minnesota Twins, The Metrodome, 501 Chicago Ave. S., Minneapolis, MN 55415.
General information: 612-375-7444.
Getting Tickets
By mail: Minnesota Twins Ticket Office, NW 8187, PO Box 66117, St. Paul, MN 55166. Indicate date, price (preferred location) and number of tickets. Check, money order, VISA, MasterCard accepted. $3 handling charge. Orders received 7 days prior to game must be picked up at the Will Call Window on the day of game.
By phone: 612-375-1116 or 800-THE-TWINS.
Ticket Prices
Club Level Reserved $13 (sold out), Lower Deck Reserved $11, Upper Deck Reserved $9, Lower Left Field General Admission $6, Upper Deck Outfield General Admission $3.

Discounts & Promotions
Special events scheduled for 17 games. Family Dates (all tickets reduced $1).
Toughest Tickets To Get
New York, Milwaukee and Oakland.
Game Times
Day games 12:15, 1:05. Night games 7:05, 7:35. Central time. Gate open 90 minutes before game, 2 hours before game for promotional events.
Broadcasts
WCCO 830 AM, WCCO TV (4) and KITN TV (29).
Other Notes
Stadium tours: 612-332-0386.
Getting To The Stadium
In downtown Minneapolis, near I-35W at Mississippi River (5th St. and Chicago Ave. S.). Commercial parking lots in area. Accessible by bus.

Critics have called the Oakland-Alameda County Coliseum a "concrete pillbox." But pitchers love the symmetrical ballpark, which has hosted seven no-hitters.

Until George Steinbrenner came along, Charles O. Finley was the most cantankerous man ever to operate a major league baseball team. He's still the most controversial.

He was arrogant, tyrannical and petty. He belittled his players in public and at the contract table. He fired managers as if he owned a pink slip factory.

He alienated fans in two cities, drove other owners to distraction with his boorish ways and conducted an open feud with the commissioner of baseball.

A decade has passed since Charlie Finley left baseball, but plenty of baseball people still rankle at the memory of his 20-year reign as owner of the Oakland Athletics.

That's why if he wants to get into the Hall of Fame any time soon, Finley is going to have to buy a ticket like everybody else.

But don't be surprised if his carnival barker's face winds up on a plaque in Cooperstown. And why not? Who's done more to spice up baseball in the last two decades?

Charlie Finley helped bring the designated hitter to the major leagues. The same with night World Series games. And brightly colored uniforms, white shoes, even mustaches.

Purists may argue the merits of these innovations — and they surely do — but it's hard to say they've hurt the game. Not when baseball attendance has nearly doubled since 1970.

Perhaps most galling to his many detractors is that Charlie Finley — tightwad, despot, mad scientist — also built the game's last great dynasty.

What about today's Athletics? Yep, they've won three American League pennants and a World Series since

Oakland
Athletics

Plenty of people still rankle at the memory of Charlie Finley's 20-year baseball escapade. But don't be surprised is he winds up in the Hall of Fame.

1988. Even with 1990's surprising loss to the Cincinnati Reds, they're the most imposing team in either league.

But they have a ways to go to match Finley's juggernaut, which swaggered its way to five A.L. West titles, three pennants and three World Series championships from 1971 to 1975.

Those A's of Reggie Jackson, Vida Blue and Catfish Hunter are still the last team to win three straight World Series. The only other team that's ever done it is the Yankees.

About the only thing they didn't do is draw very many fans. Only twice during Finley's tenure did more than one million people pass through the A's turnstiles.

That's certainly changed. In 1990, a franchise-record 2.9 million fans poured into the Oakland-Alameda County Coliseum, and attendance has been over one million for 10 straight seasons.

Not the kind of showing you'd expect from a place that's supposed to be just a hick, working-class town on the wrong side of the bay from San Francisco.

The only thing Oakland needs, though, is a better ad campaign. True, its busy seaport, three major rail lines and more than 1,000 trucking companies lend credence to a blue-collar image that's almost as old as the city's redwoods.

But it's also a biotechnology and medical center, as well as a vibrant base for financial, international trade and manufacturing firms, including mammoth Kaiser Industries.

Most of Oakland's 350,000 residents are under 50 years of age, and nearly half of them have attended college. Drab? The only place in the country with more artists is New York City's Greenwich Village. And Oakland may be the nation's last real melting pot. Thirty-four languages are spoken within its city limits.

Oakland's baseball history dates back to the turn of the century, when rugged novelist Jack London frequented its waterfront bars. As a member of the Pacific Coast League from 1903 to 1956, the Oakland Oaks won several pennants. In 1948, Casey Stengel managed an Oakland team whose players averaged 34 years of age to a championship. That got him a similar job with the New York Yankees, who won seven World Series over the next 12 years.

By the time Finley arrived in 1968, Oakland was ready for major league baseball. It just wasn't sure it was ready for the A's. Across the bay, the San Francisco Giants were one of baseball's top teams. The A's hadn't had a winning season since 1952 — and that was two cities ago, when they were in Philadelphia.

And Finley had the look of a quick-buck artist. After more than a half-century in Philadelphia, the A's had moved to Kansas City in 1955. Finley, a Chicago insurance man, bought them in 1960 and immediately spent the next seven years trying to move them again. By the time he did, K.C. was happy to see him go.

"Oakland is the unluckiest city since Hiroshima," opined U.S. Senator Stuart Symington of Missouri.

Offbeat promotions and gimmicks hadn't made a bad Kansas City team any more interesting, but that didn't stop Finley from trying them again in Oakland.

On Hot Pants Day, women wearing

you-know-what paraded down a runway on the field. After several players began growing mustaches, Finley scheduled Mustache Day and offered $300 to any other player who followed their example. They all did. On the other hand, he once canceled Fan Appreciation Day in a fit of pique over poor attendance.

In Kansas City, Finley had introduced painfully bright green-and-gold uniforms, setting a fashion trend that endured through the 1970s. In Oakland, he brought out white shoes, as well as special white caps for his coaches.

What was different from Kansas City was that these A's won. The 1968 Oakland club went 82-80, and that was just a prelude. Three years later, the A's won the A.L. West with 101 victories, their best showing in 40 years.

In 1972, they went all the way to the World Series, beating the Cincinnati Reds in seven games behind backup catcher Gene Tenace's four homers and nine RBIs. A come-from-behind victory over the New York Mets the next season helped the A's capture their second straight World Series, and they made it three in a row in 1974 against the Los Angeles Dodgers.

While Finley had been trying to get out of Kansas City, he'd also been busy signing prospects. There was Reggie, Catfish, Vida, Blue Moon, Campy and Rollie. They all blossomed in Oakland, and what a colorful, rowdy, talented bunch they were.

Reggie Jackson, a slugger with a big swing and an ego to match, hit 47 homers in 1969 and was the league's Most Valuable Player four years later. Jim "Catfish" Hunter won 21 games or more four years in a row and won

the Cy Young Award in 1974. And Vida Blue went 24-8 with a 1.42 earned run average in 1971 to bag both the MVP and Cy Young awards.

Hunter and Blue loved the Coliseum, a symmetrical 49,219-seat stadium built in 1966. Critics have called it a "concrete pillbox," but the spacious foul territory is a blessing for pitchers. Hunter threw a perfect game there in 1968 and Blue had a no-hitter two years later. In all, the Coliseum has hosted seven no-hitters in 22 years.

Finley had a showman's love for nicknames. John "Blue Moon" Odom and Bert "Campy" Campaneris came by theirs naturally, and Finley thought up Hunter's, convincing the youngster it would be a great gimmick. However, Blue, figuring his name was interesting enough, wanted no part of "True."

The A's prided themselves as much for their nonconformity as for their talent. They pioneered the hairy look — Rollie Fingers will probably be remembered as much for his handlebar mustache as for his major league-record 341 saves.

Finley called them "The Swingin' A's," and it fit. Over the years, Jackson scuffled with Odom, Mike Epstein and Billy North. Odom also traded locker room blows with Blue and Fingers.

One thing kept them going. "We had a common bond on the A's," said Jackson. "Everybody hated Charlie Finley."

There were two reasons. The first was money. Finley figured too much would dull the A's sharp edge. Jackson, Blue and Hunter each had nasty contract squabbles with him.

But mostly it was Finley's plantation-owner attitude. During the

1973 World Series, he tried to place second baseman Mike Andrews on the disabled list because he'd made two errors in a game. When the players openly denounced him, the A's owner answered by giving them cheap championship rings.

Finley switched managers like other people switch television channels. He hired 18 over 20 years, including three men twice. Dick Williams had the most success, winning two World Series in three years before quitting after the 1973 World Series. "A man can take just so much of Finley," he said.

The A's demise began in 1975 when Hunter became a free agent over a contract technicality and bolted to the Yankees. When Finley realized his other disenchanted stars would soon follow, he traded Jackson and Ken Holtzman to the Baltimore Orioles. But Commissioner Bowie Kuhn, whom Finley once referred to as "the nation's idiot," blocked his attempt to sell Blue to the Yankees and Joe Rudi and Fingers to the Boston Red Sox.

After plummeting to last place in 1977, Oakland enjoyed a brief resurgence under Billy Martin, winning the A.L. West in 1981. But by then Finley was gone, unable to compete amid the soaring salaries. He sold the team to the Walter Haas family in 1980.

If today's A's have fallen short of their predecessors, sweeping the Giants in the 1989 World Series but losing to the Dodgers in 1988 and the Reds in 1990, there are similarities.

With four straight 20-victory seasons, Dave Stewart is the game's steadiest starter, and teammate Bob Welch won the 1990 Cy Young Award with a 27-6 record. And there's no better reliever than Dennis Eckersley, who saved 48 games with a 0.61 ERA in 1990 and walked just seven men in two seasons.

The list goes on. Rickey Henderson won the league's Most Valuable Player Award in 1990, hitting .325 with 28 homers and 65 stolen bases. Jose Canseco and Mark McGwire, with 280 homers since 1987, are baseball's scariest one-two punch.

And who makes headlines like Canseco? In 1988, he became the first player to hit 40 homers and steal 40 bases in a season. In 1989, he got some well-publicized traffic tickets, was arrested for carrying a gun in his car, and installed a special 1-900 hotline number for his fans. In 1990, the A's made him the highest-paid player in the game, he fizzled in the World Series and his wife, Esther, made a stink when Manager Tony La Russa benched him in the final game.

He would have fit right in with the old swashbuckling A's. But you can bet he never would have got a $23.5 million deal out of Charlie Finley.

Reggie Jackson

Reggie Jackson belted 563 home runs during 21 seasons in the major leagues, sixth on the all-time list. He won or shared four American League home run titles.

His teams won 10 division championships, six American League pennants and five World Series. Only twice did he ever play on a losing team.

He was lethal in postseason play, batting .357 with 10 homers and knocking in 24 runs in 27 World Series games. In one of those games, he hit three straight homers.

When he finally retired in 1987, Reggie Jackson left behind a list of astonishing accomplishments. As he himself would be the first to tell you.

"I love competition," he once said. "It motivates me, stimulates me, excites me. It is almost sexual. I just love to hit that baseball in a big game."

Calling Jackson confident is like saying Madonna is perky. Bright, proud and outspoken, he loved the spotlight and had no qualms about proclaiming himself a superstar.

"The thing about Reggie is that you know he's going to produce," mused Catfish Hunter, who played with Jackson on the Oakland A's and the New York Yankees. "And if he doesn't, he's going to talk enough to make people think he's going to produce."

He usually produced. Jackson will go into the record books as one of baseball's most electrifying players, a vicious hitter whose flair for drama often defied belief.

The free agent system was made for Jackson, a hitter-for-hire who played with four different teams after breaking in with the A's in 1967. He went to the Baltimore Orioles in a 1976 trade, joined the Yankees as a free agent a year later, moved on to the California Angels in 1982, then rejoined the A's for his final season.

If he's remembered for one game, it will probably be Game Six of the 1977 World Series when he hit three straight pitches for home runs. A year later, he struck out against Bob Welch to end Game Two of the World Series but came back in the finale to crack a two-run homer off the Dodger pitcher.

The Yankees won both World Series, Jackson was nicknamed "Mr. October" and it became a Yankee

Reggie Jackson

115

Stadium ritual to chant "Reg-gie! Reg-gie! Reg-gie!"

But Jackson's best years actually came with the A's, who signed the left-handed-hitting outfielder off the Arizona State campus in 1966 for a reported $85,000.

Three years later, at the age of 23, Jackson hit a career-high 47 homers, drove in 118 runs and led the league with 123 runs scored and a .608 slugging percentage.

In 1973, he was the American League's Most Valuable Player with 32 homers and 117 RBIs and helped the A's beat the New York Mets in the World Series with a two-run homer in Game Seven.

With the A's, Jackson boasted that if he played in New York, a candy bar would be named after him. It was. After joining the Yankees, he blithely described himself as "the straw that stirs the drink."

It was a career-long arrogance that didn't set well with others. He quarreled with a host of players, feuded with managers Dick Williams and Billy Martin, and publicly lambasted owners Charlie Finley and George Steinbrenner.

Critics also note that Jackson struck out 2,597 times during his career, more than anybody else in baseball history. His lifetime batting average was just .262 and he played an undistinguished right field.

But the fans loved Reginald Martinez Jackson and they poured into ballparks to see him. He was charisma in double-knits, the ballplayer-as-showman. In promoting himself, he promoted baseball.

"Reggie's a really good guy ... He'd give you the shirt off his back," said Catfish Hunter. "Of course, he'd call a press conference to announce it."

National Parks in California
Information available by contacting directly: Channel Islands National Park (805-644-8262), Kings Canyon National Park (209-561-3314), Lassen Volcanic National Park (Mineral, CA 96063), Redwood National Park (707-464-6101), Sequoia National Park (209-561-3314), Yosemite National Park (209-252-4848).
General information available from National Park Service (Fort Mason, Bldg. 201, San Francisco, CA 94123, 415-556-4122) and U.S. Forest Service (630 Sansome St., San Francisco, CA 94111, 415-556-0122).

Bay Area Attractions
See information in San Francisco Giants chapter.

Tourism Information
Oakland Convention and Visitors Bureau, 1000 Broadway, Suite 200, Oakland, CA 94607, 800-621-0851 or 415-839-9000
Discover the Californias, California Tourist Corp., 5757 W. Century Blvd., Los Angeles, CA 90045, 800-862-2543

Oakland-Alameda County Stadium

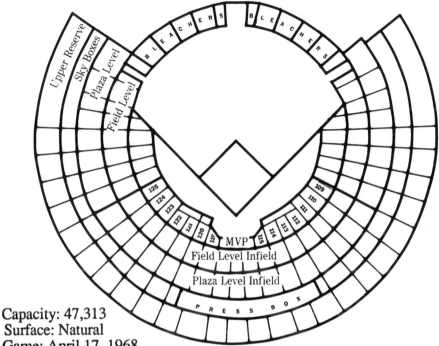

Capacity: 47,313
Surface: Natural
First Game: April 17, 1968
LF: 330 CF: 400 RF: 330

General Information
Oakland Athletics, Oakland-Alameda County
Stadium, Oakland, CA 94621, 415-638-4900.
Ticket information: 415-638-0500.
Getting Tickets
By mail: The Oakland A's, Tickets, PO Box 2220,
Oakland, CA 94621. Specify game, date, number
of tickets and location (first base or third base). $4
handling charge per order. Checks, VISA or
MasterCard. Orders received within 1 week of the
game date must be picked up at Will Call windows
on game day.
By phone: A's Ticket Office at 415-638-0500
(MasterCard and VISA accepted) or
BASS/TicketMaster at 415-762-BASS,
707-762-BASS, 408-998-BASS, 916-923-BASS.
Ticket Prices
Field level $12, Plaza level $11, Upper reserved
$7, Bleachers $4.
Discounts & Promotions
Half price admission available for all games in
Plaza level and Upper Reserved to children 14 and
under, senior citizens 65 and older, active military
and persons in wheelchairs. All Upper Reserved
tickets are half price every Tuesday night. Free
pre-game picnics on Saturdays.

Toughest Tickets To Get
New York and Boston
Game Times
Saturday and Sunday 1:05. Weekdays 12:15.
Weeknights 7:05. Friday 7:35. Pacific time.
Gates open 2 hours before game.
Broadcasts
KSFO-560 AM, KNTA 1430 AM (Spanish),
KPIX TV (5).
Other Notes
Stadium features Speed Pitch booth, Hot Shots
booth (pictures taken with life-size photos of A's).
Kingsford Picnic Plaza. Family area (section 116).
Special greetings on the scoreboard (638-4900,
ext. 555). Special tailgate section (638-4900, ext.
4949). Stadium tours: 415-638-4900, ext. 203.
Catalog of souvenirs: Oakland A's Souvenirs,
Oakland Coliseum, Oakland, CA 94621.
 A's Clubhouse (logo merchandise including
broken bats, used jerseys and souvenirs) at
415-732-5995.
Getting To The Stadium
Near Oakland International Airport, I-880 and
Hegenberger Rd. Stadium parking and overflow
parking available. Accessible by BART (subway).

Purists hate the idea of indoor baseball in the beautiful Pacific Northwest, but the Kingdome was the key factor in returning Seattle to the major leagues.

With a little luck, Ken Griffey Jr. and Alvin Davis and Erik Hanson and Randy Johnson and Mike Schooler could be part of baseball history in 1990.

If his key players perform as Manager Jim Lefebvre expects and the team can stay healthy, it should mean a winning season for the Seattle Mariners.

That's nice, you say, but so what? About half the teams in baseball have winning seasons every year. It's simple mathematics. What's the big deal?

If you're a fan of the Seattle Mariners, you know what the big deal is. You know that the Mariners' next winning season will be their first winning season.

You know that the Mariners have lost more games than they've won every year since entering the American League as an expansion team in 1977. That's 14 seasons. Long seasons.

You know they're the *only* major league team that's never had a winning season. You know they've never finished higher than fourth and have lost over 100 games three times.

You know a winning season would be a giant step for a team whose followers usually start thinking about next year sometime around the All-Star Game.

The Mariners came fairly close in 1990, finishing with a 77-85 record, second-best in their history and good enough for fifth place in the American League West.

They also drew a franchise-record 1 1/2 million fans to the Kingdome, making you wonder how the long-suffering folks of Seattle will react when the Mariners finally surge over .500.

Seattle is a sparkling, jewel-like city where spectacular scenery forms a daz-

Seattle
Mariners

The Mariners drew a franchise-record 1 1/2 million fans in 1990. Which makes you wonder what will happen when they finally have a winning season.

zling backdrop for urban wonders like the famous Space Needle.

A booming town of more than 500,000 people, Seattle began as a lumber capital, thrived as a jump-off point for the Alaskan gold rush in 1897 and grew into an aircraft manufacturing hub during World War II.

Airplanes are still big business. Boeing, which began as a tiny biplane company in 1916, now employs 85,000 people. Seattle also remains a major shipping port to the Orient.

Historic Pioneer Square honors the city's rugged origins, while the stylish Seattle Center and its monorail are legacies of a modern highlight, the 1962 World's Fair.

No mention of Seattle would be complete without a discussion of its weather, which usually gets a bum rap. Overcast skies are the rule, true, but it's hardly monsoon territory. New York, Philadelphia, Atlanta and Houston all get more rainfall than Seattle's 38 inches a year.

The weather's good enough that they've played professional baseball in the Pacific Northwest's largest city for more than a century, beginning with the Seattle Reds in 1890.

The Seattle Indians were charter members of the Pacific Coast League when it opened for business in 1903; when Emil Sick bought the the team in 1937, he changed the name to Rainiers — not after the mountain, after his beer company. The Rainiers won several pennants, including one in 1955 under local sports hero Fred Hutchinson, who went on to manage the Cincinnati Reds to the 1961 National League pennant.

One of the most curious — and briefest — chapters in Seattle's baseball history is the saga of its first major league team, the Seattle Pilots. Seattle seemed like a natural when the American League decided to add two expansion teams in 1969, but things went wrong from the start.

The Pilots played in Sick's Stadium, a cozy 30-year-old ballpark that initially held 11,500 people. Work to enlarge it to 28,500 seats went so slowly that on Opening Day several hundred fans had to wait outside while the last of the new seats were installed. For weeks afterward, people complained of splinters received from hastily built bleachers. Old plumbing was another problem. Any time the stadium was more than half full, water pressure dropped to a trickle, making every trip to the restroom an adventure.

On the field, Seattle's Tommy Harper led the league with 73 stolen bases, but otherwise the Pilots looked every bit the expansion team, losing 98 games and finishing last in the A.L. West.

Their claim to fame — other than being the only team to wear military-style gold braid on their caps — was a starring role in one of the frankest, funniest baseball books ever written, Jim Bouton's *Ball Four*. A star pitcher with the New York Yankees until his arm went bad, Bouton joined the Pilots in 1969 as a knuckleball-throwing reliever. He also kept a diary, a whimsical kiss-and-tell account of what ballplayers did before, during and after the games. The baseball establishment was outraged by Bouton's blithe tales of boozing and woman-chasing. But the public loved it, and *Ball Four* became the best-selling sports book in history.

By then, though, the Pilots also were

history. Fewer than 700,000 fans turned out that first year, which helped it become the Pilots' only year. Legal and financial problems forced the team into bankruptcy court; new owners moved the club to Milwaukee in 1970 and renamed it the Brewers.

In 1967, Seattle voters had approved bonds for a domed stadium. Undaunted by the Pilots' demise, the city went ahead with construction, and it paid off in February 1976 when the American League made Seattle the only city ever to be awarded two expansion teams.

The new club, christened the Mariners to honor Seattle's nautical heritage and owned by a group that included entertainer Danny Kaye, began play the next year in the American League's first indoor ballpark. It didn't take long, however, for purists to get misty-eyed over Sick's Stadium. The $67 million Kingdome — officially the King County Domed Stadium — holds 57,748 for baseball and the plumbing works, but critics have found little else to commend.

It's been called a mausoleum, a concrete monstrosity, a dark, dreary contrast to the beautiful Puget Sound scenery outside. Fly balls bang into overhead speakers, while pop fouls simply vanish into the Kingdome's dusky reaches. Traditionally small crowds haven't helped the ambiance. The 1979 All-Star Game is still the Kingdome's only baseball sellout, and even 1990's record attendance was the second smallest in the league.

Of course, the Mariners have had more than a little to do with that tradition. In 14 seasons, their best record was a fourth-place 78-84 in 1987, meaning Seattle fans — and baseball

essayists — have had to look long and hard for highlights.

One was Willie Horton's 300th homer on June 6, 1979. Actually, he would have had it the night before had not his high drive bounced off one of the aforementioned speakers. The Kingdome has always been a haven for home run hitters because of its short power alleys. Since 1977, the Seattle ballpark has led the majors in homers four times. Even lesser batsmen have had their moments. Larry Milbourne hit just 11 homers in 11 seasons, but two of them came in a 1978 game in the Kingdome.

Wiley Gaylord Perry played just 1 1/2 of his 22 major league seasons in Seattle, but he was with the Mariners long enough to win the 300th game of his career, a 7-3 victory over the New York Yankees on May 6, 1982, in the Kingdome. He was 43. Naturally everyone called him "The Ancient Mariner."

The only Hall of Famer ever to play for the Mariners, Perry boasted a legendary array of illegal pitches. He even wrote a book ruminating on the benefits of spit, sweat and Vaseline. Less successful was the Mariners' Rick Honeycutt, who was pitching against the Kansas City Royals in 1980 when umpire Bill Kunkel caught him doing funny things to the ball with a thumbtack taped to his finger. Honeycutt was fined $250 and banished for 10 days, the first pitcher suspended for cheating in 36 years.

Then there was Lenny Randle, who was playing third base for the Mariners in 1981 when the Royals' Amos Otis hit a slow roller down the line. Realizing he couldn't throw Otis out, Randle fell to his knees — and huffed and puffed at the ball till it rolled foul. After some head-scratching, the umpires ruled the ball a hit, saying Randle had illegally altered its course. It's still the only windblown ground ball in Kingdome history.

Seattle's Alvin Davis was the American League Rookie of the Year in 1984, while Mark Langston was the Rookie Pitcher of the Year. Langston later led the league in strikeouts three times, and Harold Reynolds stole a league-best 60 bases in 1987.

But no Mariner has ever won 20 games or led the league in saves. Seattle also has never had a league leader in batting, runs batted in or home runs.

Curiously, Seattle owns one of baseball's most productive farm systems. But the Mariners, especially during the reign of tight-fisted owner George Agyros from 1981 to 1989, have often traded potential stars when their salaries threaten to get too high. Danny Tartabull, Matt Young, Phil Bradley and Langston are some who come to mind. Others, like Floyd Ban-nister and Mike Moore, fled through free agency.

And the Mariners' own free agent endeavors have flopped more often than not. Jeffrey Leonard had a good season in 1989, but he fizzled in 1990 and so did Pete O'Brien. And those are the free agents they've landed; most don't even consider the Mariners.

But the Mariners' ship may be about to come in. Broadcasting mogul Jeff Smulyan bought the team in 1989, lowered ticket prices and vowed to make the Mariners more competitive.

Ken Griffey Jr. in 1990 not only became the first man to play on the same team with his father (Ken Griffey Sr.) but also solidified his status as a rising star, hitting .300 and leading the Mariners with 22 homers and 80 RBIs. Erik Hanson went 18-9, while Mike Schooler saved 30 games and 6-foot-10 Randy Johnson, previously best known as the majors' tallest pitcher, threw a no-hitter.

A winning season in 1991 is not out of the question. And for Mariner fans, it will be a very big deal.

The Kingdome, with the Olympic Mountains in the distance

Alvin Davis

It was early in the 1984 season. Alvin Davis had only been with the Seattle Mariners a month and was still a little nervous about his future in the major leagues.

The rookie first baseman asked Mariner traveling secretary Lee Pelekoudas whether he should go ahead and sign an apartment lease in Seattle.

Pelekoudas looked at him.

In his first 18 games with the Mariners, Davis had punished American League pitchers for 24 hits, banged seven homers and knocked in 17 runs.

"Yes, Alvin," Pelekoudas replied. "I think that would be okay."

There's not much flash to Alvin Davis. Quiet and unassuming, he's never made a fuss over recognition. He wasn't a No. 1 draft choice and he hasn't had a candy bar named after him.

But Alvin Davis, with apologies to Seattle phenom Ken Griffey Jr., is still the best ballplayer who's ever swung a bat for the Mariners.

At the age of 30, Davis already has more hits, homers and runs batted in than any other Mariner. He's the team leader in seven other offensive categories, too.

He's led the Mariners in walks five different seasons, RBIs four times, homers twice and batting twice. He's the only Seattle player to drive in over 100 runs more than once.

And when he was voted the American League Rookie of the Year in 1984, he became the first Seattle player to win one of the league's major awards. He's still the only one.

Yet Davis has made a career out of being overlooked — or at least underestimated. After he hit .395 with four homers as a junior to help Arizona State win the 1981 College World Series, the Oakland A's offered him just $30,000 to turn pro.

Davis opted to stay in college and get a degree in finance. Even though he had a better senior season, some scouts questioned his desire and Seattle offered him only $10,000 in 1982. Learning a lesson in practical economics, Davis took it.

After two seasons in the minors, Davis figured to spend most of 1984 at Salt Lake City in the Pacific Coast

Alvin Davis

123

League. Instead, the Mariners called him up after just one game when Ken Phelps, their regular first baseman, broke a finger.

In a similar situation, Hall of Famer Lou Gehrig played in 2,130 consecutive games after "temporarily" filling in for New York Yankee first baseman Wally Pipp in 1925.

Davis made almost as big a splash, belting a home run in his second at-bat and hitting safely in his first nine games. He was so hot that the A's walked him seven times in three games, while the California Angels tried a Ted Williams-style shift to counter his left-handed slugging.

By the end of the season, Davis owned a .284 average with 27 homers. His 116 RBIs were the most for an American League rookie in 34 years; his 16 intentional walks were the most for any rookie ever. Phelps, when he returned, became the Mariners' designated hitter.

Since then, Davis has been the steadiest of hitters, batting .289 and averaging 21 homers and 85 RBIs a year. In a hot streak, though, he's murderous. Twice he's homered in four consecutive games, and in 1986 he knocked in eight runs in one contest.

In 1989, after signing a three-year contract for $4.5 million, he hit 21 homers, drove in 95 runs and had a career-high .305 batting average.

Yet there are signs the Mariners still don't fully appreciate their longtime star. In 1990, they moved him to designated hitter to make room for first baseman Pete O'Brien, a 32-year-old free agent to whom for some reason they had given a four-year $7.6 million contract.

Although he wasn't happy about it, Davis quietly accepted the switch — and then made the Mariners think twice about it. O'Brien struggled to hit .224 with five homers and 27 RBIs. Davis batted .283, clubbed 17 homers and knocked in 68 runs.

Top Attractions
Museum of Flight (9404 E. Marginal Way S., 206-764-5700), Pacific Science Center (200 2nd Ave. N., 206-443-2001), Pioneer Square and Klondike Gold Rush National Park (area of First Ave., James St. and Yesler Way), Rainer Brewing Company Tours (3100 Airport Way S., 206-622-2600), Seattle Aquarium (Pier 59, 206-625-4357), Space Needle Observation Deck (Seattle Center, 206-443-2100), Woodland Park Zoo (206-789-7919).

National Parks in Washington
Information available by contacting Mount Rainer National Park (206-569-2211), Cascades National Park (206-856-5700) and Olympic National Park (206-452-4501).

Tourism Information
Seattle King County Convention & Visitors Bureau, 666 Stewart, Seattle, WA 98101, 206-447-4240.
Washington Tourism Development Division, 101 General Administration Building, Olympia, WA 98504, 206-586-2102.

Kingdome
201 S. King St.

Capacity: 57,748
Surface: Artificial
First Game: April 6, 1977
LF: 331   CF: 405   RF: 312

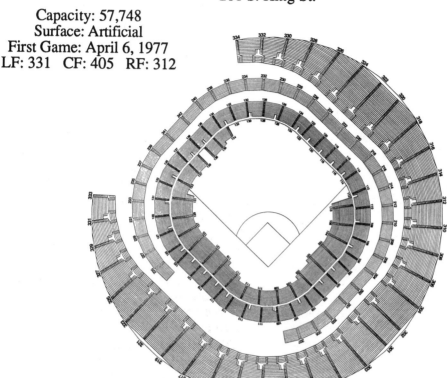

General Information
Seattle Mariners, PO Box 4100, 411 First Ave.
South, Seattle, WA 98104, 206-628-3555.
Game ticket information: 206-343-4600.
Getting Tickets
General admission tickets sold day of game only
(17,000 tickets).
Stadium ticket office: NW corner of the stadium,
8:30-5:30 Monday - Saturday, noon - 5 Sundays.
By mail: Seattle Mariners Ticket Office, PO Box
4100, Seattle, WA 98104. Specify game date,
number of tickets, price and location (first base,
third base or home plate). $2.50 handling fee per
order. Check, money order, VISA, MasterCard or
American Express accepted.
By phone: TicketMaster: 206-628-0888.
MasterCard and VISA accepted.
Ticket Prices
Box $11.50, Field $10.50, Club $8.50, View
$5.50 (14 and under $3.50), Family (100-level)
$4.50 ($2.50 for 14 and under), General
Admission $4.50 ($2.50 for 14 and under).

Discounts & Promotions
Promotions scheduled for over 20 games. Monday
two-for-one Family nights. Sunday two-for-one
Senior Days.
Toughest Tickets To Get
Boston, New York and Oakland .
Game Times
Weekdays 12:35, 5:05, 7:05, 7:35. Saturday 7:05.
Sunday 1:35, 4:35, 5:05. Pacific time. Gates open
2 hours before game.
Broadcasts
KIRO AM 71 radio and KSTW TV (11).
Other Notes
Stadium features Family Sections (5 non-alcohol
sections throughout the stadium). Stadium tours:
206-340-2100 or 296-DOME.
Getting To The Stadium
Central Seattle, south of the Space Needle, near I-5
(where joined by I-90). Stadium parking
available. Additional commercial parking.
Accessible by bus.

Arlington Stadium, which began life as a 10,000-seat minor league park called Turnpike Stadium, has been expanded over the years to hold 43,508 people.

What do Billy Martin, Whitey Herzog, Darrell Johnson and Don Zimmer have in common?

They all managed the Texas Rangers and they all won division titles. The problem, if you root for the Rangers, is that none of them did those two things at the same time.

In fact, the Rangers, now in their twentieth season in the Lone Star State, have never won any kind of championship — no World Series, no American League pennant, no A.L. West title.

The Seattle Mariners are the only other team that can admit to that. And they haven't been at it nearly as long as the Rangers, who started out in 1961 as the Washington Senators.

Unlike Seattle, though, the Rangers have been close. Since moving to Texas in 1972, they've finished second four times and tied for second one other. They've also had three third-place finishes.

The Rangers often seem to be on the rise, but they've never quite been able to take that final step. In 1974, they won 84 games, winding up just five games behind the division-champion Oakland A's. But a year later, they were 19 games back.

In 1977, Texas won a franchise-record 94 games, triggering the most successful period in the team's history. From 1977 to 1979, the Rangers averaged 88 victories. Nevertheless, they never finished closer than five games out of first.

A host of All-Stars and even a few Hall of Famers have ridden through Texas. Jeff Burroughs was the American League's Most Valuable Player in 1974 and Mike Hargrove was the Rookie of the Year. Al Oliver hit .319 over four seasons with the Rangers.

Texas
Rangers

The Rangers have had 11 managers in their 19 seasons, including some of the best in baseball. But none has brought a championship to Texas.

127

Jim Sundberg was a Gold Glove catcher from 1976 to 1981.

Ferguson Jenkins went 25-12 for Texas in 1974. He's still the Rangers' only 20-game winner, but their all-time leader is knuckleballer Charlie Hough, who won 139 games in 11 seasons before moving on to the Chicago White Sox in 1991. Gaylord Perry also spent some time in Texas, and so did Bert Blyleven and Jon Matlack.

Of course, there have been some lesser lights, too. Mario Mendoza was such a poor hitter that his lifetime .215 batting average became a standard for futility. "The first thing I look for (in the batting averages) in the Sunday papers," George Brett once said, "is who is below the Mendoza Line."

The Rangers signed high school phenom David Clyde for $125,000 in 1973, and it looked like a good deal when the 18-year-old left-handed pitcher beat the Minnesota Twins 4-3 in his very first professional game. But Clyde, perhaps rushed to the major leagues too soon, never fulfilled that promise, finishing his career just six years later with an 18-33 record.

Impatience has long been a hallmark of the Rangers. They've had 11 managers in 19 seasons, plus two interim skippers. Current Manager Bobby Valentine, hired in 1985, is the only one who's held the job more than three seasons.

Maybe that restlessness is just a byproduct of the general energy that seems to pervade Dallas-Fort Worth, or the Metroplex, as the natives call it.

Dallas first boomed as a cotton market, while Fort Worth was a cattle town. Now they're much more diverse, anchoring a metropolitan area that's approaching four million people.

Cotton is still big in Big D, but so is oil and natural gas, not to mention finance and culture. It's the Southwest's largest banking hub and among the nation's top three fashion centers. And more insurance companies are based in Dallas than in any other American city. Attractions include sprawling Fair Park, home of the Cotton Bowl and the largest state fair in the country.

Although it remains a major livestock center, Fort Worth, 30 miles to the west, has grown to include such industries as oil refineries, aircraft plants and food production facilities. It also boasts a massive park system and three of the state's finest art museums, including the Amon Carter Museum of Western Art and its collection of cowboy paintings and sculpture.

Both cities were still filled with real cowboys when professional baseball debuted in north Texas. Dallas and Fort Worth each joined the old Texas League in 1886, and both had some pretty good minor league teams. Fort Worth won six straight pennants in the 1920s, and the two cities combined to win 11 Dixie Series against the champions of the Southern Association from 1920 to 1956.

In 1965, the Dallas-Fort Worth Spurs of the American Association began playing in new Turnpike Stadium, a 10,000-seat ballpark built midway between the two cities with the expressed hope of getting a major league team.

That dream came true seven years later when the Senators, tired of fighting low attendance in Washington, moved to Texas and adopted the name of the state's legendary lawmen.

With their arrival, Turnpike Stadium was renamed Arlington Stadium, after the suburb in which it is located along Interstate 30, and enlarged to 35,694 seats. The current capacity is 43,508.

One of Arlington Stadium's two most distinctive features, a scoreboard shaped like the state of Texas, was replaced a few years ago. The other one, searing summer heat, unhappily endures. Arlington Stadium was built in a natural bowl and the stands are uncovered. As ballparks go, it's a good frying pan. That's why from June to August even the Rangers' Sunday games are at night.

That will change in a few years. Early in 1991, voters in Arlington approved a sales tax hike to finance a $165 million domed stadium. The Rangers hope the new stadium, to be built south of the current ballpark and with room for about 45,000 fans, will be ready by the 1994 season.

Of all the people who have worn a Texas uniform, nobody was more famous than the Rangers' first manager, Hall of Fame slugger Ted Williams. Unfortunately, Williams wasn't as proficient at managing as he was at hitting. The Rangers went 54-100 in 1972, barely 660,000 fans turned out to watch them, and he was gone after the season ended. Texas' parade of managers was under way.

Whitey Herzog took over in 1973, but the Rangers didn't play any better and he was fired late in the season. A fortuitous development for him, since it allowed him to become manager of the Kansas City Royals in 1975 just as they were about to win three straight A.L. West titles.

Herzog's replacement was fiery vagabond Billy Martin, who led the Rangers to a second-place finish in 1974. But Martin was fired midway through the next season after Texas skidded into fourth place; the Rangers were the only one of the five teams he managed that did not win a division title.

Arlington Stadium

that did not win a division title.

Plastics mogul Brad Corbett bought the Rangers in 1974 and eventually established himself as the George Steinbrenner of the Southwest. He spent lavishly on free agents like Doyle Alexander, Richie Zisk and Bert Campaneris, pouted when they did not play well, then sent them packing to other teams. Fans became so exasperated by his antics that they called him "Chuckles the Clown."

No season during Corbett's curious six-year reign was stranger than 1977. It began in spring training when second baseman Lenny Randle, upset at being benched, punched out Manager Frank Lucchesi behind the batting cage. Lucchesi, 50, went to the hospital with a broken cheekbone. Randle, 28, wound up in court on an assault charge. After that, the Rangers suspended him, fined him $10,000 and traded him to the New York Mets.

When Texas got off to a slow start that season, Corbett replaced Lucchesi with Eddie Stanky — who managed one game, decided he'd made a mistake taking the job, and quit. Coach Connie Ryan filled in for six games before Corbett hired Billy Hunter, his fourth manager of the season. Under Hunter, the Rangers cast their troubles aside and won 60 of their final 93 games. Turmoil and all, they finished at 94-68, their best record ever.

The next season, Hunter guided them to an 87-75 record, then he suddenly quit. Pat Corrales succeeded him, and over the next few years Corrales was followed by Don Zimmer, Darrell Johnson (who had been replaced by Zimmer with the Boston Red Sox in 1976) and Doug Rader. But none of them seemed to get more than one good season out of the Rangers, and some writers couldn't resist nicknaming the erratic club the Texas Strangers.

That business came to a halt, however, with the hiring of 35-year-old Bobby Valentine. In 1986, his first full season as manager, Valentine took the Rangers to a second-place finish behind the Minnesota Twins. And after slumping to sixth for a couple of years, Texas rebounded with 83-79 records in both 1989 and '90 for its first consecutive winning seasons since 1977-79.

Again, there are hints of greatness. Ruben Sierra had an MVP-type year in 1989, hitting .306 with 29 homers and 119 runs batted in. Rafael Palmeiro was in the 1990 American League batting race all year before finishing third at .319.

Nolan Ryan led the American League in strikeouts in 1989 and 1990. Jeff Russell saved a league-high 38 games in 1989, and wild-throwing Bobby Witt blossomed into a 17-game winner in 1990.

But the constant has been the personable but intense Valentine, a one-time prospect who turned to managing after his playing career was cut short by injuries.

He entered the 1991 season with 451 victories, nearly three times that of any other Texas manager. And he's the only Ranger skipper with more than two winning seasons.

The only thing missing is a championship. If Valentine can get one of those in Texas, it will just be one more thing he doesn't have in common with Billy Martin, Whitey Herzog, Don Zimmer and Darrell Johnson.

Ruben Sierra

It's not too hard to understand why Ruben Sierra, at the age of 25, is already considered Puerto Rico's greatest baseball hero since Roberto Clemente.

Sierra exploded on the major league scene in 1987, hitting 30 home runs and driving in 109 runs in his first full season with the Texas Rangers.

Two years later, he nearly won the American League's Most Valuable Player Award after batting .306 with 29 homers and 119 runs batted in and leading the league in four hitting categories.

In less than five major league seasons, he's led the Rangers in homers and triples twice, hits three times, and doubles and RBIs four times.

Ruben Sierra

Those are numbers that Clemente, the late Pittsburgh Pirate star, would have been proud of. Indeed, almost from the moment Sierra joined the Rangers, folks in Puerto Rico have called him the next Roberto Clemente.

It's a description that Sierra, although flattered, has been reluctant to accept.

"People say it, and it is an honor," says Sierra. "But I want to be Ruben Sierra. I want people to say I play like Ruben."

But the comparisons are inescapable. Sierra plays right field. So did Clemente. Sierra wears No. 21. So did Clemente. And Sierra looks enough like the Pirate great that people have approached him on the street and asked if he's one of Clemente's sons.

The connection goes even further. Sierra was just seven years old when Clemente died in a plane crash on December 31, 1972, outside San Juan, Puerto Rico, while taking supplies to earthquake victims in Nicaragua. But he played sandlot ball with two of Clemente's sons and learned how to hit a curveball at the Roberto Clemente Sports City in San Juan. Sierra grew up Rio Piedras, Puerto Rico, and now lives in the nearby town of Carolina, where Clemente was born.

Sierra, who signed with Texas as a 17-year-old free agent in 1982, joined the Rangers in June 1986 and hit 16 homers with 55 RBIs in only 113 games.

The next season, at the age of 20, he became the youngest switch-hitter ever to hit 30 homers in a season and led the league with 643 at-bats. Since then, he's never batted fewer than 600 times and has played in nearly 159 games a year.

In 1989, the Rangers traded for Julio Franco and Rafael Palmeiro; batting cleanup between two .300 hitters, Sierra blossomed into a superstar. He led the league in RBIs, triples (14), slugging percentage (.543) and total bases (344), and was in the top 10 in five other categories. He was only the second player in American League history to score 100 runs and have 100 RBIs in the same year.

When Robin Yount of the Milwaukee Brewers narrowly won the Most Valuable Player Award, Sierra was deeply disappointed. It was another thing he had in common with the proud Clemente, who felt he should have won more MVP awards than the one he got in 1966.

Sierra is not the Gold Glove right fielder that Clemente was, but his arm is strong enough that he had 17 assists in 1987 and 13 in 1989. And he's a shrewd if not prolific baserunner, swiping 35 bases in 41 tries since 1988.

After his 1989 heroics, 1990 was a bit of a letdown for Sierra. His .280 average was the second-highest of his career and he led the team with 96 RBIs, but his 16 homers were the fewest since his rookie season.

Still, it was a solid year, and most observers believe Sierra will do plenty more to justify the comparisons with Clemente before his career is over.

"You watch him play, and then you have to remind yourself just how young he is," says Gordon Lakey, a scout for the Toronto Blue Jays. "He is going to be the dominant player in the 1990s."

Dallas Attractions
Dallas Aboretum & Botanical Garden (8525 Garland Rd., 214-327-8263), Dallas Museum of Art (1717 N. Harwood, 214-922-0220), Dallas Zoo (621 E. Clarendon Dr.), John F. Kennedy Memorials (near Houston and Elm Sts. and Main and Market Sts.), State Fair Park (Aquarium, Cotton Bowl Stadium, Garden Center, Museum of Natural History and Science Place).
Fort Worth Attractions
Amon Carter Museum of Western Art (3501 Camp Bowie Blvd.), Botanic Gardens (3220 Botanic Dr.), Forest Park Zoo, Fort Worth Museum of Science and History (1501 Montgomery St.), Kimbell Art Museum (3333 Camp Bowie Blvd.), Modern Art Museum of Fort Worth (1309 Montgomery St.).
Arlington Attractions
Six Flags Over Texas (Arlington, 817-640-8900) and Wet'n'Wild (817-265-3013).
Tourism Information
Arlington Convention & Visitor Bureau, PO Box A, Arlington, TX 76010, 817-265-7721 or 800-433-5374 and 800-7725371 (in TX).
Dallas Convention & Visitors Bureau, 1201 Elm St., Suite 2000, Dallas, TX 75270, 214-746-6600.
Fort Worth Convention & Visitors Bureau, Water Gardens Place, 100 E. 15th St., Suite 400, Fort Worth, TX, 76102, 817-336-8791 or 800-433-5747 (in TX).
Texas Travel Information Division, PO Box 5064, Austin, TX 78763, 512-463-8585 or 800-8888-TEX.

Arlington Stadium
1700 Copeland Rd.
Capacity: 43,508
Surface: Natural
First Game: April 21, 1972
LF: 330   CF: 400   RF: 330

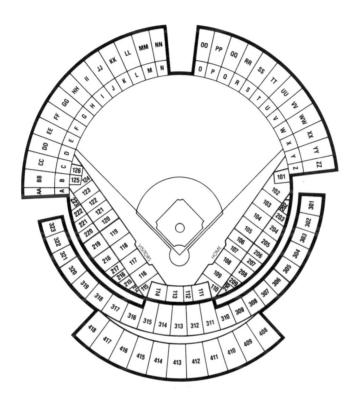

General Information
Texas Rangers Baseball Club, PO Box 1111, Arlington, TX 76004, 817-273-5222.
Ticket Information: 817-273-5100
Getting Tickets
General Admission (20,000 seats).
By mail: Texas Rangers Ticket Office, PO Box 1111, Arlington, TX 76004. Specify date, opponent, number of tickets, price and preferred location (home, first base, third base). $3 handling charge. Check, VISA, MasterCard and American Express accepted. Orders received 5 days prior to game cannot be mailed and must be picked up at Paid Will Call window (near Gate 9B).
By phone: 817-273-5100. Phone orders accepted up to 2 hours before the game.

Ticket Prices
Field and Mezzanine Box $13, Reserved Seat $12, Plaza Seat $9, Grandstand Reserved $6, General Admission $4 ($2 for child).
Toughest Tickets To Get
New York, Oakland and Boston.
Game Times
Sunday 2:05, 7:35. All other games 7:05, 7:35. Central time. Gates open 3 hours before game.
Other Notes
Catalog/Souvenirs Department, Texas Rangers Baseball Club, PO Box 90111, Arlington, TX 76004.
Stadium features non-alcohol sections. Stadium tours: 817-273-5000.
Getting To The Stadium
Midway between Dallas and Fort Worth, exit I-30 at F.M. 157 (Collins St.). Ample stadium parking.

133

Three Rivers Stadium

Wrigley Field

NATIONAL LEAGUE EAST

Chicago Cubs
Montreal Expos
New York Mets
Philadelphia Phillies
Pittsburgh Pirates
St. Louis Cardinals

Even though lights were added in 1988, afternoon ballgames remain the staple in "The Friendly Confines" of Wrigley Field.

Do you get the uncomfortable feeling that if the Chicago Cubs were a car, they'd be a Volvo? With a "Baby on Board" sign in the window?

The Cubs haven't won a World Series since Teddy Roosevelt was president. Heck, they haven't even been in one since Harry Truman held the job.

But thanks to Harry Caray, the lust for nostalgia and a couple of rare winning seasons, those cuddly Chicago Cubs are back in vogue.

They're the Reeboks, the New Kids on the Block, the Simpsons of baseball. Call the Cubs "America's Team," and the only real argument you'll get is from Ted Turner.

For decades, they were just lovable losers — the Cubbies, the anchor poor Ernie Banks had to lug around, the team whose collapse helped create the "Miracle Mets" of '69.

Since 1939, they've had just 11 winning seasons. Even when they won, something wasn't quite right. When they met the Detroit Tigers in the 1945 World Series, both teams had so many World War II rejects that sportswriter Frank Graham said, "It is the fat men against the tall men at the annual office picnic." Another writer, Warren Brown, said, "I don't think either team can win." He was right about the Cubs anyway. They lost in seven games.

In the last 10 years, the Cubs have finished above .500 only twice, but each time they've made the most of it, winning the National League East in 1984 and 1989.

And each time previously unheard-from Cub fans professed their allegiance, only to be disappointed when Chicago lost the N.L. playoffs, first to the San Diego Padres, then the San Francisco Giants.

Chicago
Cubs

Harry Caray. Nostalgic Wrigley Field. And a couple of winning seasons. The Cubs are back in vogue.

In 1990, the Cubs defended their division crown by tumbling to fifth place with a 77-85 record, then went on a free agent binge, signing slugger George Bell, starter Danny Jackson and reliever Dave Smith.

That shopping spree will undoubtedly swell the ranks of the Cub faithful, although it's hard to see how any more of them will get through the ticket gates.

In 1984, the Cubs drew over two million fans for the first time in a history that dates back to 1870. Since then, they've done it five more seasons, despite playing in a ballpark with fewer than 40,000 seats.

That ballpark, homey, ivy-covered Wrigley Field, is a very special part of the Cubs' charm. Late owner Philip K. Wrigley knew that in the 1930s when he advertised it as "Beautiful Wrigley Field," and nary a game goes by that Cub broadcasters don't invoke Ernie Banks' warm description, "The Friendly Confines."

Only in the last 15 seasons or so, however, have the Cubs and Wrigley Field been beamed into homes across the country via WGN, satellite and cable TV.

Baseball's other superstation team, the Atlanta Braves, enjoyed a faddish popularity in 1982, when millions of cable customers watched them win the N.L. West title. But they've lacked the Cubs' staying power, largely because they also lack Harry Caray.

Broadcast critics retreat to phrases like "one of a kind" and "never be another like him" when discussing Harry, who's made a career of corny jokes, shameless namedropping and dyslexic play-by-play. But there's no ignoring his appeal. Harry's

shirtsleeves style reinforces the Cubs' family image. When he gargles *Take Me Out to the Ballgame* or moans about Shawon Dunston swinging at yet another pitch in the dirt, Harry sounds like your grandfather doing the game, after a couple of beers.

Surrounded by well-kept neighborhood taverns and apartment buildings on the North Side, the Cubs represent upscale Chicago, the city that's a bustling financial, architectural and cultural center.

The Cubs are the Sears Tower, the Lincoln Park Zoo, the Chicago Art Institute. They're the Loop and Rush Street and O'Hare International, the world's busiest airport.

The Chicago of labor disputes, gangland wars and machine politics, the brawling, shot-and-a-beer Chicago, well, that's the White Sox and the South Side. That's the way both teams like it, too. Witness a sign seen in the White Sox's Comiskey Park in 1990: "Yuppie Scum — Go Back to Wrigley!"

Curiously, the Cubs were called the White Stockings when they won the National League's first pennant in 1876 and claimed five more titles from 1880 to 1886. Cubs proved to be the most durable of several later nicknames, including Colts and Orphans, that emphasized the team's youth.

The 1906 Cub team was probably the best, winning 55 of its last 65 games en route to a 116-36 mark, still the major league record for wins and winning percentage. Anchored by Mordecai "Three Finger"Brown and the well-publicized double-play combo of Joe Tinker, Johnny Evers and Frank Chance, the Cubs led the league in hitting, scoring and earned run average —

then lost the World Series to the Chicago White Sox, a team called "The Hitless Wonders" because of its .230 batting average.

With essentially the same team, the Cubs bounced back to win World Series in 1907 and 1908, beating Ty Cobb and the Detroit Tigers both times. But since then they are zero-for-seven in the Fall Classic.

The Cubs lost to the Philadelphia A's in 1910 and 1929, the last including a game in which the A's wiped out an 8-0 Chicago lead with a record 10 runs in the seventh inning. Chicago fell to the Red Sox in 1918 — Boston's last world championship — to the New York Yankees in 1932 and 1938, and to the Tigers in 1935 and 1945.

Memorable moments in Cub history include Babe Ruth's "called shot" homer off Charley Root in the 1932 World Series, a major league record 21-game winning streak in 1935 and Gabby Hartnett's "Homer in the Gloamin' " at Wrigley Field that beat the Pirates and helped Chicago clinch the 1938 pennant.

After 1939, however, the Cubs had just three winning seasons until Leo Durocher took over as manager in 1966 and promised, "One thing I can tell you. This is not an eighth-place team." Right. The Cubs finished tenth.

Durocher got them to third in 1967, though, and two years later, behind Ernie Banks, Billy Williams, Ron Santo and Ferguson Jenkins, they led the N.L. East most of the season until fading before the Mets' charge.

Before falling back into the second division, the Cubs had five straight winning seasons under Durocher. But repeated near misses only prompted jokes like: "Did you hear the Cubs are moving to the Philippines? They're going to call them the Manila Folders."

The Cubs have never lacked color. Stumpy Hack Wilson drove in a major league-record 190 runs and hit 56 homers in 1930, but was just as renowned for his drinking and erratic fielding. Still, Wilson insisted, "I never played drunk. Hung over, yes, but never drunk."

In 1960, the Cubs engineered one of baseball's most bizarre trades, swapping Manager Charlie Grimm for WGN sportscaster Lou Boudreau. That didn't work — the Cubs went 54-83 after Boudreau took over — so the next year, they instituted the College of Coaches, a revolving system in which their coaches took turns managing. Chicago's 59-103 finish in 1962, however, put an end to that little experiment.

In 1987, Andre Dawson won the dubious distinction of becoming the first member of any last-place club to be named the league's Most Valuable Player. The Cubs had been working up to it, though. Hank Sauer was MVP on a 77-77 Chicago team in 1952. Six years later, Ernie Banks became the first player on a losing club to claim the award, and in 1959 he became the first player to do it two years in a row.

When relief ace Bruce Sutter won the Cy Young Award in 1979, he also did it with a losing Cub team. But, with the exception of Three-Finger Brown, the best Cub pitcher was probably Ferguson Jenkins, who won 20 games six times in nine-plus seasons at Chicago and is still the team's career strikeout leader. He was elected to the Hall of Fame in 1990.

With an all-time roster that includes

Rogers Hornsby, Kiki Cuyler, Stan Hack and Phil Cavarretta, the Cubs have always been associated with hitting. That, of course, goes back to Wrigley Field, whose short fences and capricious winds are an entertaining element of the park's quaint atmosphere.

Built in 1914 for the Chicago Whales of the old Federal League at a cost of $250,000 and initially known as Weeghman Park, Wrigley was sold to the Cubs in 1916. It was renamed Cubs Park in 1920 and given its current name six years later.

Bill Veeck, later the owner of several major league teams, planted the original ivy at Wrigley in 1938, about the same time he oversaw construction of the hand-operated scoreboard that's still in use. Veeck also came up with the idea behind the W and L flags that fly over the ballpark to let riders on the passing El know whether the Cubs won or lost.

For years, Wrigley Field took almost perverse pride in being the only major league park without lights, even though the Cubs were all set to install them in 1941 until the Japanese bombed Pearl Harbor and the lights were donated to the war effort. Lights finally went up in 1988 after hot protests by neighborhood residents, but all but 18 Cub games a year are still played during the day.

Wrigley Field's icon status with baseball traditionalists can be an annoying reminder of Cubs chic, but there's no question it's a fun place to watch a ballgame.

One Wrigley tradition is the bleacherites' fondness for throwing home run balls by enemy batters back onto the field, a habit that can occasionally result in sore arms.

In 1975, the Pirates walloped the Cubs 22-0, and the next year Philadelphia's Mike Schmidt hit four homers in an 18-16 Phillie victory.

A 26-23 Cub victory over the Phillies in 1922 was probably Wrigley Field's wildest, but the same two teams nearly matched it on May 17, 1979, a day the wind was truly blowing out. By the time Schmidt's tenth-inning homer gave Philadelphia a 23-22 win, the Cubs and Phils had combined for 50 hits, 11 homers (three by Dave Kingman) and 15 walks. There was a six-run inning, two seven-run innings and an eight-run inning. Eleven pitchers went to the mound and only two, Ray Burris and winner Rawley Eastwick, emerged unscathed.

"The first thing you do after a game like this," said one of the victims, Phillie pitcher Ron Reed, "is see if you have any broken bones."

Ernie Banks

If his accomplishments on the field didn't already warrant a spot in the Hall of Fame, Ernie Banks would deserve to be there on attitude alone.

Rogers Hornsby, Hack Wilson and Billy Williams are among a host of sluggers who have played in Wrigley Field, but only Ernie Banks is known as Mr. Cub.

It wasn't until Ernie Banks came along that Wrigley Field became ''The Friendly Confines.'' And he made them even friendlier with his sunny suggestion, ''Let's play two!''

While Willie Mays was exuberant and Hank Aaron was workmanlike,

Ernie Banks

Banks was easygoing, so popular that Chicago fans voted him the greatest Cub ever before he retired in 1971.

He was a beacon of light in the Cubs' mediocrity of the 1950s and '60s, the first National Leaguer to win consecutive Most Valuable Player awards.

Banks was a 22-year-old shortstop for the Kansas City Monarchs of the old Negro leagues when the Cubs bought his contract for $10,000 in late 1953.

Two years later, he hit 44 homers and drove in 117 runs, and people were realizing the slender Texan with the buggy-whip swing was something special.

By the time his 19-year career was over, Banks had led the league in slugging once, home runs and runs batted in twice, fielding three times and putouts five times.

One of just a handful of men to play more than 1,000 games at two positions, Banks finished with 512 home runs, including a record 293 at shortstop, and 1,636 RBIs.

In 1958, the Cubs finished in fifth place, but Banks batted .313 and led the league with 47 homers — also still a record for shortstops — 129 RBIs and .614 slugging percentage. It was such a terrific season that he was named MVP despite Chicago's 72-82 record.

The next year was almost identical. Again the Cubs were fifth and again Banks was MVP, this time with a .304 average, 45 homers, 143 RBIs and a .596 slugging percentage.

Critics note that Banks' career batting average was an unremarkable .274 and that he was thrown out more often than he successfully stole a base. But reviews of his fielding may have been unnecessarily harsh. A 1961 knee injury forced him to spend the last 10 years of his career at first base, and Manager Leo Durocher was not the biggest fan of his defense there.

But he was a good shortstop, making just 12 errors in 1959 when he set a record with a .985 fielding percentage and winning a Gold Glove in 1960. He played 717 consecutive games at the position from 1957 to 1961.

Some of the criticism from Durocher and others may have been a backlash from Banks' enduring popularity with the fans.

"I don't think those people at Wrigley Field ever saw but two players they liked, Billy Williams and Ernie Banks," former Cub pitcher Ferguson Jenkins once remarked. "Billy never said anything and Ernie always said the right thing."

Somehow, the Cubs' failure to win a pennant during Banks' career is sometimes also offered as a negative reflection of his value to the team.

Former major league Manager Jimmy Dykes had another view. "Without Ernie Banks," Dykes once said, "the Cubs would finish in Albuquerque."

Top Attractions
Adler Planetarium (1300 S. Lake Shore Dr., 312-322-0300), Brookfield Zoo (3300 S. Golf Rd., 708-485-0263), Chicago Art Institute (Michigan at Adams, 312-443-3600), Chicago Botanic Garden (Lake-Cooke Rd., 708-835-5440), Field Museum of Natural History (Lake Shore Dr. at Roosevelt Rd., 312-922-9410), Frank Lloyd Wright Home and Studio (951 Chicago Ave., 708-848-1500), John Hancock Observatory (875 N. Michigan Ave., 312-751-3681), Lincoln Park Zoo (220 N. Cannon Dr., 312-294-4660), Museum of Contemporary Art (237 E. Ontario St., 312-280-2660), Museum of Science and Industry (Lake Shore Dr. at 57th St., 312-684-1414), Sears Tower Skydeck (Wacker Dr. at Adams St., 312-875-9696), Shedd Aquarium (1200 S. Lake Shore Dr., 312-939-2438), Terra Museum of American Art (644 N. Michigan Ave., 312-664-3939).

Tourism Information
Chicago Convention and Visitors Bureau, McCormick Place, Chicago, IL 60616, 312-567-8500.

Illinois Office of Tourism, 310 S. Michigan Ave., Suite 108, Chicago, IL 60604, 312-793-2094 or 800-223-0121.

Wrigley Field
1060 W. Addison St.

Capacity: 38,710
Surface: Natural
First Game: April 23, 1914
LF: 355   CF: 400   RF: 353

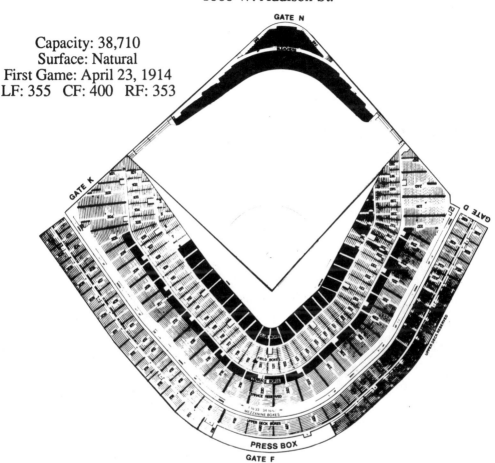

General Information
Chicago Cubs, Wrigley Field, 1060 W. Addison
St., Chicago, IL 60613.
Ticket Information: 312-404-CUBS
Getting Tickets
By mail: Chicago Cubs Ticket Office, 1060 W.
Addison, Chicago, IL 60613. Specify game date,
number of tickets and ticket price. $2 handling
charge per order. Checks accepted.
By phone: TicketMaster at 312-831-CUBS or
800-347-CUBS (outside Illinois), Monday-Friday
8-9, Saturday 8-8, Sunday 9-6.
Ticket Prices
Field Box $15, Terrace Box $11, Upper Deck Box
$11, Terrace Reserved $8, Upper Deck Reserved
$6 ($4 for 13 and under), Bleacher $6.

Discounts & Promotions
Special Events scheduled for approximately half of
games.
Toughest Tickets To Get
Montreal, New York, St. Louis, Los Angeles and
San Francisco.
Game Times
Sunday 1:20. Weekdays 12:05, 1:20, 2:20, 7:05.
Friday 2:20, Saturday 12:15, 1:20, 3:05, 7:05.
Central time. Gates open 2 hours before the game.
Broadcasts
WGN 720 AM, WGN TV (9).
Other Notes
Getting To The Stadium
North (3-5 miles) of the Michigan Ave./Loop area
of Chicago. Lake Shore Drive at Lincoln Park
area. East of the I-90 and I-94 merge point. Very
limited parking in private lots. More accessible by
subway and bus.

For its first 10 years, Olympic Stadium looked vaguely like a large doughnut, with a large hole in the middle of its roof. The convertible top was added in 1987.

Maybe it's the odd uniforms. Maybe it's the stadium that looks like a spaceship. Maybe it's the fact they don't even play in the United States.

In a sport where tradition is regarded with something akin to reverence, the Montreal Expos are so different it can be hard to take them seriously.

Ask Ron Swoboda, who was with the New York Mets in 1969 when Montreal unveiled the uniform with the stylized MEB logo — for Montreal Expos Baseball — on the front.

The blouse also had "expos" in tiny letters under the logo and calligraphic-style numbers on the back. But it was the cap with the red-white-blue crown that intrigued Swoboda.

"Where are their propellers?" he asked.

Neither is anybody going to mistake saucer-shaped Olympic Stadium for Fenway Park or Wrigley Field. Fenway has the Green Monster, Wrigley has its ivy. Olympic has the world's largest fabric retractable roof.

Then there's the whole business of the national pastime being played in Canada. We've had 20 years to get used to the idea, but there are still some who say holding a World Series in a place where it's called *Serie Mondiale* would be, um, un-American.

Montreal is different. There's Old World charm, terrific restaurants and streets that are cleaner and safer than most large American cities. There are beautiful parks, European-style churches and a modern, noiseless subway system. Only Paris has more French-speaking people, making Montreal the major leagues' only bilingual city.

But they take their baseball seriously in Quebec Province, enough so that Les Expos can make a case as the Na-

Montreal Expos

They have odd uniforms. They play in a strange-looking stadium. And most of their fans speak French. Maybe that's why baseball experts never quite know what to make of the Expos.

tional League's most consistently competitive expansion team.

True, the Mets own three National League pennants and a pair of World Series championships. But they also have 10 last-place finishes since 1962. And five next-to-lasts.

In their 22 seasons, the Expos have finished last just four times — one was a tie — and next to last four times. Their .485 winning percentage is also better than the Mets' .467.

A big reason for Montreal's success is one of the best farm systems in either league. Gary Carter, Andre Dawson, Ellis Valentine, Warren Cromartie, Steve Rogers, Tim Raines, Tim Wallach, Andres Galarraga and, more recently, Delino DeShields, Larry Walker and Marquis Grissom were all developed by the Expos.

The Canada factor notwithstanding, Montreal has a long baseball tradition. The city's first minor league team played just six games in 1890 before moving to Grand Rapids, Michigan, but since 1897 there have only been a couple of periods Montreal has been without professional baseball.

The Montreal Royals joined the International League in 1928 and won eight pennants from 1935 to 1958 as a Brooklyn Dodger farm club. Jackie Robinson, who broke baseball's color line, debuted with the Royals in 1946 and helped win one of those titles. But the best team may have been the 1948 edition led by Duke Snider, Sam Jethroe and Don Newcombe, which took the pennant by 13 1/2 games and walloped St. Paul in the Junior World Series.

Six hundred thousand Montreal faithful turned out to watch that team, but when the city made its pitch for major league ball 20 years later, there were still some skeptics. It was a hockey town, they said. It was too cold. And everybody spoke French.

The National League, however, had no trouble understanding Mayor Jean Drapeau's observation that Montreal — which had just staged the Expo '67 World's Fair and was already lobbying for the 1976 Olympics — was larger than 13 major league cities and was willing to build a 55,000-seat domed stadium.

When Montreal said the stadium would be ready by 1971, meaning the Expos would have to play in a temporary ballpark for only a couple of seasons, Canada got its first major league franchise.

Those two seasons, however, turned into eight as soaring costs and labor problems delayed completion of Olympic Stadium until 1977. And even then, it didn't have a roof. In the meantime, the Expos played in Parc Jarry, a recreational park that had held just 3,000 people until the city hastily expanded it to 30,000 seats.

Its shortcomings were immediately apparent. The uncovered single deck left fans exposed to sun, rain and snow. The setting sun beyond third base blinded first basemen, forcing them to wear sunglasses in the early innings of night games. And swimmers in a public pool just beyond the right-field fence had to be on the lookout for home runs.

Not unexpectedly, the quality of the Expos' play in their first season was on a par with that of their ballpark. They lost 110 games, including 20 in a row, and issued a league-record 702 walks.

An early Expo favorite was Coco Laboy, a 28-year-old rookie who hit 18 homers with 83 runs batted in. The downside was that he also made 25 errors at third base, second only to shortstop Bobby Wine's 31.

"Les Expos had a curious collection of players, made curiouser by the fact that their pitchers were *lanceurs*, their batters *frappeurs* and their outfielders *voltigeurs*," sportswriter Bob Verdi wrote. "But translated into either English or French, this was a club that couldn't even clear customs without committing an error."

There were moments, though, even then. Four days into that debut 1969 season, Bill Stoneman threw a no-hitter against the Philadelphia Phillies, the earliest in the history of any major league team. And Rusty Staub hit .302 with 29 homers and 79 RBIs. "Le Grande Orange" may still be the most popular player the Expos have ever had.

Despite their futility, the Expos drew 1.2 million fans that first season, and only twice since then has attendance dropped below a million. In 1976, fewer than 650,000 showed up to see a last-place team, but that figure doubled the next year when the Expos finally moved into $770 million Olympic Stadium.

The Expos' futuristic home is an intriguing place. There are two big scoreboards, including one behind the plate, and they and the public address announcer deliver information in both French and English. And try finding another ballpark with an observation deck atop a 552-foot tower, not to mention a cable car that'll take you up there.

From the outside, Olympic Stadium seems suitable for intergalactic travel.

Olympic Stadium was supposed to have a retractable roof from the start, but it was 1987 before the city installed the fabric cover, which drops from the tower like a tent. Until then, the place was like a dome with a big hole in the top.

In 1979, behind pitchers Steve Rogers and Bill Lee and sluggers Gary Carter, Andre Dawson and Larry Parrish, Montreal had its first big season, winning 95 games to finish one game back of the first-place Pittsburgh Pirates and drawing 2.1 million fans.

The Expos seemed on the verge of blossoming into one of the dominant teams of the '80s. Instead, they turned into perhaps the most enigmatic.

In 1980, Montreal finished second again, this time one game behind the Phillies, who beat the Expos twice in the last series of the season. One of the stars of that team was Ron LeFlore, who stole 97 bases in his only season with the Expos, although not without mishap. After he swiped No. 57, the Olympic Stadium scoreboard noted that the first stolen base had occurred 115 years earlier. LeFlore was reading the message when he was picked off.

The Expos claimed their first National League East title in strike-shortened 1981 but needed the makeshift split-season format to do it. After winning the second half by a half-game, they beat the Phillies in a special division playoff series before falling to the Los Angeles Dodgers in the regular league playoffs.

That was the high point of the decade. Despite adding veterans like Al Oliver, who led the league with a .331 average and 109 RBIs in 1982, and the emergence of stars Tim Raines and Tim Wallach, the Expos never quite gelled, finishing third three times from 1982 through 1985. With the disappointment came complaints that the Expos were talented underachievers. There were whispers of clubhouse strife, and players grumbled about everything from Olympic Stadium's artificial turf to the Montreal lifestyle to Canada's tax structure.

The faces began changing. Warren Cromartie went to play in Japan. Ellis Valentine, Al Oliver, Gary Carter and Jeff Reardon were traded. Andre Dawson became a free agent.

But the Expos weren't any more predictable as a rebuilding team than they were as contenders. In 1987, picked by most observers to land near the bottom of the N.L. East, they went 91-71 to come in third, four games back of the St. Louis Cardinals.

After a frustrating second-half collapse in 1989 and the loss of free agents Mark Langston, Bryn Smith and Hubie Brooks, Montreal was supposed to struggle again in 1990. But again they surprised the experts, finishing third behind the Pirates and Mets as rookies Delino DeShields, Marquis Grissom and Larry Walker combined with veterans Tim Raines and Otis Nixon to help steal a whopping 235 bases.

The Expos kept moving over the winter, too, re-signing pitching ace Dennis Martinez and dealing the 31-year-old Raines to the Chicago White Sox for two younger players, line drive-hitting Ivan Calderon and promising reliever Barry Jones.

It may be tempting to poke fun at the Expos and their uniforms, their stadium and their Canadian home. But it's awfully hard to count them out.

Tim Raines

Tim Raines may not go into the record books as baseball's most prolific base stealer — right now, that title belongs to Rickey Henderson — but nobody has been more efficient.

When Raines wants to steal a base, call an insurance adjuster. Because it's gone. Since 1979, the sturdy speedster has been thrown out less than twice in every 10 tries. No player with more than 100 career steals — not Henderson nor Lou Brock nor Ty Cobb — owns a better stolen base success rate than Raines' 85.6 percent.

Is Tim Raines the best player the Montreal Expos have ever had? Maybe. That's why it'll take some getting used to not seeing him in an Expo uniform.

After more than 10 seasons of swiping bases and hitting .300 for the Expos, the popular Raines now plays for the Chicago White Sox, thanks to an off-season trade. For some fans, though, he'll always be an Expo. And when they remember him, they'll always see that trademark lightning start and short pop-up slide.

In 1981, his rookie season, Raines stole 71 bases in 88 games to lead the National League. When he did it four years in a row, catchers got a good idea how Wile E. Coyote must feel.

He stole a career-high 90 in 1983, when he became the first player since Ty Cobb to steal more than 70 bases and drive in more than 70 runs.

But anyone who's been called the best player in the National League by both Mike Schmidt and Pete Rose must be more than a base stealer, and Raines is.

As a second baseman for the Denver

Tim Raines

Bears, he was the Minor League Player of the Year in 1980, leading the American Association with a .354 average and 77 stolen bases.

He didn't let up in the majors. Beginning in 1984, the switch-hitting Raines hit over .300 four straight years, including .334 in 1986 to win the National League batting crown.

He also sparkled on defense. Compensating for an average arm with outstanding range, he led National League outfielders with 21 assists in 1983 and with four double plays in 1985.

When his career is over, however, many fans may remember the native of Sanford, Florida, as the man who nearly made spring training obsolete.

In 1987, Raines became a free agent but, incredibly, no other team offered him a contract, an event that later brought a finding of collusion. He re-signed with Montreal but missed all of spring training and the first month of the season.

No matter. On his first day back, against the New York Mets, Raines rapped the first pitch he saw for a tri-ple. Next came a walk and two singles, then, finally, a game-winning grand-slam homer in the tenth inning. The next day, he socked another homer.

He wound up with probably his best season ever, batting .330 with a career-high 18 homers and 68 runs batted in, and leading the league with 123 runs scored.

Amazingly, most of Raines' accom-plishments have come since a drug problem that threatened to ruin his career almost before it got started.

In 1982, he admitted spending $40,000 on a cocaine habit so strong he even snorted the drug in the club-house between innings. But after off-season rehabilitation, he bounced back to hit .298 with a career-best 71 RBIs. He says he hasn't used drugs since.

"I try to never look back unless it's to learn things," Raines said. "I tell myself that you always have to look ahead."

Come to think of it, that's pretty ef-ficient philosophy for stealing bases, too.

Top Attractions
The Fur Trade in Lachine National Historic Park (514-637-7433), McCord Museum of Canadian History (690 Sherbrooke St. W., 514-398-7100), Montreal Aquarium (Ile Sainte-Helene, 514-872-4656), Montreal Botanical Garden (4101 Sherbrooke St. E., 514-872-1400), Montreal Museum of Fine Arts (1379 Sherbrooke St. W., 514-285-1600), Mount Royal Park, Old Fort and Museum (514-861-6701), Old Montreal and Old Port (514-283-5256), Olympic Park and Inclined Tower (514-252-8687), La Ronde (Ile Sainte-Helene, 514-872-6222), Underground City.

Tourism Information
Greater Montreal Convention and Tourism Bureau, 1010 Sainte-Catherine St. W., Suite 410, Montreal, Quebec, Canada H3B 1G2, 514-871-1595 (French and English).

Tourisme Quebec, PO Box 20,000, Quebec (Quebec), Canada G1K 7X2, 800-443-7000.

U.S. citizens visiting Canada will need to provide proof of citizenship (birth certificate or passport), proof of international auto insurance coverage and vehicle registration (or car rental agreement).

Olympic Stadium
4549 Pierre De Coubertin Ave.
Capacity: 43,739
Surface: Artificial
First Game: April 15, 1977
LF: 325   CF: 404   RF: 325

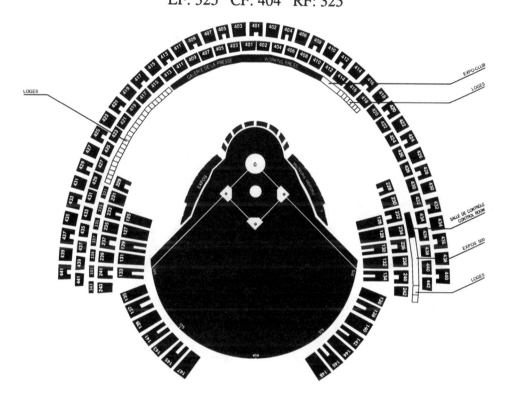

General Information
Montreal Baseball Club Ltd., PO Box 500, Station M, Montreal, Quebec, Canada H1V 3P2, 514-253-3434.
Ticket Information: 800-GO-EXPOS
Getting Tickets
Tickets held for day of game sales: 4,000 Bleacher seats
By mail: Montreal Baseball Club Ltd., Sales Department, PO Box 500, Station M, Montreal, Quebec, Canada H1V 3P2. Specify game date, ticket category and number of tickets (indicate preference of first base, third base or home). $4 handling charge. Check, VISA, MasterCard and American Express accepted.
By phone: 514-522-1910

Ticket Prices
VIP Box Seat $22, Box Seat (1st and 2nd level) $15, Box Seat (3rd level) $13, Terrace $11, Promenade $9, General Admission $5.50 ($2.50 for 15 and under, 65 and over).
Toughest Tickets To Get
New York and Los Angeles.
Game Times
Sunday 1:35. Weekdays 1:35. Weeknights 7:05, 7:35. Friday 7:35. Saturday 1:15, 1:35, 7:35. Eastern time. Gates open 2 hours before game.
Broadcasts
CFCF 600 AM, CTV (11), CBS TV (13), TSN (34).
Getting To The Stadium
In Olympic Park (northern part of city). Southeast of intersection of Highways 40 and 25. Stadium parking (10,000 spaces). Accessible by the Metro (subway).

One of the best things about Shea Stadium is that it's close to the airport. Of course, when jets roar over during games, that's also one of the worst things.

Does any team reflect the cynicism that's infiltrated the American sports scene over the last three decades better than the New York Mets?

The 1962 Mets were the worst team in modern baseball history, a team so creatively awful that a whole nation fell in love with their bumbling.

We laughed when Manager Casey Stengel sighed, "You look up and down the bench, and you have to say to yourself: 'Can't anybody here play this game?' "

To say the Mets these days are much more talented than the original team is like saying the Titanic could have used a defroster. But they aren't nearly as much fun.

In 1990, for the seventh straight season, they won more than 90 games. But not before Manager Davey Johnson got fired because of their sleepwalking play early on.

When they weren't lackadaisical, they were arrogant. Invisible early in the season, moody Darryl Strawberry followed Johnson's dismissal with the hottest streak of his career — and promptly demanded a $4.5 million-a-year long-term contract.

Then, as the Mets tried to catch the Pittsburgh Pirates in the final days of the season, he and Kevin McReynolds begged off with minor injuries. The Mets finished second, four games back. No doubt that made it a little bit easier for the Mets' brass to let Straw-beery sign a five-year $20.25 million deal with the Los Angeles Dodgers over the winter.

And does it only seem that every year some Met is undergoing treatment for drug or alcohol problems, or getting into a scuffle with a teammate or police?

Can anyone be blamed for thinking

New York
Mets

It's been a long time since the Mets were the worst expansion team in baseball history. Here's to the good old days.

the Mets want to permanently replace the Yankees as the New York team everyone loves to hate?

Okay, okay, not everyone. No question they're the Big Apple's favorite team. They've outdrawn the Yanks in attendance every year since 1983. Met fans are among the most vocal you'll find anywhere, and 1990 was the sixth straight that more than two million of them poured into Shea Stadium.

And no question they have reason to be proud. In their 29 years, the Mets have won three National League pennants and two World Series. No expansion team has done better.

Maybe the Mets' brash confidence simply mirrors that of the vibrant city they represent, the most exciting and diverse metropolis in the world.

There's no way to adequately capture New York in just a few sentences. It leads the league in the arts and fashion, in advertising and finance, in publishing and broadcasting. And don't forget taxis, skyscrapers and street vendors.

New York is roundly derided as the place in which nobody wants to live, but more than seven million people do. If its five boroughs were split up, four would rank among the nation's top 10 cities. Some 18 million people visit every year, taking in New York sites like Central Park, Broadway, Wall Street and the Statue of Liberty, not to mention the city's 25,000 restaurants.

New York, of course, has grown since 1958, but even then it was inconceivable that the nation's largest city should not have a National League team. Which was exactly the situation facing New York after the Brooklyn Dodgers and New York Giants abruptly picked up and moved to California.

Efforts to get the Cincinnati Reds,

Philadelphia Phillies or Pittsburgh Pirates to move to New York failed, and initial bids for a National League expansion team were ignored. But lawyer William A. Shea and baseball executive Branch Rickey got everybody's attention when they began talking about forming a third major league — the Continental League — that would include New York and Los Angeles.

Voila! The American and National leagues agreed to expansion, the Continental League was a memory and New York suddenly had a new baseball team.

Trouble was, the old one, the Yankees, was the most successful franchise in either league. How do you compete with that?

New York's new National League team went for instant tradition. They called themselves the Mets, short for Metropolitans, the name of New York's team in the old American Association of the 1880s. Their uniforms had the Dodgers' blue, the Giants' orange and the Yankees' pinstripes. They played in the Giants' old park, the Polo Grounds. Their new manager, Casey Stengel, had played for the Dodgers and Giants, then managed the Dodgers and Yanks.

The final bit of tradition wasn't planned, but it couldn't have been more perfect: The Mets played like the 1930s Dodgers, a team legendary for its ineptitude.

How bad were the 1962 Mets? Not so bad, as the legend goes, that the very first run they gave up came on a first-inning balk by Roger Craig in the '62 opener against the St. Louis Cardinals. But bad enough that they still lost that game 11-4.

That defeat was the first of nine in a

row for the Mets, and that was only their fourth-longest losing streak of the season. The ninth-place Chicago Cubs lost 103 games — and finished 18 games ahead of New York. Craig, the Mets' winningest pitcher, was 10-24. Their No. 2 man, Al Jackson, went 8-20.

Personifying the Mets' fumbling antics was first baseman Marv Throneberry, who led the league with 17 errors, most of them at the worst possible time. Once he hit a triple but was called out for missing first base. When Stengel rushed out to appeal, Mets Coach Cookie Lavagetto said, "Don't argue too much, Case, I think he missed second base, too."

New Yorkers have always prized winners. Combined, their teams have won 30 World Series since 1903. But the early Mets touched them in a way the staid Yankees never could. "To err is human, to forgive is a Mets fan," read one of the myriad banners that popped up at the Polo Grounds.

More than 900,000 people turned out that first year, and in 1964, the last-place Mets sold 1.7 million tickets, outdrawing the American League champion Yankees. By that time, they were in Shea Stadium, a windy, 55,601-seat stadium in Queens where roaring jets from La Guardia Airport still provide a constant counterpoint to Met rallies.

Those early fans especially loved the garrulous Stengel, who had managed the Yanks to 10 pennants in 12 years before being dumped in 1960 because he was 71 years old. Stengel had also managed some bad Dodger and Boston Brave teams, and his amused tolerance set just the right tone.

"The only thing worse than a Mets game is a Mets double header," he said.

But by the time a broken hip forced Stengel's retirement in mid-1965, there were signs of hope. The Mets rose to ninth in 1966, and the next season Tom Seaver won 16 games and was named National League Rookie of the Year.

It was 1969 before the Mets finally had a winning team. But it was a dandy. Seaver won 25 games and the Cy Young Award, leading a pitching staff that threw a league-high 28 shutouts. Tommie Agee hit 26 homers; Cleon Jones batted .340.

And the Mets, filling New York with a joy the city has never again experienced, charged past the Cubs to win their first N.L. East title, swept the Atlanta Braves in the playoffs, then showed just how amazin' they were by upsetting the powerful Baltimore Orioles in the World Series.

It was one of those special years, like 1927 and 1960 and 1975. Outfielder Ron Swoboda knew it. "This is the first time," he said. "Nothing can ever be as sweet again."

After the manager of that team, Gil Hodges, died of a heart attack in 1972, Yogi Berra took over. And the next year he nearly guided the Mets to a repeat of the miracle.

In the closest major league race of the century, the Mets won just 82 games but held on in a scramble that saw the top five N.L. East teams finish within five games of each other. Reliever Tug McGraw saved 25 games but, more importantly, coined the rallying cry, "You gotta believe," as the Mets upset the Reds in the playoffs before falling to the Oakland A's in a seven-game World Series.

With five last-place finishes in seven

years, the Mets of the late '70s and early '80s resembled those early teams, but without the charm. Only after Nelson Doubleday and Fred Wilpon bought the team from the family of original owner Joan Whitney Payson in 1980 did a recovery begin.

In 1986, after a pair of second-place finishes sparked by homegrown stars Darryl Strawberry and Dwight Gooden, Davey Johnson guided the Mets to a 108-54 record — the best in franchise history — and their second World Series victory.

During the regular season, the Mets cruised, leading the league in scoring, hitting and pitching. In postseason play, they showed their toughness, going 16 innings in the final game to edge the Houston Astros in the National League playoffs, then defeating the Boston Red Sox in a seven-game World Series saved by a stirring ninth-inning rally in Game Six.

The 1988 season looked like a rerun, as the Mets won the N.L. East by 15 games. This time it may have been too easy, though. The Dodgers surprised them in the playoffs, then did the same thing to the favored A's in the World Series.

Still, with players like Gooden, Kevin McReynolds, Howard Johnson, Vince Coleman, Hubie Brooks, David Cone and and John Franco, the Mets may have as much talent as any team in the National League.

Like the Yankees of old, they'll probably keep on marching to those 90 victories a year, winning a pennant every once in a while. They're too good not to.

But wouldn't it be a kick to see Marv Throneberry hit again?

Shea Stadium

Tom Seaver

Gen. William D. Eckert is the least remembered of baseball's eight commissioners, but in 1966 he made a ruling that changed the course of the sport for the next two decades.

The Atlanta Braves had just drafted a young pitcher off the University of Southern California campus and signed him for a reported $40,000 bonus.

But Eckert voided the contract, saying it violated baseball's rule against signing a college player during the season. After the NCAA ruled the pitcher ineligible for college play, however, Eckert decided any team except the Braves could participate in a lottery for him.

That's how Tom Seaver, instead of joining the ranks of great Braves pitchers like Warren Spahn and Phil Niekro, became the ace of the New York Mets.

In 1967, the right-handed Seaver was named National League Rookie of the Year for winning 16 games with a last-place team, and people started calling him "Tom Terrific."

It was an understatement. In a 20-year career that also included stints with the Cincinnati Reds, the Chicago White Sox and the Boston Red Sox, Seaver won 311 games and three Cy Young awards.

He struck out a National League-record 19 batters in one game, led the league in strikeouts five times and is fourth on the career list with 3,640.

He threw a no-hitter and won 20 games five times. Three times he led the league in victories and earned run average.

"Blind people come to the park just

Tom Seaver

to listen to him pitch," slugger Reggie Jackson once said.

Seaver had a 98-mph fastball that he threw with a powerful, driving motion that left his left knee perpetually dirty from scuffing the ground.

But he also had great control, never walking more than 89 batters in a season. During the same time Seaver pitched, baseball's greatest strikeout pitcher, Nolan Ryan, walked nearly 900 more batters.

With his good looks, cultural interests and clean-cut enthusiasm, Seaver drew inevitable comparisons with New York's first great right hander, Christy Mathewson. He didn't mind.

"As a pitcher, I feel I'm creating something," he said. "Pitching itself is not enjoyable while you're doing it. Pitching is work. I don't enjoy it until I can stand back and look at what I've created. That is something.''

Seaver's greatest gift, though, may have been a fierce competitive nature that he passed along to his teammates. ''There are only two places in this league,'' he said. ''First place and no place.''

Before he arrived, the Mets had finished out of the cellar just once. From 1967 until 1977, when he was traded to the Reds after a contract dispute, they were almost always in contention.

In 1969, when the Mets stunned the baseball world by winning their first World Series, and again in 1973, when they just missed, Seaver won the Cy Young Award. No. 3 came in 1975, when New York finished third despite his 22-9 record.

After 5 1/2 seasons with the Reds, Seaver returned to the Mets in 1983, only to be claimed by the White Sox the next season when New York did not protect him on its roster.

He won his 300th career victory in 1985, then wound up his career in appropriate fashion the next season with Boston. The 41-year-old Seaver won five games. And the Red Sox won their first pennant in 11 years.

Top Attractions
American Museum of Natural History (Central Park West at 79th St., 212-769-5100), Central Park (212-397-3156) and Central Park Zoo (212-408-0271), Carnegie Hall (Seventh Ave at 57th St., 212-247-7800), Empire State Building (Fifth Ave. at 34th St., 212-736-3100), General Grant National Memorial (Riverside Dr. and 122nd St., 212-666-1640), Solomon R. Guggenheim Museum (Fifth Ave. at 89th, 212-360-3513), Intrepid Sea-Air-Space Museum (Pier 86, W. 46th St., 212-245-0072), Madison Square Garden (Seventh Ave. at 31st St.), Times Square, Metropolitan Museum of Art (Fifth Ave. at 82nd St., 212-879-5500), Museum of Modern Art (11 W. 53rd St., 212-708-9480), New York Public Library (Fifth Ave. at 42nd St.), New York Stock Exchange (212-656-5168), Rockefeller Center (Fifth Ave. and 51st. St., 212-698-8676), Statue of Liberty (Liberty Island, 212-363-3200, Circle Line Boat departs from Battery Park, 212-269-5755), United Nations (First Ave. at 45th St., 212-963-7713), Whitney Museum of American Art (945 Madison Ave., 212-570-3676), World Trade Center (212-466-7397).

Tourism Information
New York City Convention and Visitors Bureau, Two Columbus Circle, New York, NY 10019, 212-397-8222.

New York State Division of Tourism, One Commerce Plaza, Albany, NY 12245, 518-474-4116 or 800-225-5697.

Shea Stadium
126th St. and Roosevelt Ave.
Capacity: 55,601
Surface: Natural
First Game: April 17, 1964
LF: 338   CF: 410   RF: 338

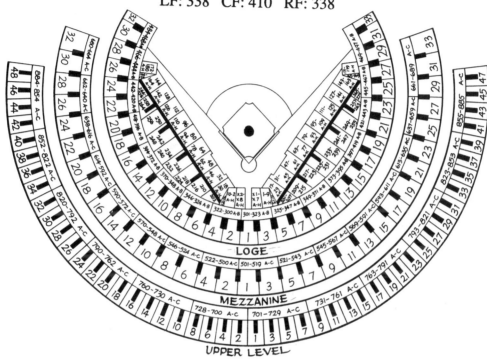

General Information
New York Mets, Shea Stadium, Flushing, NY 11368, 718-507-6387.
Getting Tickets
No day of game ticket holdbacks.
Stadium Advance Ticket Window: near Gate D. Monday-Friday 9-6, Saturday, Sunday and Holidays 9-5.
By mail: Mets Ticket Dept., Shea Stadium, Flushing, NY 11368. Specify game date, number of tickets and price. $2 postage and handling charge. Check, money order, MasterCard, VISA or American Express accepted. Allow 4 weeks for delivery.
By phone: Ticketron at 718-507-0303. MasterCard, VISA and American Express accepted.
Ticket Prices
Box $14, Upper Level Box $11, Loge and Mezzanine Reserved $11, Back Rows, Loge and Mezzanine Reserved $6.50, Upper Level Reserved $6.50.

Discounts & Promotions
Promotions for approximately 30 games. Senior citizen designated dates $1. Approximately 30 promotions.
Toughest Tickets To Get
St. Louis and Los Angeles.
Game Times
Sunday 1:40. Weekdays 1:40. Weeknights 7:40. Friday 7:40. Saturday 1:15, 1:40, 7:10. Eastern time. Gates open 2 hours before game.
Broadcasts
WFAN 660 AM, WWOR TV (9).
Other Notes
Non-alcohol seating available. No stadium tours.
Getting To The Stadium
South of La Guardia Airport, I-278 at Roosevelt Ave. Stadium parking available. Accessible by bus and subway.

Brooklyn Dodgers

Ebbetts Field has been gone for 30 years now, but the Brooklyn Dodgers left a mark on major league baseball that will never be forgotten.

Funny. Colorful. Daring. Exciting. Classy. Pick a word. They all apply to the team the rowdy, faithful denizens of Flatbush fondly called "Dem Bums."

From 1884 to 1957, the Dodgers were the pride of Brooklyn, winning three National League pennants by 1900 and nine more in baseball's modern era.

They gave the baseball world Casey Stengel, Zack Wheat, Dazzy Vance, Babe Herman, Leo Durocher, Pete Reiser, Duke Snider, Pee Wee Reese and Roy Campanella.

And in 1947, they forever changed the face of baseball by introducing a young second baseman named Jackie Robinson and breaking the game's color line.

Given that, it's only fitting that Brooklyn was a baseball hotbed even before the Civil War. One of the city's early teams, the Brooklyn Atlantics, set the tone for the zany times to come with a player named Bob "Death to Flying Things" Ferguson.

The Dodgers were initially nicknamed the Bridegrooms, then the Superbas and the Robins. Their present name originated in the 1890s, when Brooklyn traffic was such that residents were called trolley-dodgers.

Ebbets Field was built in 1913 and immediately stamped itself as different when officials discovered on Opening Day that it lacked a press box.

It was a cozy park, with a concave right-field wall that created crazy bounces, fervent fans like cowbell-clanging Hilda Chester, and the famous Sym-Phony Band, which struck up *Three Blind Mice* when the umpires took the field.

National League pennants flew in Brooklyn in 1916 and 1920. But the 1930s were the era of the Daffy Dodgers, a team of such inspired awfulness that sportswriter Edward T. Murphy once wrote: "Overconfidence may cost the Dodgers sixth place."

The classic Dodger misadventure came when Babe Herman hit a bases-loaded double and tried to stretch it to three bases. Only problem was that two other Dodgers, confused in all the excitement, were already on third when he got there. Double play.

Things changed, though, in 1941 when fiery Manager Leo Durocher guided the Dodgers to a pennant and ushered in the greatest period in Brooklyn history.

These were the scrappy Dodgers of Preacher Roe and Ralph Branca, of Dixie Walker and Carl Furillo, of Snider and Reese and Robinson and Campanella.

They won seven National League pennants over 16 years, each ending in a Subway Series with the New York Yankees and bringing the cry "Wait 'Til Next Year!" as the Yanks usually prevailed.

In 1955, however, next year finally came. Johnny Podres threw a shutout at New York in Game Seven, and Brooklyn had its first World Series championship.

It was also the only one. The lure of a bigger stadium and more television money was too much for owner Walter O'Malley, and three years later he moved the Dodgers to Los Angeles.

Ebbets Field was torn down in 1960. There's an apartment complex there now.

New York Giants

The New York Yankees were proud. The Brooklyn Dodgers were hard-nosed. And the New York Giants — well, the Giants were a whole lot of both.

Tradition? The Giants have been gone since 1958, and there are still only two teams that boast more than their nine pennants and five World Series since 1900.

Tough? How about "Iron Man" Joe McGinnity, who pitched 842 innings and won 66 games — over two years, 1903 and 1904 — and hit one batter for every 19 he faced.

For 67 years, the Giants and their horseshoe-shaped park, the elegantly named Polo Grounds, were a fixture along the Harlem River on the northern end of Manhattan.

They began play in 1883 as the New York Gothams, one of two teams owner John B. Day formed with players from the disbanded Troy, New York, franchise of the National League. Two years later, Manager Jim Mutrie was calling them "my giants," and the name stuck as they won the city's first National League pennants in 1888 and 1889.

But it was John McGraw, a pugnacious fireplug nicknamed "Little Napoleon," who turned the Giants into New York's first baseball dynasty. McGraw became manager in 1903, and the Giants captured 10 pennants in the next 29 years — winning World Series in 1905, 1921 and 1922 — and finished second 11 times.

Connie Mack managed in the majors for 53 years and had eight World Series teams, but he conceded, "There has only been one manager, and his name is John McGraw." McGraw's first two pennant winners may have been the best. The 1904 Giants won 106 games, but the stubborn McGraw refused to let them play the Boston Red Sox of the upstart American League in the World Series. The next year, they went 105-48 and knocked off the Philadelphia A's in the World Series.

McGinnity was the workhorse of these teams, but Christy Mathewson was the star. Handsome, intelligent and a perfect model for kids, he refused to pitch on Sunday. But only Cy Young and Walter Johnson had more than his 373 victories, which included 80 shutouts. Mathewson invented the screwball, and it helped him win at least 20 games in all but four of his 17 seasons.

He won most of them in the Polo Grounds, opened in 1891, rebuilt after a fire in 1911 and so named simply because the Giants' first ballpark was next to a polo field. Like most early stadiums, it was unique. A mammoth center field coexisted with the shortest pair of foul lines in the majors, both bullpens were in fair territory and the clubhouse was at the top of some stairs in deepest center.

McGraw managed through 1932, his final blaze of glory a string of four straight Giant pennants from 1921 through 1924. First baseman Bill Terry, the last National Leaguer to hit .400 (.401 in 1930), took over and New York won three more pennants over the next five years behind the hitting of Mel Ott and the pitching of Carl Hubbell.

The 1950s brought the last great Giant era, this one under tempestuous Manager Leo Durocher, and two of the most memorable moments in any sport.

Bobby Thomson's pennant-clinching homer against the Dodgers in 1951 is still the standard by which clutch hits are measured. The same can be said for Willie Mays' acrobatic snag of Vic Wertz's drive in the 1954 World Series, a play so famous it is simply called The Catch.

The Giants' final game in the Polo Grounds came in 1957. Following the cue of Brooklyn Dodgers owner Walter O'Malley, they moved west and opened the 1958 season as the San Francisco Giants.

The Polo Grounds, after getting a reprieve as a temporary home to the expansion New York Mets, was demolished in 1964 to make room for low-cost housing units.

*Since 1971, the Phillies have played
in Veterans Stadium, part of the rash
of round, multi-purpose stadiums that
broke out in the National League in the
1960s and 1970s.*

162

It's the City of Brotherly Love, the place established by William Penn and the Quakers as a refuge for those fleeing religious persecution.

It's the cradle of American democracy, the site of the signing of the Declaration of Independence, the first capital of the United States.

And it's the city in which W.C. Fields, one of its most famous natives, said he'd rather be.

For baseball fans, however, Philadelphia has two other claims to fame: the losingest team in major league history and the toughest fans this side of a soccer match.

Since their birth in 1883, when the Worcester, Massachusetts, franchise was moved to Philadelphia, the Phillies have finished last in the National League or N.L. East 28 times. They have lost 8,661 regular season games in their 108-year history. It was 32 years before they won their first pennant and 97 years until their first — and only — World Series championship.

Of the modern era's 16 original franchises, only the Cleveland Indians, with three, own fewer than the Phillies' four pennants. And the Indians have won a pair of World Series.

No wonder Philadelphia fans are surly, you say. No wonder they're so tough, as ex-Phillies pitcher Bo Belinsky put it, that they'd boo a funeral.

But the Phillie faithful's reputation for nastiness is too colorful to be blamed solely on frustration. There are too many signs they relish their obnoxiousness.

"They have Easter egg hunts in Philadelphia," said catcher-turned-quipster Bob Uecker. "And if the kids don't find the eggs, they get booed."

Philadelphia
Phillies

Phillie fans may be the toughest in all of baseball. You'd be cranky, too, if your team had won just one World Series in 108 seasons.

163

That's only a mild exaggeration. During one game in 1949, Phillie fans got so angry at one umpire's call that they rained bottles, cans and vegetables onto the field, prompting a Philadelphia forfeit.

The old Philadelphia A's also had their share of cantankerous followers. A pair of brothers, Bull and Eddie Kessler, razzed A's infielder Jimmy Dykes so badly in 1932 that Manager Connie Mack tried to get an injunction against them. When that failed, he ended up trading Dykes to protect the player's sanity. Another A's fan, Pete Adelis, was so infamous that the New York Yankees actually imported him on occasion to heckle their opponents.

Mike Schmidt is considered the best third baseman in the history of the game and in 1983 was voted by Philadelphia fans as the greatest Phillie ever. With him at third, the Phils won a World Series, two National League pennants and five N.L. East titles from 1976 through 1983.

Yet the hometown heckling of Schmidt during most of his career was legendary, an attitude that often spilled over into the sports pages of Philadelphia newspapers.

"Philadelphia is the only city in the world where you can experience the thrill of victory and the agony of reading about it the next day," Schmidt once said.

Phillie ace Steve Carlton, with 329 victories one of the three winningest left-handers in major league history, was so aggravated by the atmosphere that he spent years refusing to talk to reporters.

Maybe Philadelphia just wasn't used to that success. This is a city whose first National League club, the original

Athletics, was kicked out in 1876 for refusing to make a road trip.

The second team, the Phillies, played all of its games but few of them well. In their 1883 debut, the Phils went 17-81, finishing 23 games out of seventh place. No other Philadelphia club has matched that record for single-season futility — but not for lack of trying.

Until the late 1970s, the best Phillie era was during World War I. They won their first pennant in 1915, losing the World Series to the Boston Red Sox, and finished second three other times between 1913 and 1917.

But in late 1917 they traded pitching ace Grover Cleveland Alexander, who'd won 30 games three years in a row, to the Chicago Cubs and promptly began a string of 14 straight losing seasons. Over the next 31 years, they finished last 17 times.

The 1930 Phillies batted .315 but came in a distant eighth with a 52-102 record, largely because their pitching staff, with a 6.71 earned run average, was the worst of the century.

The Phils' best hitter in the 1930s was Chuck Klein, a left handed slugger who belted 180 homers and drove in 693 runs over a five-year period. He was named the league's Most Valuable Player in 1932 and won the Triple Crown the next year with 28 homers, 120 RBIs and a .368 average — after which Philadelphia traded him to the Cubs.

Then there was luckless Hugh Mulcahy, whose name appeared on the wrong end of the box score so many times he was nicknamed "Losing Pitcher." He went 13-22 in 1940, his best season, then fled the Phils for the military, the first ballplayer to enlist in World War II.

There were other misadventures. In 1943, William D. Cox bought the financially troubled Phillies and almost immediately was banned from baseball for betting on them. Maybe he should have pleaded insanity. The Phils lost 90 games.

The next owner, Bob Carpenter, changed the team's name to the Blue Jays for 1944 and 1945, but the move didn't do anything to change their luck. They finished last two more times.

Philadelphia baseball, in fact, may have hit its nadir in 1945. The Athletics also finished last; between them, the two teams lost 206 games and wound up a combined 86 1/2 games out of first.

Sometimes things got dangerous. In 1949, first baseman Eddie Waitkus was shot by a woman in a hotel room, an incident that inspired a key scene in Bernard Malamud's *The Natural*.

The next season, however, was the year of the ''Whiz Kids.'' Behind slugger Del Ennis and pitchers Robin Roberts and Jim Konstanty, the youthful Phils won their first pennant in 35 years, a triumph only slightly tempered by the Yankees' World Series sweep.

Gene Mauch was regarded as one of the smartest managers in baseball history, but he never got into a World Series. Maybe he should have started off with a different team than the Phillies, who lost a major league record 23 games in a row in 1961.

Mauch's 1964 Phils were much better, at least till the end of the season. With 12 games to play, they led the National League by 6 1/2 games. Then, came one of the greatest collapses in

baseball history. The Phillies lost 10 in a row, and the St. Louis Cardinals rallied to win the pennant on the final day of the season.

The Phils spent most of the years from 1883 through 1938 in Baker Bowl, a cozy ballpark whose safety record wasn't any better than the team's won-loss mark. Twelve people were killed in 1903 when the left-field stands collapsed during a game. In 1927, a similar accident in the right-field stands killed one person and injured scores of others.

Baker Bowl's dilapidated state prompted the Phillies to move into Shibe Park as tenants of the A's in 1938, and they took over the stadium on Philadelphia's north side when the American League team moved to Kansas City in 1955.

Since 1971, the Phils' home has been Veterans Stadium, part of the rash of round, multi-purpose, articifial turf stadiums that broke out across the National League in the 1960s and 1970s. The Vet, located in South Philly next to The Spectrum and John F. Kennedy Stadium, has also witnessed its share of the unusual, mostly on Opening Day.

In 1971 the ceremonial first ball was dropped from a helicopter, and Opening Day has been like something out of Barnum & Bailey ever since. Human cannonballs, paratroopers, a trapeze artist, even — in 1976 — a Paul Revere look-a-like, all have delivered the first ball. The Philly favorite, though, was Kiteman, a hang-glider pilot who crashed into the center-field bleachers one year and onto the warning track the next. When the stunt finally went off without a hitch several

Veterans Stadium

years later, the Vet was predictably filled with a chorus of boos.

Until the 1970s, the Phillie tradition of futility had been interrupted by only occasional flashes of competence. But Steve Carlton and Mike Schmidt changed that. Carlton, acquired in a trade with the Cardinals, won 27 games for the last-place Phils in 1972 and the first of four Cy Young awards. Two years later, Schmidt became the third baseman, and in 1975 Philadelphia began a string of nine straight winning seasons.

They were solid teams, carried by the bats of Schmidt and Greg Luzinksi, the gloves of shortstop Larry Bowa, catcher Bob Boone and center fielder Garry Maddox, the pitching of Carlton and Tug McGraw, and the managing of malaprop-prone Danny Ozark.

The Phils won three consecutive N.L. East titles beginning in 1976, but failure in the playoffs persuaded them to sign free agent Pete Rose in 1979, and it paid off the next season.

Under Manager Dallas Green, who replaced Ozark in late '79, Philadelphia beat Montreal twice at the end of the season to take the division by a game over the Expos, then squeezed past the Houston Astros in a five-game playoff that many still say is the most exciting ever played.

Then came the moment Phillie fans had been waiting for since sporting goods magnate Alfred J. Reach brought the team to town 97 years earlier. Schmidt hit .381 with two homers and seven RBIs and Carlton won two games as the Phils beat the Kansas City Royals in six games for their first World Series championship.

But since winning another pennant in 1983 and losing the World Series to the Baltimore Orioles, the Phillies have returned to form, going through four managers and finishing last in 1988 and 1989.

Still, there were signs of life in 1990, with scrappy Lenny Dykstra hitting .325, Dale Murphy hitting 24 homers and Terry Mulholland throwing a no-hitter. The Phils stayed in the N.L. East race for much of the year before slipping into a fourth-place tie with the Cubs at 77-85.

Maybe with some positive vibes from the fans, things will get even better. As Danny Ozark, that Philly sage of the 1970s, once philosophized: "Half of this game is 90 percent mental."

167

Mike Schmidt

Mike Schmidt was almost as famous for his love-hate relationship with the Philadelphia fans as he was for his slugging and slick play at third base.

Never mind that Schmidt hit more home runs than any other third baseman in major league history. Never mind that only Hall of Famer Brooks Robinson won more Gold Gloves at third base.

The Phillie fans booed him when he struck out. They booed him when he made an error. Once, he was even heckled by kids on a school bus as he went to pick up his daughter.

Schmidt didn't suffer these slights

Mike Schmidt

lightly, and in a 1985 newspaper article, he blasted the Veterans Stadium denizens as "an uncontrollable mob."

The story, which appeared during a road trip, seemed to guarantee the most vicious jeers yet when the Phillies returned. But he was ready for them.

When he took his position at third that night, Schmidt was wearing a long wig and preposterous sunglasses. Only the meanest spoilsports didn't join the laughter that suddenly erupted throughout the Vet.

Mostly, though, Schmidt was all business. And in his 18 years in Philadelphia — the longest any player has spent there — business was pretty darn good.

He walloped 548 homers, leading the National League eight times in that department. Twice he hit homers in four consecutive at-bats, once in one game, a feat rarer than a no-hitter.

A converted shortstop with above-average range, he won 10 Gold Gloves at third, including eight in a row, and set a league record for assists with 404 in 1974.

"He was the kind of player who, if you're lucky, comes along once in a lifetime," said Phillie President Bill Giles after Schmidt retired in 1989. "He was the best player in the history of the Philadelphia Phillies."

Yet during his career, the nononsense Schmidt was often criticized for being too cerebral. Never satisfied, he was always tinkering with his stance and his swing.

"They'd always said I thought too much," said Schmidt, who had majored in business administration at Ohio University. "But what people don't realize is that the game of baseball can just reach out, grab you and humble you.''

More often than not, that thinking paid off. In 1980, he hit 48 homers — a single-season record for a third baseman — with 121 RBIs and a .286 average to win the Most Valuable Player Award. He won it again in 1981 and 1986.

He struck out a lot, leading the National League four times, and the only time he batted over .300 was in strike-shortened 1981. But he also was the league leader in walks four seasons, and he could steal a base when needed, swiping 29 in 1975.

''If Mike Schmidt had hit .320,'' baseball author Bill James wrote in his *Historical Baseball Abstract*, ''he would have been the best player who ever lived. Even 50 points lower, he is the best third baseman.''

In 1989, millions of baseball fans across the country agreed through a very special gesture. They voted him to the National League All-Star team — one month after he retired.

Philadelphia Historic Area
Independence National Historic Park (3rd and Walnut St. and surrounding area, 215-597-8974). Betsy Ross House, First Bank of the United States, Independence Hall, Liberty Bell Pavilion, Old City Hall.

Other Attractions
Academy of Natural Sciences (19th St. and Benjamin Franklin Pkwy., 215-299-1000), Edgar Allen Poe House (532 N. 7th St., 215-597-8780) and Edgar Allen Poe National Historic Site (313 Walnut St.), The Franklin Institute (Science Museum and Planetarium) (20th St. and Benjamin Franklin Pkwy., 215-448-1200), Pennsylvania Academy of Fine Arts (Broad and Cherry Sts., 215-972-7600), Philadelphia Museum of Art (26th St. and Benjamin Franklin Pkwy., 215-763-8100), Philadelphia Zoo (34th and Girard Ave., 215-243-1100).

Little League Baseball Museum
See information in Pittsburgh Pirates chapter.

Tourism Information
Philadelphia Convention and Visitors Bureau, 1515 Market St., Philadelphia, PA 19102, 215-636-3300 or 800-321-WKND.

Pennsylvania Bureau of Travel Marketing, 453 Forum Building, Harrisburg, PA 17120, 717-787-5453 or 800-VISIT-PA.

Veterans Stadium
Broad and Patterson Sts.
Capacity: 62,382
Surface: Artificial
First Game: April 10, 1971
LF: 330   CF: 408   RF: 330

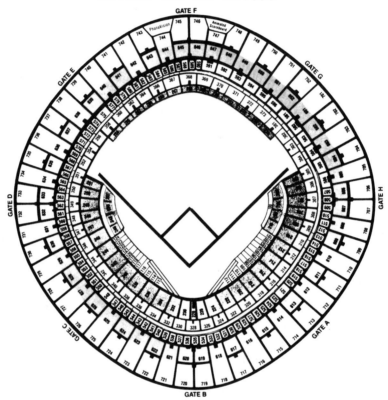

General Information
Philadelphia Phillies, PO Box 7575, Philadelphia, PA 19101, 215-463-6000.
Ticket Information: 215-463-1000.
Getting Tickets
No tickets held back for day of game sales.
By mail: The Phillies Tickets, PO Box 7575, Philadelphia, PA 19101.
By phone: 215-462-6108. VISA MasterCard and American Express accepted.
Ticket Prices
Field Box (200 level) $10, Terrace Box (300 level) $9, Loge Box (500 level) $9, Reserved (600 level) $6.50, Reserved (700 level) $4.
Discounts & Promotions
Promotions scheduled for approximately 30 games.
Toughest Tickets To Get
New York.

Game Times
Sunday 1:35. Weekdays 12:35, 7:35. Friday 7:35. Saturday 7:05. Eastern time. Gates open 90 minutes before game, 2 hours before game on Saturday and Sunday.
Other Notes
Phillie Phanatic does a musical routine during the 5th inning break and 7th inning stretch. No stadium tours for general public.
Phillies Home Video, PO Box 7575, Philadelphia, PA 19101.
Catalog of souvenirs: Phillies Merchandising Department at 215-463-6000.
Getting To The Stadium
South of central/historic Philadelphia, east of intersection of I-95 and I-76. Parking plentiful. Accessible by subway.

Philadelphia Athletics

Their passing has never been lamented with that of the Brooklyn Dodgers and New York Giants, but the Philadelphia Athletics were also one of baseball's fabled franchises.

From 1901 to 1954, the Athletics won nine American League pennants — second only to the New York Yankees — and five World Series.

The A's produced a string of Hall of Famers, including hitters like Home Run Baker, Jimmy Foxx and Al Simmons, and pitchers like Rube Waddell and Lefty Grove.

They also had the most respected manager in the game's history, Connie Mack, who ran the team from its inception until his retirement in 1950 at the age of 88.

No other major league manager has more career victories than Mack's 3,776. Of course, nobody's come very close to his 4,025 losses, either.

Which indicates, quite correctly, that when the A's weren't good, they were bad. Real bad. They finished last 19 times, including 11 seasons in which they piled up at least 100 losses.

That's enough to get most managers fired several times over, but Mack owned 25 percent of the team at the start and eventually became the majority stockholder.

He was as much a Philadelphia fixture as the Liberty Bell, a tall, dignified man who managed in a dark suit, tie and derby with a scorecard rolled up in his hand.

His very first team finished second. The next year, after Baltimore Manager John McGraw dismissed them as "white elephants," the A's won the pennant and cheerfully adopted that animal as their mascot.

From 1902 through 1914, Philadelphia won six pennants and three World Series, beating the Chicago Cubs in 1910 and McGraw's New York Giants in 1911 and 1913.

The latter teams boasted the $100,000 infield — a buck went a lot further then — of Stuffy McInnis, Eddie Collins, Jack Barry and Home Run Baker. The early A's most colorful character, though, was Rube Waddell. A child-like alcoholic who jumped the team to chase fire engines, wrestle alligators or watch minstrel shows, Waddell nevertheless had four straight 20-victory seasons. Years later, Mack still insisted he was the best left hander he'd ever seen.

The A's second great dynasty was 1929-31, when they won 104, 102 and 107 games en route to three straight pennants and capped the first two seasons with World Series victories over the Cubs and St. Louis Cardinals.

Jimmy Foxx, perhaps the strongest hitter baseball has ever seen, and Al Simmons, nicknamed "Bucketfoot Al," for his unorthodox stance, led the offense. Foxx socked 100 homers over those three years; in 1932, he belted 58. Simmons hit .381 in 1930 and .390 the next year, leading the league both times.

The pitching mainstay was Lefty Grove, a 300-game winner who led the American League in earned run average nine times and winning percentage five times, despite not reaching the majors until he was 25. Historian Bill James has called him "the greatest pitcher of all time, period."

But between these powerhouse clubs and again in later years, the A's were a hapless lot, largely because of attendance and money problems that prompted Mack to periodically sell off his stars. In 1915, they began a string of seven straight last-place seasons, including a 117-loss fiasco in 1916. Ten more bottom-of-the-heap finishes from 1935 to 1950 helped spell their end in Philadelphia.

Shibe Park, the A's home since it was built in 1909 as the majors' first concrete-and-steel ballpark, was renamed Connie Mack Stadium in 1952. But two years later, the Mack family sold the team to businessman Arnold Johnson, and an era ended when he decided to seek greener pastures in Kansas City.

Connie Mack, outlasting his old team by just two seasons, died in 1956.

*Three Rivers Stadium opened in
1970, ushering in the greatest period in
Pirate history. Over the next 10 years,
Pittsburgh won two World Series, two
National League pennants and six N.L.
East titles.*

Quick, can you name the winningest pitcher in the history of the Pittsburgh Pirates?

Okay. You don't even have to be quick. Take your time. Talk it over with a friend if you like.

But unless you're the most diehard of Pirate fans or can remember when President William Howard Taft was in the White House, you're going to have a tough time naming the top three, let alone No. 1.

Yes, Vern Law won a Cy Young Award in 1960 with a fine 20-9 record and a National League-leading 18 complete games. And forkballing Elroy Face won an amazing 17 straight games in relief in 1959.

Then there was Harvey Haddix, who pitched 12 perfect innings against the Milwaukee Braves on May 26, 1959, only to lose everything in the thirteenth on an error, a walk and Joe Adcock's run-scoring double.

None's the answer to our quiz, though. Bob Friend, the workhorse right hander of the 1950s and '60s? He's tops in losses with 218, but his 191 victories rank only No. 4 on the Pirate win list.

Tied for second at 194 are Babe Adams and Sam Leever, pitching stalwarts on the Pirate teams in the early part of this century but now just the faintest of memories.

The winningest Pittsburgh pitcher is Wilbur Cooper, another product of the Model T era. The left-handed Cooper won 202 games from 1912 to 1924, including four 20-victory seasons in his last five with the Pirates.

But he's not in the Hall of Fame, and neither are any of the others. In fact, of the 11 Hall of Famers who spent all or most of their careers with the Pirates, none are pitchers.

Pittsburgh
Pirates

Most of the Pirates' greatest hitters are in the Hall of Fame. Most of their pitchers are trivia questions.

The Pirates, in a tradition that continues today with the likes of Bobby Bonilla, Barry Bonds and Andy Van Slyke, have always been best known for their muscular, free-swinging hitters.

It's tempting to say that's right in step with Pittsburgh's swaggering, sweaty, hard-hat history. The city where the Allegheny and Monongahela rivers meet to form the Ohio has been a steel and iron center since the early 1800s, and the later development of nearby oil, coal and natural gas deposits only enhanced its blue-collar image.

But today's Pittsburgh is a gleaming city whose Golden Triangle skyscrapers have helped render its grimy, smoky reputation obsolete. Businesses range from H.J. Heinz to Rockwell International. And the industry has spawned a rich, cultural heritage in such institutions as the Carnegie Institute, Carnegie Music Hall and Carnegie Museum of Natural History.

Still, it was a rough-and-tumble mill town when the Pirates — then called the Alleghenies, after the nearby mountains — began play in the American Association in 1882. Five years later, they joined the National League. In 1890, they were so bad — a franchise-worst 23-113 and 66 1/2 games out of first — they were nicknamed the Innocents.

For the most part, though, the Pittsburgh franchise has had more good moments than bad. The Pirates — so named in 1891 because of the way they spirited away a player the Philadelphia A's had failed to protect — own five World Series titles, nine National League pennants and six N.L. East championships.

The winning began in earnest with the addition of their first and greatest star, Honus Wagner, who joined the Pirates in 1900 when the Louisville franchise folded. Wagner was a stocky, barrel-chested shortstop with long arms — the joke was he could tie his shoes without bending over — who hardly looked like the best player in the league.

But from 1900 to 1911, ''The Flying Dutchman'' won eight batting titles, leading the league in stolen bases five times and runs batted in four times. He's still among the career leaders in hits, doubles, triples and stolen bases. Wagner was also one of the best-liked players of his time, in stark contrast to ferocious Ty Cobb, the only player to enter the Hall of Fame ahead of him.

If, like many baseball fans, you consider the World Series the perfect annual ending to the world's best sport, you can thank Barney Dreyfuss.

It was Dreyfuss, the Pirates' owner, who invited the American League-champion Boston Pilgrims to play his team, which had just won its third straight pennant, in the first modern World Series in 1903. The Pirates lost the best-of-nine series in eight games, but a tradition was born.

After winning a club-record 110 games, Pittsburgh was back in the World Series in 1909, defeating the Detroit Tigers and Cobb in seven games for its first Series victory.

The Pirates' slugging tradition blossomed in the 1920s. Seven starters on the team that beat the Washington Senators in the 1925 World Series hit .300 or better, including Hall of Famers Kiki Cuyler, Max Carey and Pie Traynor. Until Mike Schmidt came along, Traynor was generally considered the top third baseman in National League history.

Two years later, the Pirates fell in the Series to the best New York Yankee team of all time, but not before introducing Lloyd "Little Poison" Waner, who hit .355 in his rookie year. His older brother, Paul "Big Poison" Waner, led the league with a .380 average and 131 RBIs in 1927.

Paul Waner was almost as famous for his drinking as for his hitting, much of which reportedly occurred while he was hung over. "I see three baseballs," he once said, "but I only swing at the middle one."

The Waners are the only brother combination in the Hall of Fame.

From 1909 until mid-1970, the Pirates made their home in Forbes Field, named after Revolutionary War General John Forbes and located in the shadow of the University of Pittsburgh's 42-story Cathedral of Learning. Boasting electric lights, telephones, elevators and ramps instead of stairs, the concrete-and-steel stadium was such a wonder that early admirers called it the Hialeah of ballparks.

In the beginning, it was also big: 360 feet down the left-field line, 376 feet to right and 462 to center. But in 1925, the addition of new stands shortened the right-field line to 300 feet. On May 25, 1935, Babe Ruth took advantage by hitting three homers — the last of his career. The next year, another left-handed hitter, Chuck Klein of the Philadelphia Phillies, slammed four homers in one game at Forbes.

In 1947, Forbes became friendlier for right-handed hitters as well, when the Pirates moved the left-field fence in 30 feet to accommodate newly acquired slugger Hank Greenberg. But

"Greenberg Gardens" quickly became known as "Kiner's Korner" in honor of the man who really took advantage of it.

Although it's become fashionable to disparage his feats in recent years, no slugger has had a streak like Ralph Kiner put together in the years after World War II. From 1946 to 1952, he led or tied for the league lead in home runs. Kiner's 369 career homers don't seem like a lot today, but he hit them all in just 10 years. Over his career, he had 7.1 homers for every 100 at-bats; only Babe Ruth did better.

It was Kiner who inspired pitcher Fritz Ostermueller's famous, pre-free agent comment, "Home-run hitters drive Cadillacs, single hitters drive Fords."

Despite Kiner's long-ball prowess, he played on the worst teams in Pittsburgh history. From 1946, when they were bought by a syndicate that included entertainer Bing Crosby, to 1957, the Pirates finished last five times and in seventh place five more. A horrendous 42-112 season in 1952 left them 54 1/2 games out of first.

But after General Manager Branch Rickey rebuilt the farm system in the early '50s, acquiring future stars Roberto Clemente, Dick Groat and Bill Mazeroski, the Bucs began the climb back to respectability.

In 1960, they were more than respectable, winning their first pennant in 33 years and upsetting the Yankees on the most dramatic hit in World Series history, Mazeroski's game-winning homer in the bottom of the ninth of Game Seven.

That team also had big Dick Stuart, whose predecessor at first base, Dale Long, set a major league record by homering in eight consecutive games in 1956. Stuart was an able slugger, belting 66 homers one season in the minors. But he's probably better remembered for the atrocious fielding that earned him the nickname "Dr. Strangeglove."

With the 1970s came the move to Three Rivers Stadium, a little-praised multi-purpose, artificial turf ballpark that nevertheless was the scene of the Pirates' most prosperous period.

This was the era of Clemente, Willie Stargell and Al Oliver, of the gaudy gold-and-black "Lumber Company" teams of cocky Dave Parker and Bill "Mad Dog" Madlock. It began with Clemente hitting .414 in the 1971 World Series — the first to include a night game — and ended with Stargell socking three homers for the "We Are Family" club in the '79 Series.

Both times the Pirates rallied to beat the Baltimore Orioles. In between, with pitching from Dock Ellis, Steve Blass, Jim Rooker, Jerry Reuss and John Candelaria, they won three other N.L. East titles, finishing second three times and third once.

Only a few years later, amazingly, Pittsburgh was on the brink of losing the Pirates because of drastically sagging attendance caused by poor play.

Two things happened, however, to turn things around. First, a local group, with a loan from the city, bought the team to keep it in town. Then General Manager Syd Thrift engineered trades that brought prospects Bobby Bonilla, Andy Van Slyke and Doug Drabek to Pittsburgh, and the draft produced the likes of Barry Bonds and John Smiley.

In 1988, just two years after their third straight season in the N.L. East cellar, the Pirates surprised everybody with a second-place finish.

And in 1990, despite a flurry of injuries, they held off the New York Mets to post a 95-67 record and win their first N.L. East title in 11 years. Bonds and Bonilla finished one-two in the Most Valuable Player race, while Drabek went 22-6 to claim the Cy Young Award. The Pirates also drew two million fans for the first time in their history. Only a playoff loss to the eventual world champion Cincinnati Reds kept it from being a perfect season.

But with Bonilla, Bonds and Van Slyke carrying on Pittsburgh's slugging tradition, the Pirates know the hits will keep on coming. And if Drabek can become more memorable than Wilbur Cooper, so may some more pennants.

Roberto Clemente

During much of his career, Roberto Clemente was accused of being moody, quick to take offense at slights real or imagined, and a incurable hypochondriac.

He was a proud man who didn't mind saying he thought his accomplishments, such as four National League batting titles, often went unappreciated.

He won the league's Most Valuable Player Award in 1966 with 29 homers, 119 runs batted in and a .317 batting average, and was convinced he should have won more.

His teammates liked him, but even they sometimes whispered that perhaps he was more concerned about Roberto Clemente's welfare than that of the Pittsburgh Pirates.

Curiously, his outspoken nature, quite a contrast from that of other black and Latin ballplayers of the 1960s, may have been the very thing that obscured Clemente's feats while he was playing.

At the other extreme, his special election to the Hall of Fame in March 1973 was obviously part of an emotional response to his death in a plane crash three months earlier.

It doesn't take a very long glance through the record books, however, to determine that Roberto Clemente deserves his place among baseball's elite.

In 18 seasons in the majors, he batted .317 with 240 homers, 1,305 RBIs and exactly 3,000 hits. A right-handed hitter known for fierce line drives, he hit .300 or better 13 times, including a career-high .357 in 1967 and .312 in 1972 at the age of 38.

Roberto Clemente

He also was tough in the clutch, batting .310 in the 1960 World Series against the New York Yankees and .414 with a pair of homers in 1971 against the Baltimore Orioles.

Clemente's prowess in right field may have been even more impressive. He won 12 consecutive Gold Gloves, and Pirate pitcher Steve Blass once said, "With him, it was like having four outfielders."

What really set him apart, though, was a throwing arm that some still say was the best that baseball's ever seen. It's certainly what prompted the Pirates to snatch the young Puerto Rican from the Brooklyn farm system for $4,000 in 1954 when the Dodgers left him unprotected.

He led the league in assists a record five times, including 27 in 1961, and there are countless stories of his gunning down surprised players at second base or even first. Bill Mazeroski swears Clemente once even threw a runner out on a bunt when the Pirates had a trick play on.

"He was the most complete ballplayer I ever saw," said former Los Angeles Dodger General Manager Al Campanis.

Some of the personality knocks on Clemente may have been deserved, but the hypochondria charge was probably a bad rap. A 1956 traffic accident left him with a chronic bad back, and even though critics said he missed too many games, he never played in fewer than 102 in a season.

His quest for recognition perhaps satisfied by the various awards, Clemente settled another criticism by taking more of a leadership role in his later years. The Pirates responded with N.L. East titles in his final three seasons.

He got his 3,000th hit in the last game of the 1972 season. Three months later, on December 31, 1972, he was helping deliver supplies to Nicaraguan earthquake victims when his plane crashed into the ocean off Puerto Rico, killing all aboard.

He was the first Hispanic player elected to the Hall of Fame.

Little League Baseball Museum
(approximately 4 hours east of Pittsburgh or 3 hours west of Philadelphia; PO Box 3485, South Williamsport, PA 17701, 717-326-3607).
Open 9-5 Monday-Saturday, noon-5 Sunday.
Admission $4 adult, $2 62 and over, $2 14 and under or $10 family.

Top Attractions
The Carnegie Museum (Museum of Art, Museum of Natural History) (440 Forbes Ave., 412-622-3172, Duquesne Incline (cable car ride) (1220 Grandview Ave., 412-381-1665), Monongahela Incline (205 W. Carson, 412-231-5707), Fallingwater (Frank Lloyd Wright house; Mill Run near Ohiopyle, 412-329-8501), Pittsburgh Zoo (Highland Park, 412-665-3639).

Tourism Information
Greater Pittsburgh Convention and Visitors Bureau, Four Gateway Center, Pittsburgh, PA 15222, 412-281-7711 or 800-821-1888.

Pennsylvania Bureau of Travel Marketing, 453 Forum Building, Harrisburg, PA 17120, 717-787-5453 or 800-VISIT-PA.

Three Rivers Stadium
600 Stadium Circle
Capacity: 58,729
Surface: Artificial
First Game: July 16, 1970
LF: 335   CF: 414   RF: 335

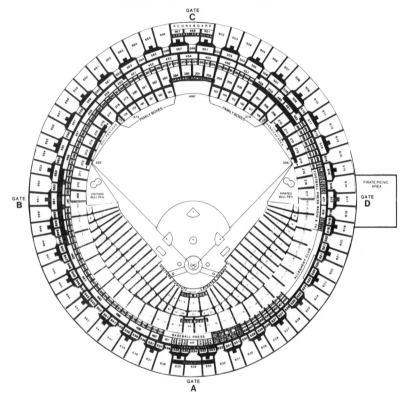

General Information
Pittsburgh Pirates, PO Box 7000, Pittsburgh, PA 15212, 412-323-5000.

Getting Tickets
Stadium ticket office: Gate A
By mail: The Pittsburgh Pirates, PO Box 7000, Pittsburgh, PA 15212. Specify date and price of tickets. $2.50 postage and handling charge. Check or money order accepted.
By phone: 800-BUY-BUCS. American Express, VISA, MasterCard and Discover Card accepted.

Ticket Prices
Club Box $12, Mezzanine Box $8.50, Terrace Box $8, Family Boxes $6.50 (no drinking, no smoking), Reserved $6.50, General Admission $5 ($2.50 for 12 and under).

Discounts & Promotions
Promotions scheduled for approximately half of the games.

Toughest Tickets To Get
New York

Game Times
Sunday 1:35. Monday-Saturday 7:35. Eastern time. Gates open 90 minutes before game.

Broadcasts
KDKA 1020 AM, KDKA TV (2), BLL (cable).

Other Notes
Pirate Cove picnic area for groups. Baseball Boardwalk (level one concourse, batting and pitching cages).
Pirates Clubhouse Store Catalog, Three Rivers Stadium, 600 Stadium Circle, Pittsburgh, PA 15212

Getting To The Stadium
Literally, where the Ohio, Monongahela and Allegheny Rivers converge. Across the Duquesne Bridge from central Pittsburgh area. Stadium parking available. Accessible by bus.

Busch Stadium and the Gateway Arch were key elements in St. Louis' successful efforts to revitalize its downtown area during the 1960s.

Is there a better baseball town in the United States than St. Louis? Most people who know about such things say no, and it's hard to argue with them.

The Cardinals were so bad in 1990 that Whitey Herzog, their manager for 10 years, quit midway through the season and they finished last for the first time since 1918.

Yet nearly 2.6 million fans poured through the turnstiles in Busch Memorial Stadium to watch the Cards play — this in a metropolitan area of barely 2.3 million people.

St. Louis' track record in other sports is, well, a bit embarrassing. In the last 25 years, the city has lost a pro football team, a pair of pro basketball teams and two pro soccer teams. And the hockey team, the Blues, was headed out of town in 1983 until the NHL vetoed the sale.

But St. Louisans are crazy about baseball. During the summer, red is the primary color in the Gateway City. Cardinal caps, T-shirts and jackets are everywhere. And just try turning on a local sports talk show without hearing someone wonder why the Cards didn't hit and run in the fourth last night or when they're going to call up that latest phenom from Louisville.

Actually, the Cardinals' popularity goes beyond St. Louis. Thanks in part to geography, Branch Rickey and Guiglielmo Marconi, they may be baseball's greatest regional team.

They certainly were the first. Until the late 1950s, the Cards were the only National League team west of the Mississippi River and south of the Mason-Dixon line, creating a natural following in the Midwest and South.

Under Rickey, St. Louis' general manager in the 1920s and '30s, the Cardinals put together the majors' first

St. Louis Cardinals

St. Louisans are crazy about baseball. So are a lot of other people in the Midwest and South. The Cardinals may be baseball's greatest regional team.

farm system, buying and operating dozens of minor league teams in small towns across the country.

That built rural fan interest even more, and so did radio. In parts of Arkansas, Illinois, Iowa and Nebraska, tuning in Cardinal broadcasts is a tradition. The grandsons of men who listened to Dizzy Dean describe Cardinal games now listen to Jack Buck; in between, their fathers heard Harry Caray and Joe Garagiola. The Cardinals' 50,000-watt flagship station, KMOX, can be heard in 44 states at night, and St. Louis has more than 130 radio affiliates in 11 states.

Of course, things might be different if the Cardinals didn't give their fans something to be excited about. Sure, 1990 was a washout, the Cards' 70-92 record their worst since 1978. But there haven't been many seasons like it at 250 Stadium Plaza.

The Cardinals own 15 National League pennants, three fewer than the Dodgers. And only the New York Yankees boast more modern world championships than St. Louis' nine. Fourteen players or managers who made their names with the Cardinals are in the Hall of Fame. St. Louis players have won 14 Most Valuable Player and two Cy Young awards.

Today, St. Louis is a major industrial city, the home of McDonnell-Douglas, General Dynamics, Ralston-Purina and, of course, Anheuser-Busch. It's sophisticated, with the country's second-oldest symphony and unique attractions like the Missouri Botanical Gardens and its 12,000 different plants and trees. Distinctive German, Irish and Italian neighborhoods give the city a cosmopolitan feel. And the shimmering Gateway Arch is a sig-

nature every bit as memorable as New York City's Statue of Liberty or San Francisco's Golden Gate Bridge.

But in 1881, it was still a rough river town, the kind of place where a guy might start a baseball team because there was a ballpark near his saloon and it seemed like a good way to get some customers. That's what Chris Von der Ahe did.

Von der Ahe's St. Louis Browns, the original Cardinals, dominated the American Association, then a major league, by winning four straight pennants from 1885 to 1888. They beat the National League's Chicago White Stockings in the 1886 World Series, but lost to the Detroit Wolverines the next season and the New York Giants in 1888.

Their oddest postseason appearance, however, was their first, a nomadic, sloppily played World Series with the White Stockings in 1885.

First of all, after a game in Chicago and three in St. Louis, the teams played one in Pittsburgh and two in Cincinnati. The owners boosted the gate by letting fans crowd onto the field, then kept all the ticket proceeds, neither of which gave the players much incentive. By some accounts, there were more than 100 errors in the seven games.

The first game was a tie, and the second ended in a St. Louis forfeit when Manager Charles Comiskey pulled his team off the field to protest an umpire's calls. The two teams later agreed to disregard the forfeit, but Chicago Manager Cap Anson changed his mind after St. Louis won the seventh game. After all that, each team wound up with three wins and a tie.

The Browns moved into the National

League in 1892 after the American Association folded. For awhile they were known as the Perfectos. After they changed their stocking color to red in 1899, a sportswriter began calling them the Cardinals. The new nickname became official a year later.

The most successful era in Cardinal history began in 1926, when St. Louis won its first National League pennant and stunned the Yankees in the World Series behind two victories and a famous seventh-game save from veteran Grover Cleveland Alexander.

Over the next 20 years, the Cardinals won eight more pennants and were world champions in 1931, 1934, 1942, 1944 and 1946.

Their first great star was Rogers Hornsby, the best hitter in National League history. His lifetime .358 mark is second only to Ty Cobb, he led the league in batting seven times, including a modern-era record .424 in 1924, and he won two Triple Crowns and a pair of MVP awards. He also managed the Cards in that 1926 championship year. Hornsby, however, also was second only to Cobb in orneriness, the main reason he spent the final 11 years of his career with five different teams.

There were other Cardinal heroes. Sunny Jim Bottomley, a first baseman, drove in 12 runs in one game in 1924, a major league record. Outfielder Chick Hafey, who won the 1931 batting title, was the first Hall of Famer to wear glasses.

During the Great Depression years of the 1930s, many people found fun and inspiration in the Cardinals' rowdy, eccentric Gas House Gang teams — so named because their usually dirty uniforms looked like those of service station or "gas house" mechanics.

Third baseman Pepper Martin was an Oklahoma-born prankster who liked to drop water-filled balloons out of hotel windows when he wasn't stealing bases headfirst or batting a record .418 in three World Series. Hard-hitting outfielder Joe Medwick was removed from a 1934 World Series game for his own safety after he slid hard into a Detroit infielder and angry Tiger fans began hurling rotten vegetables and bottles at him.

The king, though, was Dizzy Dean. It's impossible to describe Dean's impact on baseball in just a few words, but from 1932 to 1936 he averaged 24 wins, with a fabulous 30-7 mark in 1934, and led the league in strikeouts four times.

Most of all, the pride of Lucas, Arkansas, was a one-of-a-kind character. He was born Jay Hannah Dean, but often told reporters his name was Jerome Herman Dean. He was comically brash. After he threw a three-hitter in the first game of a double-header, his brother, Paul, tossed a no-hitter in the nightcap. "If I'd known Paul was going to pitch a no-hitter," said Dizzy, "I'd a pitched one, too." When he was hit in the head by a ball while pinch-running in the 1934 World Series, a newspaper headline the next day said, "X Rays of Dean's Head Show Nothing."

Dean's career was cut short when a line drive in the 1937 All-Star Game broke his toe and he hurt his arm trying to come back too soon. But he found a new career in broadcasting, where his homespun style was an immediate hit. Educators critized his

*A bronze statue of Stan Musial greets
visitors to Busch Stadium.*

mangled English, but he simply replied, "A lot of people who don't say 'ain't' ain't eating."

Stan Musial brought his unique peek-a-boo stance to the Cards in 1941, and they won four pennants in the next five years. From 1942 to 1944, St. Louis averaged 105 victories a season, the best three-year period for any National League team. Musial won three MVP awards in the '40s, as well as three of his seven batting titles. Pitcher Mort Cooper and shortstop Marty Marion also were MVPs.

In 1944, they beat the American League's St. Louis Browns four games to two in the only all-St. Louis World Series and the last Series to be played entirely in one ballpark.

That was Sportsman's Park, which the two teams shared from 1920 until the Browns moved to Baltimore in 1954 and the field was renamed Busch Stadium after Cardinal owner Augie Busch. Built in 1909, Sportsman's Park was best known for a screen erected atop its cozy 310-foot right-field wall in 1930. Philadelphia slugger Jimmy Foxx would have had 70 homers in 1932, instead of 58, had it not been for that screen. If it had been up in 1927, Babe Ruth would have hit 56 homers, not 60.

The Cardinals moved into Busch Memorial Stadium in 1966, two seasons after they broke an 18-year drought by winning the pennant and surprising the Yankees in the World Series.

St. Louis' return to dominance — the Cards beat the Boston Red Sox in the 1967 World Series and won another pennant in '68 — coincided with their belated development of black stars. Two were Curt Flood, whose 1970 suit against baseball's reserve clause paved the way for today's free-agent system, and Bill White, now president of the National League.

But the best were Hall of Famers Lou Brock and Bob Gibson. Stolen from the Cubs in a 1964 trade for pitcher Ernie Broglio, Brock set season and career stolen base records en route to Cooperstown. The intense, hard-throwing Gibson won two Cy Youngs and an MVP, winning 20 games five times and posting a league-record 1.12 earned run average in 1968, when he somehow lost nine games against 22 victories.

Under Manager Whitey Herzog in the 1980s, the operative word was speed. Paced by Vince Coleman, Ozzie Smith and Willie McGee, the Cardinals ran, ran, ran, leading the league in stolen bases from 1982 through 1988. They also beat the Milwaukee Brewers in the 1982 World Series and won pennants in 1985 and 1987.

The Cards now are a team in transition. Busch died in 1989, Herzog, McGee and Coleman left the next season, and new Manager Joe Torre, a former Cardinal catcher, is taking a long look at youngsters like Todd Zeile, Ray Lankford and Bernard Gilkey.

If they click and if key veterans like pitchers Joe Magrane and Jose DeLeon return to winning form, you can bet St. Louis fans will keep packing Busch Stadium.

Stan Musial

Stan Musial once held about 50 major league or National League records, but Hollywood will probably never make a movie about his life.

He wasn't funny like Dizzy Dean or tragic like Lou Gehrig. Once you got past his nickname, "Stan the Man," there wasn't anything particularly colorful about him at all.

He just went out and did his job like any good son of a Polish miner from western Pennsylvania would do. And his job was hitting baseballs.

"What he was was a ballplayer," Bill James wrote in his *Historical Baseball Abstract*. "He didn't spit at fans, he didn't get into fights in nightclubs, he didn't marry anybody famous. He hustled."

Musial started out as a pitcher, going 18-5 in the Florida State League in 1940 before hurting his arm. So he moved to the outfield the next year and hit .379 with 26 homers in the West Virginia League.

His arrival with the Cardinals in late '41 didn't draw much attention in the midst of Joe DiMaggio's 56-game hitting streak and Ted Williams' .406 average.

And some of those who did notice ridiculed his left-handed peek-a-boo batting crouch. Pitcher Ted Lyons said it looked like "a small boy looking around the corner to see if the cops are coming," and pitcher Fred Hutchinson predicted Musial would never make it.

But St. Louis won four pennants in his first five seasons, finishing second in 1945 while he was in the military. He was the National League Most Valuable Player in 1943, 1946 and 1948, and finished second four other times.

"What's the best way to pitch to Stan Musial?" teammate Joe Garagiola once asked. "That's easy. Walk him and then try to pick him off first base."

Musial wasn't flashy, just consistent. He won seven National League batting titles, the last in 1957 when he hit .351 at the age of 36. Five years later, as a 41-year-old grandfather, he batted .330.

"I just throw him my best stuff," said Brooklyn Dodger pitcher Carl Erskine, "then run over to back up third base."

Musial wasn't much of a home run hitter until 1948, when he suddenly belted 39, but he then hit 20 or more in each of the next seasons. He once hit

Stan Musial

five homers in a double header, and he won the 1955 All-Star Game with a twelfth-inning blast.

In 1951, so the story goes, New York Giant Manager Leo Durocher was explaining to rookie Willie Mays how to play each St. Louis hitter. But he skipped the third batter, and Mays asked about him.

"The third hitter is Stan Musial," Durocher replied. "There is no advice I can give you about him."

He played in 24 All-Star games, making the team as an outfielder in the first part of his career, then switching to first base and doing it again.

By the time he retired in 1963, Musial owned a .331 lifetime average, 475 homers, 725 doubles, 177 triples, 1,949 runs and 1,951 runs batted in.

His 3,630 career hits were once second only to Ty Cobb and he's still fourth on the all-time list. It was no small irony that when Musial collected No. 3,000 in 1958, the Cardinals' manager was the once-skeptical Fred Hutchinson.

The gentlemanly Musial remains the most popular player ever to wear a Cardinal uniform, as evidenced by the bronze statue of him that stands outside Busch Memorial Stadium.

Former Baseball Commissioner Ford Frick may have summed up Stan the Man's impact best when he said: "Here stands baseball's perfect warrior. Here stands baseball's perfect knight."

The Sporting News (1212 N. Lindbergh Blvd., 314-997-7111). Lobby with sports memorabilia; tour of archives and other memorabilia by appointment. Lobby open 8:30-5 weekdays.
St. Louis Sports Hall of Fame (Busch Stadium, between gates 5 and 6, 314-421-FAME). All sports but emphasis primarily on Cardinals; memorabilia and movie. Open 10-5 daily. Admission $2 adults, $1.50 ages 5-15.

Top Attractions
Anheuser-Busch Brewery (13th and Lynch Sts., 314-577-2626), Gateway Arch and Museum of Westward Expansion (314-425-4465), Grant's Farm Tours (10501 Gravois, 314-843-1700), Missouri Botanical Gardens (4344 Shaw Blvd., 314-577-5100), National Bowling Hall of Fame (111 Stadium Plaza, 314-231-6340), National Museum of Transportation (3015 Barrett Station Rd., 314-965-7998), St. Louis Art Museum (Forest Park, 314-721-0067), St. Louis Science Center (Forest Park, 314-289-4444), St. Louis Union Station (1820 Market St., 314-421-6655), St. Louis Zoological Park (Hwy. 40 and Hampton Ave., 314-781-0900), Six Flags Over Mid-America (314-938-5300).

Tourism Information
St. Louis Convention & Visitors Commission, 10 S. Broadway, Suite 300, St. Louis, MO 63102, 314-421-1023 or 800-247-9791.
Missouri Division of Tourism, Truman State Office Building, PO Box 1055, Jefferson City, MO 65102, 314-751-4133.

Busch Stadium
250 Stadium Plaza
Capacity: 54,224
Surface: Artificial
First Game: May 16, 1966
LF: 330   CF: 414   RF: 330

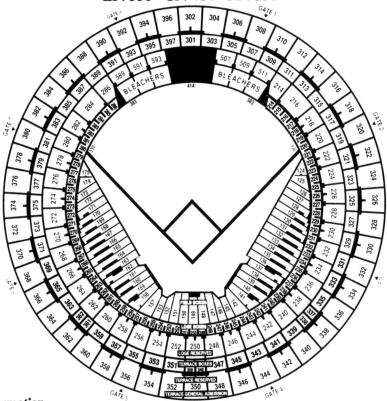

General Information
St. Louis Cardinals, 250 Stadium Plaza, St. Louis, MO 63102, 314-421-3060.

Getting Tickets
Bleacher tickets sold 2 hours before game.
By mail: St. Louis Cardinal, Ticket Sales, PO Box 8787, St. Louis, MO 63102. Specify price, number of tickets and date. $4 handling charge. Check, money order, VISA and MasterCard accepted.
By phone: 314-421-2400. $4 handling charge. VISA and MasterCard accepted. Orders must be placed 24 hours before game.

Ticket Prices
Box Seat $11, Reserved Seat $8.50, General Admission Reserved $5, Bleachers $4.

Discounts & Promotions
Promotions scheduled for over 15 games. Senior Citizen and Fan Specials (discounts on selected games).

Toughest Tickets To Get
Chicago.

Game Times
Sunday 1:15, 7:05. Weekdays 12:35, 3:05, 7:35. Friday 7:35. Saturday 12:15, 1:15, 7:05. Central time. Gates open 90 minutes before game.

Broadcasts
KMOX 1120 AM, KPLR TV (11).

Other Notes
Stadium features Centerfield Picnic Area (group reservations).

Getting To The Stadium
Just west of the Gateway Arch in downtown area, where I-70, I-55 and Highway 40 converge. Commercial parking lots in area of stadium.

St. Louis Browns

If it wasn't for Bill Veeck, the St. Louis Browns would be remembered only as the most hapless team in the history of major league baseball.

The Browns spent 52 seasons in the American League, finishing last or next-to-last in 22 of them. Eight times, they lost 100 games or more. They won just one pennant.

But on August 19, 1951, Veeck, who had bought the team earlier in the year, did something that forever secured the Browns a special place in baseball folklore. He sent a midget up to bat in a major league ballgame.

Veeck was baseball's premier showman, a guy who wasn't afraid to liven up the game with a good gag. And he figured a 3-foot-7-inch pinch-hitter was good for a chuckle or two. He was right.

The midget, Eddie Gaedel, walked on four pitches — Veeck had threatened to shoot him with a rifle if he swung — and when he left the field for a pinch-runner, Sportsman's Park rang with laughter.

Baseball officials denounced the stunt as an insult to the game's integrity. But that was okay with Veeck, who enjoyed tweaking authority almost as much as entertaining fans. When A.L. President Will Harridge later ruled Gaedel ineligible, Veeck impishly wondered if the ban might also apply to Phil Rizzuto, the New York Yankees' 5-foot-6 shortstop.

By the time Veeck arrived, the Browns' franchise was already 50 years old. Most fans know that the Baltimore Orioles trace their ancestry to the Browns. But few probably realize the ballclub actually began as the Milwaukee Brewers in 1901.

After just one season, however, the American League team moved south and became the Browns, a name originally used by St. Louis' National League club, the Cardinals.

The Browns finished second in 1902, but for most of their existence they were overshadowed by the Cards — and with good rea-son. The Cardinals won pennants, the Browns tried to get out of the second division.

St. Louis' lone American League pennant came in 1944, when many major league teams were weakened by the absence of star players fighting in World War II. The World Series was an all-St. Louis event won by the Cards in six games, largely because of the Browns' 10 errors.

The Browns' best season may have been 1922 when they went 93-61 and finished a game behind the champion Yankees. Hall of Famer George Sisler hit .420 and stole 51 bases, while Kenny Williams led the league with 39 homers and 155 runs batted in.

Branch Rickey once managed the Browns; so did Sisler, Rogers Hornsby and Gabby Street. When one-armed outfielder Pete Gray made it to the majors in 1945, it was with the Browns.

But it's Veeck's tenure for which the Brownies will be fondly remembered. He brought Satchel Paige, then 45, back to the majors, a move that was loudly decried as just another stunt until the legendary pitcher won 18 games in three years. Then there was Bobo Holloman, who was headed to the minors in 1953 until he threw a no-hitter. So the Browns kept him — and watched him finish the year 3-7 with a 5.23 ERA. He never pitched in the majors again.

Veeck and the Browns also were responsible for Grandstand Managers' Day. That was August 24, 1951, when fans were given cards reading ''yes'' and ''no'' and allowed to vote on strategy during the game. It worked. The Browns beat the Philadelphia A's 5-3.

Again baseball's hierarchy was not amused. Veeck was eventually forced out in St. Louis, and the Browns were moved to Baltimore in 1954. But he never lost his sense of fun.

''I try not to break the rules,'' he once explained with a grin, ''but merely to test their elasticity.''

Riverfront Stadium

Dodger Stadium   190

NATIONAL LEAGUE WEST

Atlanta Braves
Cincinnati Reds
Houston Astros
Los Angeles Dodgers
San Diego Padres
San Francisco Giants

Home runs rocket out of Atlanta-Fulton County Stadium, aka "The Launching Pad." At an elevation of 1,057 feet, it's the highest ballpark in the major leagues.

The Atlanta Braves, who trace their origins to the 1871 Boston Red Stockings, are the only team to have suited up every year since the birth of major league baseball.

Only the most uncharitable of people would add that the Braves have also usually suited up the worst major league team. It only seems that way.

Sure, there have been a few low moments in the Braves' 25 years as the Deep South's only major league team. Some of them spectacularly so.

Who can forget the day owner Ted Turner put on a uniform and managed the National League team? Or promotions like Headlock and Wedlock Night?

If you're a Braves fan, perhaps it's only right that one of their radio and television sponsors is a well-known headache powder.

But it would be a mistake to dismiss any team that's turned out sluggers like Hank Aaron and Dale Murphy and a one-of-a-kind pitcher like Phil Niekro.

Yes, the Braves haven't always been proficient. You can count their winning seasons in Atlanta on both hands, with four fingers left over. But that's not the same as dull.

Atlanta-Fulton County Stadium, aka The Launching Pad, has witnessed a no-hitter, the last four-homer game by one player and that little piece of history on April 8, 1974.

Perhaps the Braves are just a mirror of their home, since there's also quite a bit more to Atlanta, one of the nation's most progressive cities, than appears at first glance.

C'mon, the first thing you thought of was *Gone With the Wind*, right? Don't worry about it. Ted Turner likes the movie so much himself he bought an Atlanta theater so he could always see

Atlanta
Braves

You can count the Braves' winning seasons on both hands and have four fingers left over. Still, events like Headlock & Wedlock Night have kept things interesting.

193

Rhett and Scarlett on the big screen.

But a lot's happened in Atlanta since Gen. William T. Sherman burned most of the city to the ground on his march to the sea during the Civil War. So much so that some call it the New York of the South, even if the Yankee connotation still kind of rankles.

For Coca-Cola, this is it, the world headquarters. Same for Delta Air Lines. The federal Centers for Disease Control, which keeps track of the nation's illnesses, is also based in the Georgia capital. Atlanta is the largest railroad center in the South, and William B. Hartsfield Atlanta International Airport is the third-busiest in the world.

Local attractions range from Six Flags Over Georgia and Stone Mountain to the homes of the late civil rights leader Dr. Martin Luther King and author Joel Chandler Harris.

Professional baseball in Atlanta, in fact, dates back to the days of Harris' beloved characters, Uncle Remus and Br'er Rabbit. The city's first pro ballclub took the field in 1885, eventually becoming one of the minor leagues' great franchises, the Atlanta Crackers.

For most of their existence, the Crackers played in the Southern Association and their home was Ponce de Leon Park, once described as "the most magnificent park in the minor leagues."

It was also one of the biggest. A magnolia tree in deep center field was so far from home plate — over 450 feet — that muscular Eddie Mathews, a Hall of Famer who played for the Crackers in 1950-51, was the only hitter to ever reach it on the fly. Atlanta showed off its potential in 1947 when

the Crackers, then owned by Coca-Cola, drew 404,000 fans. In 1964, work began on $18 million Atlanta-Fulton County Stadium after an anonymous major league team said it was willing to head south.

That team was the vagabond Braves, who had moved from Boston to Milwaukee in 1953 and drawn a record 2.2 million fans in their 1957 world championship season before apathy began setting in. In 1965, the Braves' final year in Milwaukee, fewer than 500,000 customers turned out. The next season, three times that number pushed through the turnstiles in Atlanta.

What they saw was a humdrum fifth-place team that seemed to set the tone for the Braves' next 2 1/2 decades in Atlanta, which has never hosted a World Series.

The '69 Braves, behind knuckleballer Phil Niekro's 23 victories and Hank Aaron's 44 homers, won the National League West before falling in the playoffs to New York's "Miracle Mets."

In 1982, Dale Murphy and Bob Horner combined for 68 of the Braves' league-leading 146 homers and Atlanta bagged a second division title, only to lose the playoffs again, this time to the St. Louis Cardinals.

But aside from those flashes of glory and a second-place finish in 1983 that lured over two million fans into the stadium, most of the Braves' highlights have been of the individual variety.

Phil Niekro was an icon in Atlanta, winning 20 games three times and throwing a no-hitter for the Braves before retiring in 1987 at the age of 48. He finished with 318 career victories — 301 of them after he turned 29.

Mostly, though, Atlanta has been a hitter's town, perhaps because at 1,057 feet it's the major leagues' highest city. Balls rocket out of Atlanta-Fulton County Stadium, a circular, multi-purpose, natural-grass ballpark south of downtown.

In seven seasons with Baltimore, Davey Johnson hit 66 homers. In 1973, his first year with the Braves, he belted 43, still a record for second basemen.

Before being traded to the Philadel-phia Phillies last season, boy-next-door Dale Murphy hit 20 homers or more a dozen times in Atlanta, winning Most Valuable Player awards in 1982 and 1983.

Rico Carty and Ralph Garr won batting titles with the Braves. On July 6, 1986, against the visiting Montreal Expos, Bob Horner became only the eleventh major leaguer to hit four homers in a game, and the first since Mike Schmidt in 1976.

It's probably only proper that a

Atlanta-Fulton County Stadium

home run also accounted for the greatest moment in Atlanta sports history, which occurred April 8, 1974.

That, of course, was Hank Aaron's 715th homer, which broke the career mark set by Babe Ruth and made Mets pitcher Al Downing the answer to a trivia question.

Aaron was a quiet legend in Atlanta, but rising Braves like pitcher John Smoltz and outfielder Ron Gant are already as visible as "Hammerin' Hank" ever was nationally.

That's because of WTBS, the first superstation, which has beamed Braves games to all corners of the United States via satellite and cable TV systems since the mid-1970s.

Owner Ted Turner has gone so far as to proclaim them "America's Team." But then Turner, himself once nicknamed "Captain Outrageous," has never been the bashful type.

"If only I had a little humility, I'd be perfect," he once said.

Almost immediately after buying the Braves in 1976, Turner was suspended for tampering with Gary Matthews, a San Francisco outfielder.

When high-priced free agents failed to help the team in 1977, Turner tried managing for a day. The Braves lost their seventeenth game in a row, and National League President Chub Feeney found a rule prohibiting Turner from doing it any more.

The Braves have had other characters. When pitcher Pascual Perez drove around Atlanta, he drove around Atlanta. He got lost one day en route to the ballpark and circled the city several times on Interstate 285 before realizing something was amiss.

Another pitcher, Terry Forster, was so portly that comedian David Letterman called him a "fat tub of goo" on national television. Appearing on Letterman's show later, Forster admitted, "It just snacked up on me."

The merriment has often carried over to Braves promotions, some of the weirdest in baseball.

There have been ostrich races and bathtub races, even a Farrah Fawcett look-a-like contest. Headlock and Wedlock Night featured a mass wedding at home plate, followed by pro wrestlers. Wet T-Shirt Night was won by a Methodist minister's daughter.

Braves fans have learned to take such foolishness in stride. When the *Atlanta Journal-Constitution* ran a slogan contest in 1990, one twisted entrant suggested: "Braves Baseball — Year of the Blood Sacrifice."

As a prophecy, it may have been too kind. The Braves' 65-97 record wasn't as bad as their previous two seasons, but it was still the worst in either league and marked their fourth last-place finish in five years.

Still, there's reason for hope.

New General Manager John Schuerholz, the architect of several good Kansas City Royal teams, signed third baseman Terry Pendleton and first baseman Sid Bream over the winter to bolster Atlanta's defense. Despite shaky numbers in 1990, Tom Glavine, John Smoltz and Steve Avery still look like the core of a potentially fine pitching staff. And the farm system has produced solid hitters in Ron Gant, Jeff Blauser and David Justice.

Don't worry, though. There will always be a place for the odd in Atlanta. In 1990, Smoltz injured himself trying to iron his shirt. He was wearing it at the time.

Hank Aaron

When a player not only is in the Hall of Fame but also holds the major league record for home runs, it's hard to picture him as unappreciated.

But during his 23-year career, Hank Aaron always seemed to be playing in the shadows of more colorful stars, like Willie Mays and Ernie Banks and Mickey Mantle and Ted Williams.

Even now, 15 years after Hammerin' Hank called it quits with 755 career homers, there's an amazing tendency by some to downplay his accomplishments.

Well, they say, he set the record in 12,364 at-bats, while Babe Ruth hit his 714 homers in just 8,399. And he played nearly half his career in homer-happy Atlanta-Fulton County Stadium.

Of course, that Aaron got those extra at-bats in a career that lasted just one season longer than Ruth's says a little something about his durability. And almost all of Ruth's career was played in Yankee Stadium, one of the best parks for left-handed hitters in either league.

There wasn't anything flashy about Henry Aaron. Ruth was brute force, all shoulders and forearms, when he went deep. Aaron used his wrists and a deceptively quick bat.

For more than two decades, the man from Mobile, Alabama, just went out and did his job. He played a sparkling right field, filling in on the infield in a pinch. And he hit. And hit. And hit.

"Throwing a fastball by Henry Aaron," pitcher Curt Simmons once said, "is like trying to sneak the sunrise past a rooster."

Aaron won two batting titles and led the National League four times each in homers, runs batted in, slugging and doubles. He hit 40 homers or more eight times, drove in at least 100 runs in 11 seasons and batted .300 or better 14 times.

He was the league's Most Valuable Player in 1957, with 44 homers, 132 RBIs and a .322 batting average, but had a half-dozen other seasons equally as impressive.

There's no question The Launching Pad helped Aaron. He belted 335 homers during nine seasons in Atlanta and admittedly took advantage of the smaller park.

Hank Aaron eyes home run No. 715 on April 8, 1974, at Atlanta-Fulton County Stadium.

"I didn't get all the publicity that some other players get," Aaron said. "...So eventually I decided, well, I'm going to go for the home run."

But consider: He was already 32 when the Braves left Milwaukee. If he'd played his peak years in Atlanta-Fulton County Stadium, says baseball authority Bill James, Aaron "absolutely would have hit more than 60 home runs in a season."

He stepped into the record books on April 8, 1974, when he drove a fourth-inning fastball from the Los Angeles Dodgers' Al Downing over the left-field wall in Atlanta for his 715th career homer.

His father greeted him at home plate and the Braves' fans went wild. Others, however, never quite forgave him for erasing Ruth's previous mark of 714.

Aaron understood.

"I never wanted them to forget Babe Ruth," he said. "I just wanted them to remember Aaron."

Top Attractions
Atlanta International Raceway (404-946-4211), Botanical Gardens (Piedmont Park, 404-876-5858), Capitol (Capitol Square, 404-656-2844), CNN Center (1 CNN Center, Marietta St. at Techwood Dr., 404-827-2400), Georgia's Stone Mountain Park (404-498-5600), Carter Presidential Center (One Copenhill, 404-420-5100), High Museum of Art (1280 Peachtree St., NE, 404-892-3600), Martin Luther King Jr. National Historic Site (449 Auburn Ave. NE, 404-524-1956), Six Flags Over Georgia (I-20 W, 12 miles west of downtown, 404-739-3400), White Water Park (404-424-9283), Zoo Atlanta (Grant Park, 404-624-5678).

Tourism Information
Atlanta Convention & Visitors Bureau (233 Peachtree St., Suite 200, Atlanta, GA 30303, 404-521-6600).

Georgia Department of Industry and Trade, PO Box 1776, Atlanta, GA 30301 (404-656-3590 or 800-446-1448).

Atlanta-Fulton County Stadium

521 Capitol Ave.
Capacity: 52,007
Surface: Natural
First Game: April 12, 1966
LF: 330   CF: 402   RF: 330

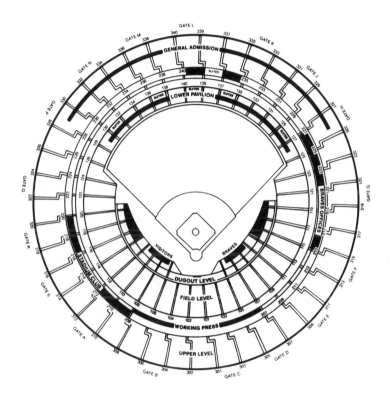

General Information
Atlanta Braves, PO Box 4064, Atlanta, GA 30302, 404-522-7630.
Getting Tickets
General Admission held for day of game sales.
Stadium ticket booth: Gate G, 8:30-5:00 Monday-Saturday, 1-5 Sunday.
By mail: Braves Ticket Office, PO Box 4064, Atlanta, GA 30302. Specify date, number of tickets and type of ticket. $3 handling charge. Check, VISA, MasterCard and American Express accepted. Allow 2 weeks for delivery. Orders received within 7 days of game will be held at the Will-Call Window.
By phone: TicketMaster 404-249-6400 or 800-326-4000. MasterCard, VISA or American Express accepted. Subject to a per ticket service charge. Orders less than 1 week prior to game will be held at the stadium.

Ticket Prices
Club Level and Dugout Level $11, Field Level $9, Upper and Pavillion Level $6, General Admission $4 ($1 for under 12).
Toughest Tickets To Get
Chicago, New York and Los Angeles.
Game Times
Sunday 2:10, 8:05. Weekdays 2:10, 5:40, 7:40. Friday 7:40. Saturday 7:10. Eastern time. Gates open 2 hours before game.
Broadcasts
WSB 750 AM, WTBS-TV (17).
Getting To The Stadium
Southeast of central Atlanta, where I-75/85 intersects I-20. Parking plentiful. Accessible by bus (no stadium access by subway).

Until they moved into modern River-front Stadium (above) in 1970, the Reds' home was cozy Crosley Field, which seated fewer than 30,000 fans.

First.

It's a word that pops up quite a bit when you talk about the Cincinnati Reds.

And not only because of 1990, when they led the National League West from wire to wire, then stunned the favored Oakland A's in the World Series.

From the time they took the field in 1869 as the first officially professional team — and went 130 games without a loss — the Reds have been baseball trailblazers.

Today's uniforms, although double-knit and so tight you can tell if a player has a tattoo, trace their origins to the cricket-style knickers that Cincinnati introduced in 1869.

The idea of admitting women to games at no charge existed as early as the 1870s, but it was the Reds who in 1886 became the first team to regularly schedule Ladies Day.

In 1934, a handful of adventurous Cincinnati players flew to a game in Chicago. No big deal today, but that made them the first major league team to travel by plane.

The Reds, giving broadcast legend Red Barber his start, were one of the first ballclubs to air their games on radio. And on August 26, 1939, they played the Dodgers in Brooklyn in the first televised game.

Cincinnati's most famous first, however, may have saved baseball during the Great Depression. It certainly contributed to the game's boom over the last 50 years.

On May 24, 1935, President Franklin D. Roosevelt pushed a button at the White House, some 600 lights flicked on at Crosley Field, and the Reds hosted the Philadelphia Phillies in the majors' first night game.

Cincinnati
Reds

When the 1990 season came to a close, the Reds were world champions. But then, they're used to being out in front of the pack.

Actually, night baseball had been played as early as 1880 — one year after Thomas Edison invented the light bulb — and there'd even been two previous night exhibition games in Cincy.

But the big leagues balked until Reds General Manager Larry McPhail decided more people would come to the ballpark if games were played when they didn't have to work.

Twenty thousand fans showed up for that first night game, nearly one-tenth of what the Reds had drawn in all of 1934, and by the late 1940s every major league park except Wrigley Field had lights.

The pioneer spirit has always been alive in Cincinnati, a transportation and industry hub tucked in the rolling, forested hills along the Ohio River.

Henry Wadsworth Longfellow once called it the "Queen City of the West," and the elegant, yet hard-working influence of the European immigrants who settled it in the 1800s still lingers. Cincinnati makes more machine tools than any other city in the nation. As the headquarters of soap-maker Proctor & Gamble, it also helps clean up when the job is done.

The Cincinnati Zoo is the second-oldest in the country, and the city's Taft Museum boasts the works of Rembrandt, Goya and Gainsborough. And while Chicago has its pizza, Philadelphia its cheese steaks and Baltimore its crabcakes, Cincinnati is famous for chili, a hearty delight usually served with spaghetti and cheese.

Beer is also a Cincy staple, thanks to the city's heavy German flavor, and it played a role in one notorious incident in the Reds' formative years.

Founded as an amateur team called the Red Stockings in 1866, the Reds joined the National League as a charter member a decade later. But in 1880, the league banned Sunday baseball and beer sales. The renegade Reds refused to go along, and the league promptly kicked them out. It was 10 years before they returned.

Scandal also tainted the first great Cincinnati team of the modern era. The Reds defeated Chicago in the 1919 World Series, only to learn later that some of the White Sox had taken money to throw the games. Maybe it wasn't that much of a surprise, since gamblers also tried to bribe the Reds. But Cincinnati's Edd Roush, the National League batting champ, always argued that the Reds would have won even if the Series had been on the up-and-up.

Despite their long history, most of the Reds' nine National League pennants and five world championships have come in just the last 30 years. In addition to 1990's World Series triumph, they beat the Detroit Tigers in 1940, the Boston Red Sox in 1975 and the New York Yankees in 1976. In 1939 and 1961, they lost to the Yanks, in 1970 to the Baltimore Orioles and in 1972 to the A's.

But in even the leanest of years, colorful, often great players have dotted Cincinnati rosters.

Johnny Vander Meer lost more games than he won over a 13-year career, but any time someone throws a no-hit game his name pops up. That's because nobody else has ever tossed two in a row like he did in 1938.

Fred Toney was another Reds pitcher who made no-hit history. On May 2, 1917, he and the Chicago Cubs' Hippo Vaughn locked up in the majors' only nine-inning double no-hitter. Cincinnati won in the tenth on a pair of singles and an error.

Jim Maloney threw a no-hitter against the Astros on April 30, 1969. The next day, Houston's Don Wilson returned the favor against Cincinnati.

The Reds also boast the youngest major leaguer ever. Joe Nuxhall, a product of the World War II player shortage, was just 15 years old when he pitched two-thirds of an inning against the Cardinals on June 10, 1944. The youngster gave up five runs on two hits and five walks. It took Nuxhall eight years to return to the majors, but then he stayed for 15 more. Now he's a Reds broadcaster.

But think Cincinnati baseball, and you have to think sluggers. One of the best was Hall of Famer Ernie Lombardi, a huge, easygoing man nicknamed ''Schnozz'' for an obvious reason and possibly the slowest person ever to play the game. A ferocious line-drive hitter, he was one of just two catchers ever to lead the National League in batting. In 1938, he did it with a .342 average, despite hitting into a league-record 30 double plays.

Few teams have muscled up like the 1956 Reds (or Redlegs, as they called themselves from 1953 to 1959 because of McCarthyism and the Red Scare), who belted a league-record 221 homers. Five players,including rookie Frank Robinson, socked at least 28. Cincinnati had sleeveless uniforms then and the epitome of that team, big Ted Kluszewski, disdained an undershirt so opposing pitchers could get a good look at his threatening biceps.

Cincy fans have always loved their teams, but they may have gotten carried away in 1957 when they stuffed the All-Star Game ballot boxes and elected Reds to start at every position but first base for the National League.

Such was the national outrage that Commissioner Ford Frick replaced Reds Wally Post and Gus Bell with Willie Mays and Hank Aaron. The next year, players, coaches and managers did the voting, and balloting wasn't returned to the fans until 1970.

From 1912 through early 1970, the Reds played at Crosley Field, with fewer than 30,000 seats the smallest ballpark in the majors. Initially named Redland Field after the first park built on the site, Crosley Field featured 360-foot foul lines and a distinctive incline in front of the left-field wall that served as a warning track. When a nearby creek flooded in early 1937, two pitchers rowed a boat over the outfield fence. Later that year, Crosley Field became the first (again) major league park with an artificial surface when the Reds dyed the sun-scorched grass green.

On June 30, 1970, the Reds moved into $48 million Riverfront Stadium, a gleaming multi-sport facility with artificial turf that sits on the banks of the Ohio River in downtown Cincinnati.

And whereas the previous decade had been blighted by the lopsided 1965 trade of slugger Frank Robinson to Baltimore for pitcher Milt Pappas and two other players, the 1970s marked the most successful era in Reds history.

Under Manager Sparky Anderson, the Big Red Machine dominated the decade, breezing to six National League West titles, four N.L. pennants and two World Series championships. Only once did they finish lower than second.

There were plenty of individual

honors, too. Strong-armed catcher Johnny Bench won Most Valuable Player awards in 1970 and 1972, all-purpose Pete Rose claimed one in 1973, second baseman Joe Morgan was a back-to-back winner in 1975 and 1976, and George Foster slugged his way to one the following year.

Rose, nicknamed "Charlie Hustle" for his aggressive play, finished his playing career in 1986 with a major league-record 4,256 hits, most of them with the Reds. He hit in 44 consecutive games in 1978, a National League record.

Bench and Morgan, as well as short-stop Davey Concepcion and center-fielder Cesar Geronimo, were also annual Gold Glove winners. That helped Anderson — dubbed "Captain Hook" for his quick use of relievers Clay Carroll, Pedro Borbon and Rawley Eastwick — get the most out of a steady if unspectacular pitching staff.

In one of the best World Series ever, the Reds beat the stubborn Red Sox four games to three in 1975, bouncing back from a 12-inning 7-6 loss in Game Six that many say is the best World Series game of all time. Then Cincy blitzed the Yankees in four straight the next year, the first National League team in 54 years to win consecutive World Series.

The '80s were a series of near-misses for the Reds, who had five second-place finishes, including 1981 when they had the best overall record in the National League but finished second in each half of the strike-torn season. Actuatlly, the Reds usually seemed to make more news off the field, whether it was owner Marge Schott putting a picture of her dog on the cover of the Reds' media guide or — on a more serious note — Pete Rose being banned from baseball for gambling.

But under new Manager Lou Piniella in 1990, the Reds raced to a 33-12 start and never looked back on the way to their first N.L. West title in 11 years. Barry Larkin, Chris Sabo, Eric Davis and Paul O'Neill led the league's best-hitting offense, while relievers Randy Myers and Rob Dibble combined for 50 saves to anchor the pitching.

Cincinnati shut down the muscular Pittsburgh Pirates to win the National League playoffs in six games, but that was a mere warmup for what they did to Oakland in the World Series.

Unheralded Billy Hatcher battered the American League's top pitching staff for nine hits, while Sabo and Davis drove in five runs apiece. The A's, meanwhile, got just one run off Series MVP Jose Rijo in 15 1/3 innings and none at all against the Reds' bullpen in 12.

And Cincinnati shocked the defending champions with a four-game World Series sweep that left the A's and just about everyone else in baseball in a daze.

It shouldn't have. It just meant the Reds were first.

Again.

Johnny Bench

His bazooka arm was so good that he once picked a runner off second, threw another out at third and gunned down a batter trying to bunt — in one inning.

He was the most dangerous hitter on a team packed with them, slamming 389 career home runs, including the most ever for a National League catcher, 327.

After just three full seasons in the majors, with Rookie of the Year and Most Valuable Player awards already under his belt, it was obvious he was headed for the Hall of Fame.

But was Johnny Bench — with competition like Yogi Berra, Roy Campanella and Mickey Cochrane — the best catcher to ever play the game? Cincinnati Manager Sparky Anderson certainly thought so. In 1976, when someone asked him to compare the New York Yankees' Thurman Munson to Bench, Anderson's reply was lightning-quick.

"Don't ever embarrass anyone," Anderson said, "by comparing him to Johnny Bench."

Catchers are supposed to be slow and bulky, but Bench was the picture of grace from the moment he joined the Reds in 1967 as a confident 19-year-old from Binger, Oklahoma.

He revolutionized catching, using a special hinged mitt to popularize the one-handed catching style so common today.

It helped that Bench had enormous hands — he could grasp seven baseballs with just one of them — and an arm so good that he went 30-1 as a high school pitcher.

"Every time Bench throws," remarked Baltimore General Manager

Johnny Bench

Harry Dalton, "everybody in baseball drools."

He won 10 straight Gold Gloves. That he also quickly became one of baseball's most feared batters was pure gravy.

In 1970, at the age of 22, Bench batted .293 with 45 homers and 148 RBIs to win his first MVP award. That season held such promise that some critics never quite forgave him for never doing better.

But two years later Bench was named MVP again after hitting .270 with 40 homers and 125 RBIs, and from 1970 to 1977 he drove in more than 100 runs six times.

In 1976 he was the World Series MVP, batting .533 with a pair of homers and six RBIs in the Reds' four-game sweep of the Yankees. He hit at least one homer in all four World Series he played in, and in all but one of six National League playoffs.

Durability was another strong suit. Bench caught more than 120 games in each of his first 10 seasons in the majors. Only a handful of catchers had more than his career total of 1,739 games behind the plate.

"A catcher and his body are like the outlaw and his horse," Bench once said. "He's got to ride that nag till it drops."

Ted Williams sized Bench up correctly when the youngster approached him during spring training in 1969 and asked for an autograph.

Wrote Williams: "To Johnny, a Hall of Famer, for sure."

College Football Hall of Fame (25 miles north of Cincinnati, 513-398-5410). Exhibits include photographic displays and memorabilia, theaters and games. Open 10-5 daily. Admission $3.50 adult, 2.25 child.

Louisville Slugger Factory Tours (Hillerich & Bradsby Co., Louisville, KY, 502-585-5226). Tours 8-11 and 1-3 weekdays, beginning on the hour. Free. Call for prerecorded directions.

Top Attractions
Bicentennial Riverfront Park, Cincinnati Art Museum (Eden Park, 513-721-5204), Cincinnati Zoo (3400 Vine St., 513-281-4701), Contemporary Arts Center (115 E. 5th ., 515-721-0390), Ft. Ancient, Museum of Natural History, Taft Mansion and Museum (316 Pike St., 513-241-0343), Harriett Beecher Stowe Home.

Amusement and Water Parks
Americana Amusement Park (513-539-7339), The Beach (513-398-SWIM), Kings Island (513-398-5600), Surf Cincinnati (513-742-0620).

United States Air Force Museum (one hour north in Dayton, Wright-Patterson Air Force Base, 513-255-3286). Open 9-5 daily. No admission charge.

Tourism Information
Cincinnati Convention & Visitors Bureau (300 W. 6th St., Cincinnati, OH 45202, 513-621-2142).

Ohio Division of Travel & Tourism (PO Box 1001, Columbus, OH 43266, 800-BUCKEYE).

Riverfront Stadium
100 Riverfront Stadium
Capacity: 52,952
Surface: Artificial
First Game: July 30, 1970
LF: 330   CF: 404   RF: 330

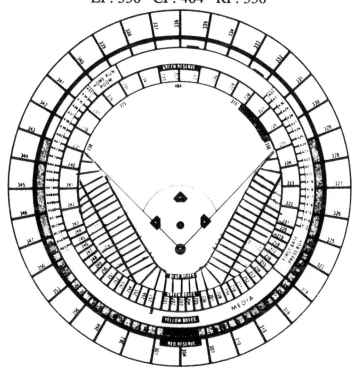

General Information
Cincinnati Reds, Riverfront Stadium, Cincinnati, OH 45202, 513-421-4510.

Getting Tickets
Seats in Top Six Rows on sale 4 hours before game.

By mail: Cincinnati Reds, Box 1970, Cincinnati, OH 45201. Specify date of game, number of tickets and price. $2 handling charge per order. Check or money order accepted. Orders received within 5 days of game will not be mailed; tickets will be held at the Will Call window (near Gate 13, west side of stadium).

By phone: TicketMaster at 513-421-REDS or 800-877-1212 (outside Cincinnati). Service charge on tickets.

Ticket Prices
Blue Box Seat $10, Green Box Seat $9, Yellow Box Seat $9, Red Box Seat $8, Green Reserve Seat $7, Red Reserve Seat $6, Top Six Rows Seat $3.50.

Discounts & Promotions
Promotions scheduled for 23 games. Senior Citizen, Teen, Family and College Dates (selected dates for half-price tickets when purchased in advance only).

Toughest Tickets To Get
Chicago and St. Louis, particularly on weekends.

Game Times
Sunday 1:05, 2:15, 8:05. Weekdays 12:35, 7:35. Friday 7:35. Saturday 1:15, 2:15, 7:05. Eastern time. Gates open 90 minutes before game.

Broadcasts
WLW 700 AM, WLWT TV (5).

Other Notes
Stadium tours: 513-352-5400.
Cincinnati Reds Gift Shop, Fifth and Elm Sts., Cincinnati, OH 45202.

Getting To The Stadium
Central Cincinnati, in the vicinity of the merge point of I-75, 71 and 471. Parking plentiful in (underground) and around stadium. Accessible by bus.

The Astrodome's firsts included air conditioning, cushioned seats and a mechanically rotated grandstand. Eventually, it also produced the world's first artificial grass, Astroturf.

Some teams are identified by their tradition of success — or lack of it — some by a certain style of play, still others by a history of memorable players.

The Houston Astros, however, no matter how many World Series they win or Hall of Famers they produce, will forever be identified with where they play.

The Superdome is bigger. The SkyDome and Olympic Stadium boast roofs that can be opened and closed, and the one at the Metrodome is held aloft by a cushion of air.

But the Astrodome was the first domed stadium, the one that changed baseball forever, for better or worse, by bringing it indoors and putting it on a carpet.

Baseball executive Branch Rickey, who set a couple of trends himself by inventing baseball's farm system and integrating the major leagues, knew a pioneer when he saw one.

''The day the doors on this park open,'' he said shortly before his death in 1965, ''every other park in the world will be antiquated.''

At first glance, the Astrodome seems just another flashy example of the passion for size and the future that's gripped Houston since World War II. In 1950, Houston had fewer than 600,000 residents; now there are almost three times that, making it the fourth-largest city in the country.

Oil, of course, prompted that boom, and the Texas city has struggled to diversify its economy since the bottom fell out of the crude market in the early 1980s.

There's still plenty of hustle and bustle. Thirteen Fortune 500 companies wheel and deal out of Houston, and the $761 million Johnson Space

Houston Astros

It's not the biggest. It's not the fanciest. And hardly anyone still calls it the "Eighth Wonder of the World." But the Astrodome was the first, the one that changed baseball forever.

Center keeps an eye on NASA flights.

Despite being 50 miles from the Gulf of Mexico, Houston prides itself as one of the country's busiest seaports. The Texas Medical Center, with more than 500,000 employees, is a high-tech medicine hub.

The Astrodome, however, has always been more than another specimen of Texas' bigger-is-better credo. It was, in fact, Houston's ticket to the major leagues.

Baseball has been around Houston almost as long as oil wells. From 1917 to 1958, the Houston Buffaloes were members of the Texas League, playing most of that time in Spanish-style Buff Stadium. Dizzy Dean won 26 games for Houston in 1931, and fellow Hall of Famers Joe Medwick and Chick Hafey also made stops there.

A Houston group bid for several existing major league teams in the 1950s, but things didn't get serious until the National League, threatened by the planned Continental League, agreed to add two expansion teams.

On October 17, 1960, after Judge Roy Hofheinz unveiled a model of a proposed domed stadium at a meeting of league owners, one of those franchises was awarded to Houston.

"I knew with our heat, humidity and rain, the best chance for success was in the direction of a weatherproof, all-purpose stadium," said Hofheinz, a former Houston mayor.

He got the idea after visiting the Colosseum in Rome during the '50s and learning that slaves had dragged a papyrus awning over the amphitheater on hot days. A major drawing card for Buff Stadium had been air-conditioned restrooms; just think if the whole stadium could be cooled!

Of course, by the time the Astrodome opened on April 9, 1965, with a price tag of $31.6 million, the Houston franchise already had a few innings behind it.

For starters, when the Astros began play in 1962, they were called the Houston Colt .45s, nicknamed for the famous six-shooter. After three seasons, the name was changed because of a royalties dispute with the Colt Firearms Co., and Hofheinz said the Harris County Domed Stadium would be called the Astrodome.

On the field, the Colts were slightly better than their fellow expansionists, the hapless New York Mets, but only occasionally as entertaining.

They played their first three seasons in Colt Stadium, a temporary, single-deck ballpark next to the Astrodome construction site. Colt Stadium was a mosquito-ridden oven that once sent 100 people to the first-aid room with heat exhaustion during an afternoon double header. Perhaps that's why, in 1963, it became the site of the first major league Sunday night game. The bad news for the players was that it was also one of the most poorly lighted parks in the league.

Colt Stadium witnessed two no-hitters in its brief history, and one of them was a little special. On April 23, 1964, Houston's Ken Johnson became the first major leaguer to lose a complete-game no-hitter, 1-0 to the Cincinnati Reds, the result of a pair of errors.

With the possible exception of New York's Yankee Stadium, no ballpark's debut has been as eagerly anticipated as the Astrodome's. Even President Lyndon B. Johnson and his wife, Lady Bird, showed up for the opener, an exhibition with the Yankees that the Astros won 2-1 in 12 innings.

And why not? The Astrodome's firsts included air conditioning (price tag: $4.5 million), cushioned seats and a mechanically rotated grandstand. The dome was 710 feet wide and 208 feet tall. Its 4,596 skylights were a record for any building, and its $2 million, 474-foot-long scoreboard was the biggest and noisiest in baseball.

"It isn't much," Houston pitcher Jim Owens told the Yanks' Jim Bouton, "but we call it home."

Nowhere else could Lindsey Nelson have broadcast a game from a gondola above second base, as he did in the Astrodome on April 28, 1965.

Stan Musial took a look at the place and marveled: "I got started too early in baseball. In air conditioning, I could have lasted 20 years longer."

Of course, Musial also avoided the Astrodome's little problem with flyballs. Outfielders simply couldn't see them. During day games, flyballs all but disappeared against those shiny new skylights. Neither sunglasses nor orange baseballs seemed to help, so Hofheinz ordered the skylights painted.

Trouble was, the Astrodome's grass began dying. Watering didn't work, and neither did new turf. Eventually, the Astros spray-painted the yellowing grass, too.

The Astros took their problem to the Monsanto Chemical Co., which responded with a zippered carpet of green nylon grass that was virtually indestructible. On Opening Day 1966, Houston used groundskeepers dressed as spacemen and armed with vacuum cleaners to introduce what it proudly called Astroturf.

Its impact was immediate. Fielders didn't have to worry as much about bad hops on Astroturf, but they also had to play deeper because it made balls roll so much faster. Critics likened it to a giant pool table.

"If horses don't eat it," said Phila-

The Astrodome

delphia Phillie infielder Richie Allen, "I don't want to play on it."

But others did. By 1968, artificial surfaces had been approved by five other major league teams who realized the quick-drying turf could also help prevent rainouts.

It took awhile for the Astros to get as much ink for their teams as for their stadium, despite heroes like Jimmy Wynn and Don Wilson. Wynn, nick-named the "Toy Cannon," was the first Houston player to hit three homers in one game in the Astrodome and the first to hit one into the upper deck. Houston pitchers have thrown eight no-hitters, an amazing number for a franchise that's not yet 30 years old, and Wilson had two of them.

Despite challenges in 1969, 1972 and 1979, Houston didn't win its first pennant until 1980, when Joe Niekro went 20-12 and J.R. Richard was 10-4 before a mid-season stroke that ended his career. The Astros won the N.L. West in a one-game playoff with the Los Angeles Dodgers, then took the Phillies to five games — four of which went extra innings — before losing what some say was the best National League playoff series ever.

Rolling to a franchise-best 96-66 record, the Astros took the N.L. West again in 1986. Cy Young Award win-ner Mike Scott clinched the division in the most dramatic of fashions, with a no-hitter against the Giants. But again the Astros lost the National League playoffs, this time in six games to the Mets.

Because of the Astrodome's Texas-size dimensions — 340 feet down the lines, 390 to the power alleys — the Astros have had most of their success by emphasizing pitching and slashing,

speedy hitters like Cesar Cedeno.

That looks like it will continue, if only because the Astros have lost the only sluggers from what was the league's worst-hitting team in 1990. Franklin Stubbs became a free agent, and Glenn Davis was traded to the Bal-timore Orioles. Problem is, pitchers Danny Darwin, Dave Smith, Juan Agosto and Larry Andersen are gone, too, thanks to free agency and trades.

But shortstop Eric Yelding, catcher Craig Biggio and outfielder Steve Fin-ley fit the swift Astro mold, and out-fielder Eric Anthony and first baseman Luis Gonzalez could provide some pop. If Mike Scott and new pitchers Pete Harnisch and Curt Schilling pro-duce, the Astros could improve on 1990's fourth-place tie with the San Diego Padres.

It's hard to believe the Astrodome is 26 years old. Half the stadiums in major league baseball today are newer and even though a $60 million renova-tion in 1987 left it snazzier than ever, you almost never hear it called the "Eighth Wonder of the World" any more.

But it'll always be special. The place where a scoreboard first blared "Charge!" The place where the Astros first trotted out those garish Hawaiian-style softball uniforms. The place where a game once was rained out be-cause streets outside were flooded.

And its legacy will live as long as any player is befuddled by a bloop hit's crazy hop over his head or a line drive that caroms out of the corner like a cue shot.

"It will revolutionize baseball," for-mer executive Gabe Paul once said of the Astrodome. "It will open a new area of alibis for players."

J.R. Richard

From Larry Dierker to Joe Niekro to Nolan Ryan to Mike Scott, the Houston Astros have always had pitching. Good pitching. Often excellent pitching.

But no Astro pitcher has ever intimidated the National League, left it in such utter awe, as flamethrowing right-hander J.R. Richard did in the 1970s.

And none left the National League — indeed, all of baseball — quite so saddened as Richard did when his career came to an abrupt, tragic end in 1980.

His numbers alone qualify Richard as the stuff of legends. He won 107 games and lost just 71 in 10 seasons with the Astros and was 84-55 over the last five.

In 1976 he went 20-15 with a 2.75 earned run average, then won 18 games in each of the next seasons and led the league with a 2.71 ERA in 1979.

He's still the only National League right-hander to strike out more than 300 batters in a season, getting 303 in 1978 and 313 the next season. And his career average of 8.37 strikeouts per game trails only Ryan, Sandy Koufax and Sam McDowell.

Richard may not have been the most talented pitcher in the league or the smartest. But few had the same terrifying combination of size, speed and wildness.

At 6 feet, 8 inches and 237 pounds, Richard's appearance alone was enough to make most batters rethink their choice of careers. His big motion didn't help, either.

"He is so close to the plate when he finishes his windup," Richie Hebner

J.R. Richard

once said, "that I'm thankful he didn't eat onions before the game."

Add his 98 mph fastball and a 93 mph slider, and the situation got pretty lopsided. It was enough to make 300-game winner Don Sutton peevish.

"I'm sick of hearing about J. Rodney Richard," Sutton once said. "We all know what he can do with his stuff. But what I'd like to see is what he can do with my stuff."

The little matter of Richard's control — or its absence — added just the right touch of danger.

Three times he led the league in walks allowed, including 151 in 1976. Once he walked 11 batters in a game and still won. Another time, he won despite six wild pitches.

In 1980, Richard was 30 years old. With a 10-4 record and a 1.89 ERA, the onetime schoolboy star from Ruston, Louisiana, appeared en route to his best season ever. He even tossed a pair of scoreless innings in his first All-Star game.

But the man who had pitched over 200 innings each of the five previous years suddenly complained of fatigue and began leaving games early. Doctors couldn't find much wrong, and there were whispers he was malingering.

On July 30, however, as he was warming up in the Astrodome, Richard collapsed and was rushed to the hospital. A blood clot had formed in his pitching shoulder and moved to his brain. He'd had a stroke.

Through rehabilitation, he overcame partial paralysis on his left side and even made a couple of comeback tries in the minors. The once-overpowering Richard managed to get his fastball back to 90 mph, but the Astros felt he could no longer move well enough to field his position.

He never pitched another inning in the major leagues.

Top Attractions
Astroworld/Waterworld (near Astrodome), Battleship *Texas* and San Jacinto Battleground State Park (22 miles E of downtown), Childrens Museum (3201 Allen Pkwy.), Contemporary Arts Museum (5216 Montrose Blvd.), Hermann Park Zoo, Houston Arboretum and Nature Center, Houston Museum of Natural Science (Hermann Park), Lyndon B. Johnson Space Center (25 miles SE of downtown, 713-483-4321), Museum of Fine Arts (1001 Bissonnet).

Tourism Information
Greater Houston Convention & Visitors Council, 3300 Main St., Houston, TX 77002, 713-523-5050 or 800-231-7799 and 800-392-7722 (in TX).
Texas Travel Information Division, PO Box 5064, Austin, TX 78763, 512-463-8585 or 800-8888-TEX.

The Astrodome
8400 Kirby Dr.
Capacity: 54,816
Surface: Artificial
First Game: April 12, 1965
LF: 330   CF: 400   RF: 330

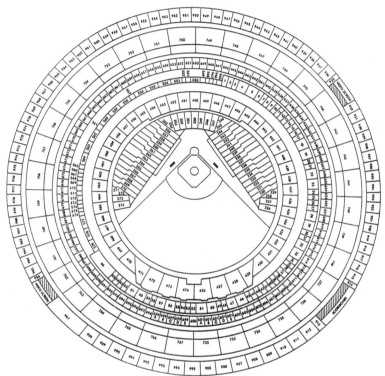

General Information
Houston Astros, Box 288, Houston, TX 77001, 713-799-9500.

Getting Tickets
Pavilion seats (general admission) and standing room tickets held for day of game sales.

By mail: Houston Astros Tickets, PO Box 1691, Houston, TX 77251. Specify game date, number of tickets, location and ticket price. $4 handling charge. Check, money order, American Express, Discover, MasterCard and VISA accepted.

By FAX: 713-799-9525.

By phone: Teletron at 713-629-3700 or 800-275-1000. American Express, Discover, MasterCard and VISA accepted.

Ticket Prices
Field Box $12, Mezzanine $10, Loge $8, Upper Box Terrace $7, Upper Box $6, Upper Reserved $5, Pavilion (General Admission) $4 ($1 for children).

Discounts & Promotions
Youth clinics, senior citizen and military discount games.

Toughest Tickets To Get
Los Angeles, New York, San Francisco, Chicago and St. Louis.

Game Times
Sunday 1:35, 7:05. Weekdays 1:35. Weeknights 6:05, 7:35. Friday 7:35. Saturday 7:05. Central time. Gates open 90 minutes before game.

Broadcasts
KPRC 950 AM Radio; KXYZ 1320 AM Radio (Spanish) and KTXH TV (20).

Other Notes
Stadium tours: 713-799-9595 (11:00, 1:00 and 3:00 daily).

Getting To The Stadium
Southwest on I-610 Loop, between Alternate 90 and 288. Stadium parking. Accessible by bus.

Dodger Stadium somehow lacked water fountains when it opened in 1962. That problem was corrected, however, and today the stylish ballpark is the standard by which all others are measured.

There's a strong temptation to call the Los Angeles Dodgers the ideal team for a city that has turned make-believe into a billion-dollar business.

Their manager clowns around with Hollywood celebrities, their players seem to do more TV commercials than Ed McMahon and their stadium is a field of dreams come true.

The Dodgers are so glittery they make Liz Taylor look like a bag lady. Their uniforms are stylish, their jaws are square and they've probably never had a cavity.

Maybe it's their own fault. The Dodgers have worked so hard over the years to cultivate their image as baseball's perfect team that the image has taken over. Which, of course, makes them an easy target for the non-believers among us. Too good to be true, we say. All special effects, no plot. Dodger in the Sky? Save it for Spielberg.

Except there is the little matter of those five World Series championships since 1959, more than any other major league team during that period. How about the nine National League pennants and the seven N.L. West titles over the same time? No other franchise can match that kind of success. Stars? Try seven Cy Young Award winners and four Most Valuable Players.

The Dodgers do more than just look good. Yes, they sometimes approach caricature. But from the moment they arrived in California in 1958, the Dodgers have been a model baseball franchise.

They've had just two managers: taciturn Walter Alston, who took over in 1954 in Brooklyn and stayed under 23 consecutive one-year contracts, and boisterous Tommy Lasorda, who's run

Los Angeles
Dodgers

The Dodgers look so good that they often approach caricature. But five World Series championships, nine pennants and seven division titles give plenty of substance to the glitter.

the show for the last 14 years. That's stability.

Their farm system has turned out pitchers Sandy Koufax, Don Drysdale, Don Sutton, Fernando Valenzuela and Orel Hershiser, speedsters Willie Davis, Maury Wills and Davey Lopes, and hitters Tommy Davis, Frank Howard, Steve Garvey, Ron Cey and Pedro Guerrero. That's production.

They play in Dodger Stadium, a place that's as modern today as when it opened in 1962, a place so beautiful it's been called baseball's Taj Mahal. That's a ballpark.

In a city where entertainment is a given, they've drawn over three million fans a season a record eight times and over two million 26 times. That's success.

Over the last three decades, Los Angeles has gotten so used to winning that many fans don't even stick around to see the Dodgers do it. Leaving after the seventh inning to beat the traffic is a cherished Dodger Stadium tradition. And watch the stadium empty out earlier if a loss seems imminent.

Maybe the City of Angels used up all of its patience waiting for the Dodgers to arrive. There was minor league baseball in Southern California before there were movies. In 1893, Los Angeles even hosted Stockton in a night game played under kerosene lamps. And the Los Angeles Angels and the Hollywood Stars were long-time members of the Pacific Coast League.

But even as motion pictures and balmy weather were turning the old Spanish mission town into one of the nation's largest cities, the major leagues showed only sporadic interest. The St. Louis Browns planned to move to Los Angeles after the 1941 season, but World War II spoiled those plans. Eleven years later, an L.A. group wanted to buy the Browns and bring them west, but the deal fell apart when the city wouldn't approve the L.A. Coliseum for baseball. So the Browns moved to Baltimore and became the Orioles.

By 1957, Los Angeles wanted baseball in the worst way, and when the hapless Senators indicated they were ready to leave Washington, it looked as if the city was going to get it.

That's when Walter O'Malley stepped in. New York had balked at helping O'Malley build a new stadium for his Brooklyn Dodgers, so he was willing to shift the star-studded team to Southern California. Los Angeles jumped at the chance and was rewarded with a world championship a year later as the Dodgers defeated the Chicago White Sox in the 1959 World Series in six games.

And they *were* still the Dodgers. The team had used a variety of nicknames in Brooklyn, but Dodgers — after that borough's trolley-dodging inhabitants — was the one that had endured. And O'Malley wasn't going to risk losing any more East Coast fans than he had to by changing the name.

In their first four years in Los Angeles, the Dodgers played in one of the strangest ballparks ever. Actually, the L.A. Coliseum wasn't a ballpark at all, and that was the problem. It had been built for the 1932 Olympics, and it turned out to be a great place for football. When a baseball diamond was squeezed in, though, things got weird. The right-field fence was 440 feet away, which sure cut down on left-handed slugger Duke Snider's fun, while the left-field wall was just 251 feet distant, if that word can be used here. Even a 40-foot-high net called the Chinese Screen did little to stop cheap homers. The bizarre configuration prompted broadcaster Lindsey Nelson to remark: "They had room at the Los Angeles Coliseum for 93,000 people and two outfielders."

The Coliseum certainly had plenty of seats. A crowd of 93,103 fans who saw a Dodger game there on May 7, 1959, is still the largest in baseball history. Each of the Dodgers three home World Series games that year also drew over 92,000. Some of those seats, though, were 65 rows deep. TV host Art Linkletter echoed the disgust of many when he quipped: "My tickets in the Coliseum are Seat 67, Aisle 72, Highway 99."

By Opening Day 1962, however, Dodger Stadium was ready at a cost of nearly $24 million, the first ballpark to be constructed entirely with private funds since Yankee Stadium in 1923.

O'Malley built it in Chavez Ravine, an area of gullies east of downtown Los Angeles that the city gave him in exchange for Wrigley Field, the city's minor league park that O'Malley had bought in 1957.

When it opened, Dodger Stadium somehow lacked water fountains, but that problem was quickly rectified, and it quickly became the palace by which all modern ballparks are measured.

"Sometimes I'd go into Dodger Stadium just to be alone," said Jim Lefebvre, the manager of the Seattle Mariners, who played for the Dodgers in the 1960s. "The game might start at 8 and I'd get there at 1 and sit in the stands and look at the field. It was that beautiful."

The stadium sits at the center of 300 landscaped acres with a panoramic view of downtown Los Angeles. There's room for 16,000 cars on 21 terraced parking lots that are color-keyed to seating areas.

Inside, each of the 56,000 seats has an unobstructed view of the classic natural grass and red-brick clay playing field, and only one of the six levels has more than 25 rows of seats.

The stadium's big Diamond Vision screen was the world's first giant full-color video board when it was unveiled in 1980. Palm trees beyond the outfield fence provide a serene balance to the electronic wizardry.

The Dodgers celebrated their new stadium in grand style, using speed and pitching to dominate the National League over the next few years. From 1963 to 1966, Los Angeles won three pennants and two World Series. Only a playoff loss to the San Francisco Giants in 1962, a season in which MVP Maury Wills stole 104 bases and Don Drysdale won the Cy Young Award, kept the Dodgers from a fourth pennant.

The Dodgers' most impressive team of that era may have been the 1963 club, which won the pennant by six games, then held the hard-hitting New York Yankees to just four runs in a stunning World Series sweep. Sandy Koufax, with a 25-5 record and a 1.88 earned run average, won the Cy Young and MVP awards.

In 1974, Los Angeles played its final World Series for Walter Alston, losing to the Oakland A's in five games but unveiling the nucleus of a team that would make three more post-season appearances over the next seven years.

The Dodgers gave Tommy Lasorda a pennant in his first year as manager in 1977 before falling to the Yankees in the World Series. Then they did the same thing the next season.

Those may have been the best-balanced Los Angeles Dodger teams ever, leading the league in homers and earned run average both seasons. In '77, Steve Garvey, Ron Cey, Reggie Smith and Dusty Baker each slugged at least 30 homers.

As much as anyone, Garvey typified the Dodgers' glamor-boy image. A former Dodger batboy, he was handsome, polite to a fault and so popular that a junior high school was named after him. Fans wore T-shirts that read: "Steve Garvey Can't Help It If He's Perfect."

His teammates, however, sometimes questioned Garvey's sincerity, and his image was tarnished when his apparently idyllic marriage broke up. A few years later, after he had moved on to San Diego, two women sued him for paternity. This time, the T-shirts read: "Steve Garvey Is Not My Padre."

But Garvey could play. In 1981, he hit .359 in post-season play for a gutty Dodger team that wiped out memories of the World Series near-misses in '77 and '78. First, Los Angeles came back from two games down to beat the Houston Astros in a special N.L. West playoff caused by the mid-season strike. Then the Dodgers erased a 2-1 deficit against the Montreal Expos to take the league playoffs in five games. Finally, after losing the first two games at home, they bounced back against the Yankees to win the World Series in six.

The 1988 season was equally satisfying, especially after consecutive 73-89 finishes, the Dodgers' worst in two decades. Cy Young winner Orel Hershiser threw a record 59 consecutive scoreless innings and Kirk Gibson was the league's MVP as Los Angeles won the N.L. West, upset the New York Mets in the playoffs and knocked off the heavily favored A's in the World Series.

Things could be looking up again. After riding young right-hander Ramon Martinez's 20-6 season to a second-place finish in 1990, the Dodgers added a host of new faces through trades and free agent signings.

Center fielder Brett Butler will provide some speed and defense, and pitchers Kevin Gross and Bob Ojeda could bolster the rotation. Then there's Darryl Strawberry. Seeing the moody ex-Met right fielder in the same uniform that Sandy Koufax and Steve Garvey once wore may make you wonder what's wrong with your picture.

Still, it's hard to argue with a guy who averages 31 homers and 92 RBIs a year. If Lasorda can make the Straw Man willing to bleed Dodger blue, there could be another pennant in La-La Land.

Sandy Koufax

He pitched in the major leagues for 12 seasons. The first six, he won 36 games and lost 40. The final six — well, they're why Sandy Koufax is in the Hall of Fame.

He came to the Dodgers in 1955 as the rawest of left-handed pitchers, a homegrown Brooklyn bonus baby with a murderous fastball and only an occasional idea of where it was going.

He left in 1966 with five consecutive earned run average titles, four no-hitters, one perfect game, three Cy Young awards and one Most Valuable Player award.

For five amazing seasons, from 1962 to 1966, Sandy Koufax was simply the best pitcher in either league. That he was also among the classiest just made it nicer.

He won 20 games three times during that span and never lost more than nine. Six times in his career he struck out more than 200 batters, three times more than 300.

The Dodgers won three pennants in those years — and would have had a fourth if he hadn't missed two months with a finger injury in 1962 — and two World Series.

Someone once asked Gene Mauch, who managed 26 years in the major leagues, if Koufax was the best left-hander he'd ever seen. "He was the best right hander, too," replied Mauch.

From the moment he joined the Dodgers, Koufax threw hard with his whiplash, over-the-top motion. Real hard.

"Either he throws the fastest ball I've ever seen, or I'm going blind," Richie Ashburn, who hit .308 in 15 major league seasons, once said.

But wildness, not to mention a pretty tough Dodger pitching staff, kept him in the background until 1961. Then catcher Norm Sherry suggested he relax and mix in a few off-speed pitches. He went 18-13 and struck out 269 batters, then a National League record.

"I became a good pitcher when I stopped trying to make them miss the ball and started trying to make them hit it," said Koufax, who walked only 58 batters in 1963 and finished his career

Sandy Koufax

221

with three strikouts for every walk.

That he also had the league's best curve and a very good change-up made things doubly tough for hitters. Twice he struck out 18 batters in a game.

After a 14-7 season in 1962, he went 25-5 the next year with a 1.88 ERA, 306 strikeouts and a league-record 11 shutouts. Then he beat the Yankees twice in the Dodgers' four-game World Series sweep.

"I can see how he won 25 games," said Yankee catcher Yogi Berra. "What I don't understand is how he lost five."

In 1964, Koufax's ERA dropped to 1.74 and he had a 19-5 record. The next season, he was 26-8, fanned 382 batters and threw his final no-hitter, a 1-0 perfect game against Chicago in which the Cubs' Bob Hendley tossed a one-hitter. He finished with two shutouts in Los Angeles' World Series victory over the Minnesota Twins, despite sitting out the opening game to observe Yom Kippur.

After a much-publicized contract holdout with fellow pitcher Don Drysdale, Koufax also cruised through the '66 season, winning 27 and losing nine, with a 1.73 ERA.

Then, to the shock of the baseball world, he retired. Koufax was only 30, but he'd pitched those final two magnificent seasons with an arthritic left elbow, and he wanted to leave "while I could still comb my hair."

Six years later, on the first ballot he was eligible, Sandy Koufax became the youngest player ever inducted into the Hall of Fame.

Top Attractions
California Museum of Science and Industry (700 State Dr., 213-744-7400), Forest Lawn (1712 S. Glendale Ave., 213-254-3131), George C. Page Museum of La Brea Discoveries (tar pits, 5801 Wilshire Blvd., 213-936-2230), Griffith Observatory (2800 E. Observatory Rd., 213-664-1191), Hollywood Bowl (2301 N. Hollywood Ave., 213-850-2000), Los Angeles County Museum of Art (5905 Wilshire Blvd., 213-937-2590), Los Angeles County Natural History Museum (900 Exposition Blvd., 213-744-DINO), Los Angeles Zoo (5333 Zoo Dr, 213-666-4090), Museum of Contemporary Art (250 S. Grand Ave., 213-626-6222), Venice Beach and Boardwalk.

Hollywood
Hollywood sign (Mount Lee), Hollywood Wax Museum (6767 Hollywood Blvd., 213-462-8860), Mann's Chinese Theatre (hand and foot cement prints, 6925 Hollywood Blvd., 213-461-3331), Walk of Fame (along Hollywood Blvd.).

Tourism Information
Greater Los Angeles Visitors and Convention Bureau, 515 S. Figueroa Ave., Los Angeles, CA 90071, 213-689-8822.

Discover the Californias, California Tourist Corp., 5757 W. Century Blvd., Los Angeles, CA 90045, 800-862-2543.

Dodger Stadium
1000 Elysian Park Ave.

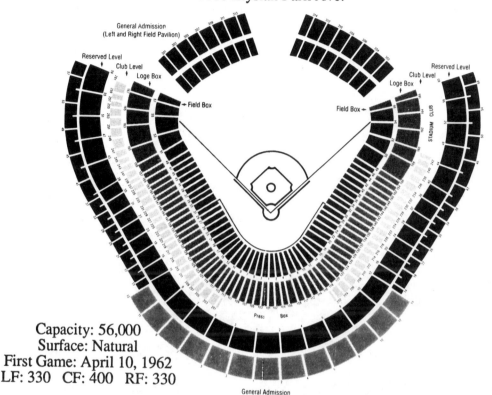

Capacity: 56,000
Surface: Natural
First Game: April 10, 1962
LF: 330   CF: 400   RF: 330

General Information
Los Angeles Dodgers, Dodger Stadium, 1000 Elysian Park Ave., Los Angeles, CA 90012, 213-224-1500.
General Information (games and events): 213-224-1491.
Ticket Information: 213-224-1400.
Ticket outlet information: 213-480-3232 or 213-642-4242.
Getting Tickets
By mail: Ticket Manager, Los Angeles Dodgers, PO Box 51100, Los Angeles, CA 90051. $3 handling and mailing charge per order.
Ticket Prices
Box Seats $10, Reserved Seats $7, General Admission $5 ($3 for 12 and under on day of game only).

Discounts & Promotions
Promotions scheduled for nearly half of games. Children, Senior Citizen and Service Personnel (in uniform) Tickets $3 for select locations when purchased at the stadium 2 hours before game.
Toughest Tickets To Get
New York and San Francisco.
Game Times
Sunday 1:05. Monday-Friday 7:35. Saturday 7:05. Pacific time. Gates open 90 minutes before game.
Broadcasts
KABC 790 AM, KWKW 1330 AM (Spanish), Fox TV (11).
Other Notes
Souvenirs and publications by mail: FMI, Dodger Stadium, 1000 Elysian Park Ave., Los Angeles, CA 90012.
Getting To The Stadium
At intersection of Ventura (101), Pasadena (110) and Golden State (5) Freeways. Ample parking. Game ticket color corresponds to parking location. Lot opens 2 hours before game. Accessible by bus (information at 213-626-4455 or 714-635-6010).

*San Diego/Jack Murphy Stadium,
named after a sports editor who helped
bring major league sports to San
Diego, may be the best multi-purpose
stadium in baseball.*

Ray Kroc was livid. He had just paid millions of dollars for the San Diego Padres, and his new employees were performing more like fry cooks than professional ballplayers.

Kroc wasn't used to that. He had bought a little hamburger restaurant in Des Plaines, Illinois, in 1955 and turned it into McDonald's, the largest fast-food restaurant chain in the world. He was used to results.

But here it was, the eighth inning of San Diego's 1974 home opener with the Houston Astros, and the Padres were playing every bit as badly as the 9-2 deficit indicated.

Kroc couldn't stand it any longer. He grabbed the public address microphone, and suddenly 39,000 fans heard his voice boom through San Diego Stadium.

"Ladies and gentlemen, I suffer with you," said Kroc, who became even more embarrassed when a streaker picked that moment to dash across the playing field.

Kroc ordered security guards to arrest the naked man, but that didn't make him feel any better about the other problem.

"This is the most stupid ballplaying I've ever seen!" the Padres' new owner blared to the crowd.

Kroc later apologized, but the outburst was typical of a showmanship that obviously tickled the San Diego faithful. The Padres didn't play any better that season than in 1973 — they went 60-102 — but their attendance jumped 76 percent.

The Padres have never enjoyed more than occasional success on the diamond, boasting just six winning seasons and one pennant since their debut as a National League expansion team in 1969.

San Diego
Padres

Okay, so the Padres have enjoyed only occasional success. But you can't ignore a team that's given baseball taco-colored uniforms, a mime in a chicken suit and a broadcaster who sounds like Norm Crosby.

But any franchise that's enhanced American culture with taco-colored uniforms, a mime in a chicken suit and a broadcaster who talks like Norm Crosby cannot be ignored.

The Padres have always seemed to have a fondness for the slightly goofy, be it a pitcher who resembled Harpo Marx or a slugger nicknamed after a sandwich.

That's not exactly true. In their first five years, they weren't that interesting. Just bad. In 1969, they lost 110 games and finished 29 games out. Not out of first — out of fifth.

Their original owner, C. Arnholt Smith, had also owned the city's Pacific Coast League team — also called the Padres — which listed such stars as Bobby Doerr, Vince DiMaggio and Ted Williams among its alumni.

Until the Navy established a base there in World War I, San Diego wasn't much more than a sleepy fishing village with typically balmy California weather.

Today, with more than one million residents, San Diego is the sixth-largest city in the United States. It remains a strong military town and there's other industry, but the big business is tourism. Sights range from the famous San Diego Zoo to Mission San Diego de Alcala. An average 350 days of sunshine each year and some 70 beaches and parks also make it a mecca for joggers and other physical fitness enthusiasts.

By the 1960s, Smith figured the city was ready for major league baseball, and the National League agreed, especially since the city had a new $28 million stadium and a built-in rivalry with the Los Angeles Dodgers.

The Padres' main attraction in their early years was Nate Colbert, an Astro castoff who averaged 27 homers a year from 1969 to 1974. Nobody's had a better day at the plate than Colbert did in 1972, when he clubbed five homers and drove in 13 runs in a double header with Atlanta.

But when he took a look at the Padres' sagging attendance figures, Smith may have wished he'd bought Sea World instead of a bad baseball team. He put the Padres on the market in early 1974, and a buyer was ready to move the team to Washington, D.C., when Ray Kroc made an eleventh-hour bid to pay cash and keep the Padres in San Diego.

The team still struggled on the field; it wasn't until 1978 that San Diego enjoyed its first winning season. But things were starting to get more interesting.

In 1974, a curly-haired left hander named Randy Jones went 8-22 for the Padres. In 1975, he captured the city's imagination by winning 20 games. The next year he captured the Cy Young award with a 22-14 record and a 2.74 earned run average. All that despite a 73 mph fastball that prompted Mike Schmidt to say, "If I were a pitcher, I'd be embarrassed to go out to the mound with stuff like that."

San Diego began its tradition of great relief pitchers in 1977 by signing mustachioed free agent Rollie Fingers, who responded with 35 saves that season and 37 the next, both league bests.

From 1974 to 1980, the Padres' best hitter was Dave Winfield, who had played basketball at the University of Minnesota and was drafted in three professional sports. Winfield hit .276 with 34 homers and 118 RBIs in 1979, but he left San Diego two years later to sign with the New York Yankees.

There were other highlights. In 1980, San Diego set a National League record when three Padres — Gene Richards, Ozzie Smith and Jerry Mumphrey — stole over 50 bases each.

To many baseball fans, Willie McCovey will always be a San Francisco Giant. But the big first baseman played for the Padres from 1974 to 1976, hitting 52 homers and earning the nickname — naturally — Big Mac.

Like a lot of owners in the 1970s, Kroc signed some free agents in an effort to fix his team in a hurry. Some, like Fingers, worked out. Others didn't. Outfielder Oscar Gamble hit 31 homers for the Chicago White Sox in 1977 and 19 for the Texas Rangers and Yankees in 1979. The year in between, however, he managed just seven at San Diego.

"I signed Oscar Gamble on the advice of my attorney," a disgusted Kroc said later. "I no longer have Gamble and I no longer have my attorney."

Another veteran who passed through San Diego was spitball artist Gaylord Perry, stopping just long enough during a 314-victory career to win the 1978 Cy Young award with a 21-6 record and a 2.72 ERA.

Gradually, the Padres were playing better. And they also were dressing — well, differently. Solid-colored uniforms were the rage of the 1970s, and a flashy yellow-and-brown ensemble was San Diego's contribution. The Padres dumped the getup in 1985, however, no doubt figuring it was hardly any way for the defending National League champions to appear in public.

The Padres unveiled new uniforms for 1990, scrapping their traditional brown in favor of navy blue, including pinstripes at home. It may not make anyone forget about the Yankees but does seem more compatible with the stylish stadium in which they play.

Renamed Jack Murphy Stadium in 1981 after a sports editor who had helped bring major league sports to San Diego, the Padres' ballpark is perhaps the best multi-purpose stadium in the majors. Until Chicago's new Comiskey Park went up, it was the last stadium to be built with natural grass, and there aren't many fields lovelier. The scoreboard, which includes a Diamond Vision screen, is also tops.

The Padres' home also was the birthplace of a personality who's probably more well-known than any of their players, "The Famous Chicken."

In 1974, Ted Giannoulas was a college student when a radio station hired him to wear a chicken costume and pass out candy eggs at the zoo for $2 an hour. He turned the gig into regular appearances in the stands at Padre games, and fans took a liking to his antics. One night, Padres President Ballard Smith suggested he take the act on the field, and suddenly a costumed Giannoulas was nervously ad-libbing with an umpire and introducing his trademark raised-leg salute.

"The place went nuts. Ballard told me to get out there and do more," said Giannoulas, who's made a 17-year career out of gags involving eye charts and whammy spells. "Management seemed to enjoy it, and I know Ray Kroc did because it was amusing and it took the fans' minds off all the losing."

By 1984, though, losing was no longer a problem. Under Manager Dick Williams, the Padres came up with the right mix, adding veterans Steve Garvey, Graig Nettles and Goose Gossage to homegrown Tony Gwynn, Kevin McReynolds and Eric Show. The result was a 92-70 record and San Diego's first N.L. West title.

Garvey hit .400 and Gwynn .368 as the Padres rallied from a two games-to-none deficit to beat the favored Chicago Cubs in the playoffs. But San Diego couldn't handle the Detroit Tigers in the World Series, falling in five games.

In recent years, the Padres have been disappointing, repeatedly falling short despite such talents as hitters Jack Clark and Benito Santiago and pitchers Ed Whitson and Bruce Hurst.

The most memorable thing about 1990, to the Padres' chagrin, was comedienne Roseanne Barr's mangling of *The Star-Spangled Banner* before a game in San Diego.

Favored to win the N.L. West, the Padres instead limped home in fourth, costing General Manager Jack McKeon his job and prompting a team shakeup that sent Joe Carter and Roberto Alomar to the Toronto Blue Jays in a trade for Tony Fernandez and Fred McGriff.

Still, Gwynn, the Padres' star right fielder, has kept interest alive with four batting titles, and reliever Mark Davis won the 1989 Cy Young award with 44 saves before bolting to free agency.

Then there's Jerry Coleman. As long as he's behind the mike, the Padres will never be dull. The former Yankee infielder is legendary for such on-air malaprops as "Rich Folkers is throwing up in the bullpen," and "With one out here in the first, Dave Clark looks a lot better than the last time he pitched against the Padres."

In a wacky reversal of the usual process, the Padres took Coleman out of the broadcast booth in 1980 and named him manager. San Diego went 73-89, however, and the next season he was back doing play-by-play.

Just as well. The airwaves would be a much poorer place without such gems as this Colemanism:

"There's a fly to deep center field. Winfield is going back, back, back. He hits his head against the wall! It's rolling toward second base!"

It's hard to ignore San Diego/Jack Murphy Stadium's mammoth left-field scoreboard.

Tony Gwynn

In 1979, Jack McKeon took in an exhibition game between the San Diego Padres and San Diego State University because he'd heard the Aztecs had a can't-miss prospect.

The prospect, an infielder named Bobby Meacham, eventually did make the major leagues, but McKeon soon found himself much more interested in another youngster.

"I'm there to watch Meacham, and this other kid is hitting a double, a triple, and running the bases like crazy," said McKeon. "I finally turned to one of our scouts and asked, 'Who the hell is that guy? He looks like the best player on the field.' "

Twelve years later, that guy — Tony Gwynn — is one of the best players in the major leagues, a four-time National League batting champion who also owns three Gold Gloves.

He was a two-sport star at San Diego State, a second-team all-league guard who once handed out 18 assists in a basketball game, as well as a baseball All-American.

The then-San Diego Clippers, in fact, selected Gwynn in the tenth round of the 1981 National Basketball Association draft, but at 5-foot-11 he decided his future lay on the diamond. The day before the NBA lottery, the Padres made him their third-round pick in the major league draft, and he's done nothing to make them regret it.

After hitting .348 for three minor league teams in 1 1/2 seasons, Gwynn joined San Diego in 1982. Except for an injury rehabilitation the next year, he's been whacking line drives there ever since.

At the age of 24, Gwynn batted

Tony Gwynn

.351 in 1984 to lead the National League in batting and the Padres to their only National League pennant.

When McKeon predicted the next year that Gwynn would regularly hit .320 or better, the low-keyed Padre right fielder was embarrassed — then did just that in three of the next five seasons.

Gwynn's best year so far has been 1987, when he hit .370 — the best in the league since Stan Musial's .376 in 1948 — and stole a career-high 56 bases.

Speed has always been a part of Gwynn's game, even though he carries nearly 200 pounds on his stocky frame. He's stolen 25 bases or more in six seasons and once swiped five in one game, tying a league record.

There was a time when Gwynn felt his defensive skills were overlooked, but that was before he was named the league's best-fielding right fielder in 1986, 1987 and 1989. In '86, he led the league with 337 putouts and had 19 assists.

Still, if Tony Gwynn makes the Hall of Fame, it will be because of his bat. When he hit .336 in 1989, he became the first National League to win three consecutive batting titles since Musial in 1950-52.

Gwynn works at it, studying videotapes of his swing, taking extra batting practice before games, even haunting batting cages during the off-season to keep himself sharp.

Even so, he admits he doesn't entirely understand his talent.

"Sometimes I sit here and try to figure out how the hell I'm doing what I do," Gwynn said. "The answer is, I don't know. After all is said and done, I've just been blessed with the ability to hit the ball."

Balboa Park
Aerospace Museum (619-234-8291), San Diego Hall of Champions, San Diego Museum of Art (619-232-7931), San Diego Zoo (619-234-3153), Natural History Museum (619-232-3821), Spanish Village Art Center and other museums and exhibits.

Other Attractions
Coronado Island (Hotel Del Coronado), Old Town State Historic Park (619-237-6770), San Diego Museum of Contemporary Art (700 Prospect St. La Jolla, 619-454-3541), Scripps Aquarium (8602 La Jolla Shores Dr., La Jolla, 619-534-4085), Sea World (1720 S. Shores Rd., 619-226-3901).

Tourism Information
San Diego Convention and Visitors Bureau, 1200 Third Ave., Suite 824, San Diego, CA 92101, 619-232-3101.

Discover the Californias, California Tourist Corp., 5757 W. Century Blvd., Los Angeles, CA 90045, 800-862-2543.

San Diego/Jack Murphy Stadium
9449 Friars Rd.
Capacity: 59,022
Surface: Natural
First Game: April 8, 1969
LF: 327   CF: 405   RF: 327

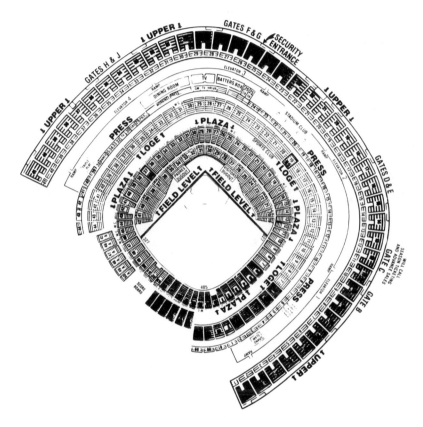

General Information
San Diego Padres, PO Box 2000, San Diego, CA 92112, 619-283-7294.
Game information: 619-280-INFO.
Getting Tickets
Advance ticket window: Gate C, Monday-Friday 9-6.
By mail: San Diego Padres, PO Box 2000, San Diego, CA 92120. $3 handling per order. Check or money order accepted.
By phone: 619-283-SEAT. VISA and MasterCard accepted.
Ticket Prices
Field, Press, Plaza and View Boxes $11, Loge and View Reserved $9.50, General Admission $5.

Discounts & Promotions
Promotions scheduled for 30 games.
Toughest Tickets To Get
Los Angeles, New York and Chicago.
Game Times
Sunday 1:05. Weekdays 1:05, 7:05. Friday and Saturday 7:05. Pacific time. Gates open 2 hours before game.
Broadcasts
KFMB 76 AM, XEXX (Spanish), KUSI-TV (51).
Getting To The Stadium
Near intersection of I-8 and I-805. Access easiest from Friars Rd. Stadium parking plentiful.

Nights at windswept Candlestick Park can be so chilly that the Giants, tongue firmly in cheek, once awarded Croix de Candlestick *pins to fans who braved the cold.*

Remember the famous scene in that old Steve McQueen movie, *Bullitt*, where he chases the bad guys up and down the hills of San Francisco in a souped-up Mustang?

Sure you do. There were so many roaring engines, squealing tires and cars flying through the air, the tickets should have come with Dramamine.

Still one of the best movie chases ever, it gives you an idea of the wild ride the San Francisco Giants have taken over the last 30 years.

Talk about ups and downs. In their first 14 seasons in the City by the Bay, the Giants never had a losing record, a better streak than they ever enjoyed in New York.

The next 14, however, must have made them feel like the '62 Mets reincarnated. Ten times they lost more than they won, including a franchise-high 100 games in 1985.

Even when things have gone well for the Giants, they've left their fans feeling vaguely dissatisfied. They do own a pair of National League pennants and three N.L. West titles since moving west in 1958. But they're still looking for that first World Series championship.

And it seemed like they spent a lifetime in the 1960s finishing second or third behind the St. Louis Cardinals and — much, much worse — the Los Angeles Dodgers.

The Giant record book is sprinkled with the names of Hall of Famers like Willie Mays, Willie McCovey and Juan Marichal, not to mention other stars like Orlando Cepeda and Bobby Bonds. Current sluggers Will Clark, Kevin Mitchell and Matt Williams could also make a bid for Cooperstown before they're through.

But like San Francisco itself, the

San Francisco
Giants

The Giants have had plenty of ups and downs since moving to San Francisco in 1958. They've won a couple of pennants. And they've had to play in Candlestick Park.

Giants are dogged by the feeling that even with their colorful tradition, they may always be in somebody else's shadow.

California's first major city and still one of the country's most picturesque, San Francisco is an international financial hub and a cultural center renowned for both its tradition and an individualism that spawned both the beat and hippie movements. Signature landmarks range from the Golden Gate Bridge to the Transamerica Building to Fisherman's Wharf.

When an outsider thinks California, though, the sunny, booming sprawl of trendsetting Los Angeles is what invariably comes to mind, a fact that chagrins all good San Franciscans.

You probably won't make any points by reminding them that Los Angeles is also the principal reason San Francisco got major league baseball in the first place.

Records show there was baseball in the Bay Area as early as 1860. The San Francisco Seals — for whom Joe DiMaggio had a 61-game hitting streak in 1933 — were proud members of the Pacific Coast League for over 50 years.

But San Francisco didn't enter the major league picture until Walter O'Malley decided it would be better if another team came along when he moved his Brooklyn Dodgers to California in 1958. He staked out Los Angeles and suggested Horace Stoneham, owner of the New York Giants, take San Francisco.

The Giants had a storied history in New York, but Stoneham eyed the dwindling crowds in the Polo Grounds, his worn-out ballpark, and backed up the moving van.

When a reporter accused him of taking the Giants away from the children of New York, Stoneham replied: "I feel bad about the kids, but I haven't seen many of their fathers lately."

Their first two years in San Francisco, the Giants played in Seals Stadium, a downtown ballpark that seated fewer than 23,000 fans, less than half the Polo Grounds' capacity. Still, they drew 1.27 million in 1958, almost twice the total their final year in New York.

After a fifth-place finish in 1960, their first season in Candlestick Park, the Giants began an 11-year streak in which they only once finished lower than third.

In 1962, the Giants caught the Dodgers on the last day of the season, then beat them in a three-game playoff to finish with a 103-62 record and win their first pennant on the West Coast.

It was an amazing offensive team. Willie Mays slammed a league-high 49 homers and drove in 141 runs, while Orlando Cepeda had 35 homers and 114 RBIs, Felipe Alou 25 homers and 98 RBIs and Willie McCovey 20 homers.

San Francisco took the Yankees to seven games in the World Series and trailed 1-0 with two on and two out in the ninth of the finale when McCovey hit what he called "hardest ball I ever hit." But it was a line drive right at Yankee second baseman Bobby Richardson for the Series' final out.

When he was inducted to the Hall of Fame in 1986, McCovey noted that people had asked how he wanted to be remembered. "I tell them I'd like to be remembered as the guy who hit the line drive over Bobby Richardson's head."

As they had been in New York, the

Giants and Dodgers were natural geographic rivals. Their annual pennant duels — and mutual dislike — only intensified the situation.

In 1965 and 1966, the Giants finished second to the Dodgers by a combined 3 1/2 games. Neither San Francisco's Juan Marichal nor Los Angeles' Don Drysdale was slow to knock down enemy batters, and both seasons were marked by beanball wars.

Marichal, a high-kicking right hander, was the Giants' ace, debuting with a one-hit shutout in 1960 and winning more games than any other pitcher from 1963 through 1969. But he may be best remembered for whacking Dodger catcher John Roseboro over the head with a bat in 1965, drawing a nine-day suspension and a then-record $1,750 fine.

Despite Marichal's stellar career, which included a no-hitter, he never won a Cy Young award. The only Giant who has? Mike McCormick, a journeyman who was on his second tour with San Francisco when he went 22-10 with a 2.85 earned run average in 1967.

Bobby Bonds hit 33 homers with 102 RBIs in 1971 as San Francisco won its first N.L. West title, but the Giants lost the playoffs to the Pirates and it was 16 years till their next division championship.

As their stars aged, were traded away or both, the Giants slumped during the '70s. They couldn't have picked a worse time, since across the bay the Oakland A's were winning three straight World Series.

The A's had put a dent in San Francisco crowds since arriving from Kansas City in 1968, and when the Giants finished fifth in 1974, attendance plunged to under 520,000.

A third problem was one that still exists: Candlestick Park. Is there another ballpark in the National League that is so universally maligned?

No visiting broadcaster enters Candlestick's blustery, bone-chilling confines without repeating Mark Twain's judgment on nippy San Francisco summers.

The $24.6 million stadium was star-crossed from the outset, its construction marred by disputes between Stoneham and his contractor, grand jury investigations and a Teamsters strike.

It was advertised as the first major league stadium to be built entirely of reinforced concrete. That wasn't of much consolation, though, on Opening Day 1960 when the foul poles were discovered to be in fair territory.

Nothing was as bad as the weather, however. The same Candlestick Point location that provided a great view of the bay also exposed the ballpark to nasty, unpredictable winds. During the 1961 All-Star Game, one gust was so strong it knocked the Giants' 165-pound Stu Miller off the mound, and he was called for a balk.

Candlestick boasted a special heating system for 20,000 reserved seats, but even it was no match for night temperatures that often dropped to 40 degrees. One fan even sued, complaining that his freezing feet had forced him to flee his seat during several exciting rallies.

The Giants have tried to upgrade conditions. A $16.1 million renovation in 1971 helped reduce the winds by turning Candlestick into a 58,000-seat bowl, and an additional $30 million was spent on improvements in 1987.

They've also tried humor, awarding their hardier fans a few years back with *Croix de Candlestick* pins.

Owner Bob Lurie saved the Giants in 1976 when he bought the team as it was about to be moved to Toronto, and he has vowed to keep them in the Bay Area. But it's no secret he wants out of Candlestick when the lease expires in 1994. And voters in both San Francisco and Santa Clara have turned down new stadium proposals in the past two years.

Attendance rebounded after Lurie's arrival, but times on the field were generally lean until General Manager Al Rosen and Manager Roger Craig were hired in 1985 to overhaul the team.

They did. Just two years after a last-place 62-100 finish, the Giants won the N.L. West in 1987 before losing the playoffs to the Cardinals.

In 1989, they got a step closer, as a record two million fans saw them take the division again and knock off the Cubs in the playoffs for their first National League pennant in 27 years.

Most Valuable Player Kevin Mitchell led the league with 47 homers and 125 RBIs, while Will Clark hit .333 with 23 homers and 111 RBIs and Scott Garrelts had a league-best 2.28 ERA.

But they came up second-best once more, although this time in a World Series that will always be recalled more for the killer earthquake that struck shortly before Game Three than for the A's four-game sweep.

Could 1991 be the season the Giants take their recent cycle of odd-year progress all the way and give San Francisco its first world championship?

Maybe. After 1990's third-place finish, San Francisco went on a free agent binge, spending $33 million on reliever Dave Righetti, starter Bud Black and outfielder Willie McGee. Add them to a nucleus that includes Matt Williams, who knocked in 122 runs in 1990 to become San Francisco's third straight league RBI leader, and the Giants at least may be poised for a run similar to that of those '60s teams.

The question is, where will they make it?

Willie Mays

Normally, the kid from Alabama had a good-natured grin as big as his talent, the kind of guy who made you feel good just watching him take the field.

But Willie Mays was frustrated. He'd torn up the minors — .353 at Trenton, then .477 at Minneapolis — and here he was, finally, with the New York Giants. And he was 0 for 12.

As he dug in against Boston Braves ace Warren Spahn, probably the top left-handed pitcher in the National League, the 20-year-old Mays wondered if he was ready for the big time.

Three pitches later, he knew. So did everybody else, as he sent a Spahn curveball soaring over the left-field roof at the Polo Grounds for his first major league hit.

By the time Willie Mays retired 22 years later in 1973, he had 3,282 additional hits, a reservation in the Hall of Fame and a strong case as the best all-around player who ever lived.

He hit 660 career homers, second only to Hank Aaron and Babe Ruth. He led the National League in homers and stolen bases four times each, and he was the first player to hit 300 homers and steal 300 bases.

He won Most Valuable Player awards in 1954 and 1965, and in 1961 he slammed four homers in a game, a feat so rare it eluded both Aaron and Ruth and has occurred just twice since.

Twice he hit 50 homers in a season, one of just two National Leaguers to do so, and he won a batting title in 1954 with a .345 average.

Mays was also without peer defensively, a center fielder with speed, instinct and a marvelous throwing arm, all of which helped him make a record 7,095 putouts.

He'll be forever remembered for The Catch, that over-the-head snag of Vic Wertz's 450-foot blast in the 1954 World Series, but it was his whirling

Willie Mays accepts the 1965 National League Most Valuable Player Award.

throw back to the infield to keep two runners from advancing that made the play special.

But the easy-going enthusiasm with which Mays did everything is what set him apart. The fans loved the "Say Hey Kid" — so named after the way he greeted friends — and so did his teammates.

"He lit up the room when he came in," said Leo Durocher, his first manager. "He was a joy to be around."

Said another longtime manager, Charlie Grimm: "Willie Mays can help a team just by riding on the bus with them."

Mays was not oblivious to his innate showmanship, and he later acknowledged that his cap always flew off when he ran because he wore it a size too small.

"When I was 17 years old, I realized I was in a form of show business," he once said. "It's like being an actor on the Broadway stage. He doesn't phrase his part exactly the same way every day. He thinks up new things. So I played for the fans and I made sure each fan that came out would see something different each day."

When Willie Mays was elected to the Hall of Fame in 1979, there were hundreds of National League pitchers who knew it was just a formality. One of them was Warren Spahn.

"I'll never forgive myself," Spahn said with a smile. "We might have gotten rid of Willie forever if I'd only struck him out."

Bay Area Attractions
Alcatraz (415-546-2805), Angel Island (415-546-2805), Cable Car Barn and Museum (1201 Mason St., 415-474-1887), California Palace of the Legion of Honor (Clement St. and 84th Ave., 415-750-3614), Chinatown (415-391-2000), Fisherman's Wharf (415-391-2000) and Ghirardelli Square (415-775-5500), Golden Gate Bridge (415-974-6900) and Golden Gate Park (Gardens, Asian Art Museum, Natural History Museum, Steinhart Aquarium), Jack London Waterfront (30 Jack London Sq., Oakland, 415-893-7956), Oakland Museum (1000 Oak St., 415-273-3401), Old Mint (Fifth and Mission Sts., 415-974-0788), San Francisco Museum of Modern Art (401 Van Ness Ave., 415-863-8800), San Francisco Zoo (Sloat Blvd. and 45th St., 415-735-7061).

National Parks in California
See information in Oakland Athletics chapter.

Tourism Information
San Francisco Convention and Visitors Bureau, 210 Third St., Suite 900, San Francisco, CA 94103, 415-974-6900.
Discover the Californias, California Tourist Corp., 5757 W. Century Blvd., Los Angeles, CA 90045, 800-862-2543.

Candlestick Park
Capacity: 58,000
Surface: Natural
First game: April 12, 1960
LF: 335   CF: 400   RF: 335

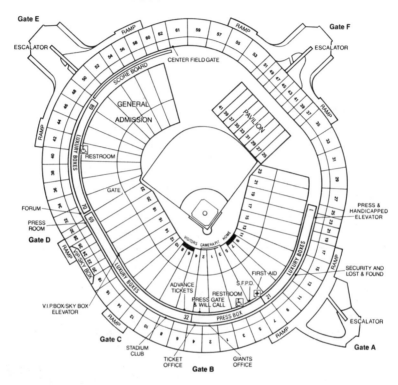

General Information
San Francisco Giants, Candlestick Park, San Francisco, CA 94124, 415-468-3700.
Ticket Information: 415-467-8000.
Getting Tickets
By mail: Ticket Office, San Francisco Giants, Candlestick Park, San Francisco, CA 94124.
Specify game date, seat category and number of tickets.
By phone: BASS/TicketMaster at 415-762-BASS, 408-998-BASS, 916-923-BASS, 707-762-BASS, 209-226-BASS, 209-466-BASS.
Ticket Prices
MVP-Lower Box $12.75, Lower Box $12, Upper Box $11, Lower Reserved $10, Upper Reserved $8, Pavilion (No smoking, no drinking) $5, General Admission $2.50 ($1 for 14 and under except Sundays, Holidays and Concert dates, must be accompanied by adult).
Discounts & Promotions
Special Events for approximately 30 games.

Toughest Tickets To Get
Los Angeles, New York, Cincinnati and Chicago, particularly on weekends.
Game Times
Sunday 1:05, 1:35, 5:05. Weekdays 12:35. Weeknights 7:05, 7:35. Friday 7:35. Saturday 1:05. Pacific time. Gates open 2 hours before game.
Broadcasts
KNBR-68 AM, KLOK-1170 AM (Spanish), KTVU TV(2).
Getting To The Stadium
Between San Francisco International Airport and downtown area on Highway 101, bay side. Limited parking in main lot (fills 1-2 hours before game); unpaved spillover lots. Special lot for RVs on the east side of main lot. Accessible by MUNI bus (415-631-MUNI for information), by BART via MUNI transfer and by SAM TRANS (415-761-8000 for information; 348-8858 in peninsula area and 367-1500 in South Bay area).

The Ballparks Room at the National Baseball Hall of Fame and Museum.

The National Baseball Hall of Fame and Museum.

Baseball Hall of Fame

Baseball may not have been born in the picturesque upstate New York village of Cooperstown as popular folklore has it — but it should have been.

According to legend, Abner Doubleday created baseball one summer day in 1839, using a stick to draw a diamond in the dirt of a Cooperstown cow pasture.

The tale grew out of a report by a special commission that was created in 1905 to study the game's origin. The main evidence was a letter from a man named Abner Graves, who claimed to have witnessed the event.

The commission ignored the facts that Doubleday, later a Union general in the Civil War, was a 20-year-old cadet at West Point in 1839 and that he died in 1893 without ever having said a word about inventing the national pastime.

Baseball officials accepted the yarn — it was certainly more palatable than the theory that baseball evolved from the English game of rounders — and when the National Baseball Hall of Fame and Museum opened on June 12, 1939, it was in Cooperstown.

That location is reason enough to give the Doubleday myth a forgiving wink. Could there be a more fitting home for baseball's shrine than quiet, nostalgic Cooperstown?

The village of 2,300 people sits at the foot of glimmering Otsego Lake, about halfway between Schenectady and Binghamton, like something out of a Norman Rockwell painting. Victorian homes and mammoth shade trees line the neat, orderly streets, conjuring up images of boys racing along on Western Flyers, their dogs close behind.

There's one stoplight — and no freeway or fast-food restaurant for miles.

Main Street is pure Americana, a cozy thoroughfare of quaint shops and brick storefronts filled with autographed balls, historic bats and gloves, and weathered caps.

The Hall of Fame is at the end of the street, a stately brown-brick building that in any other town would be the post office or courthouse or perhaps a school. But this is Cooperstown. Here, it's baseball's Mecca.

The Hall of Fame was the product of separate efforts to establish a National Baseball Museum and celebrate the 100th anniversary of the game's accepted Doubleday origin. In 1936, baseball writers elected the Hall of Fame's first five members: Ty Cobb, Babe Ruth, Honus Wagner, Christy Mathewson and Walter Johnson.

Today, there are 211 members, including legends like Cy Young, Lou Gehrig, Lefty Grove, Joe DiMaggio, Ted Williams, Willie Mays, Mickey Mantle and Hank Aaron; pioneers like Candy Cummings, the man who invented the curve ball; Negro league stars like Satchel Paige and James "Cool Papa" Bell; umpires like Bill Klem and Tommy Connolly; and baseball executives like Branch Rickey and Bill Veeck.

All are honored on bronze plaques in the Hall of Fame Gallery, but the greatest tribute is the baseball memorabilia that virtually overflows the museum's four floors.

There's the ball found in Abner Graves' house in 1935 that was used to substantiate the Doubleday legend.

There's Babe Ruth's locker, as well as the bat and ball from his 60th homer in 1927. There are Shoeless Joe Jackson's shoes. And the uniform Ted Williams wore in 1960 when he hit a home run in the final at-bat of his career.

Life-size wood sculptures of Ruth and Williams greet visitors at the entrance, along with scoreboard graphics providing directions. One exhibit uses film, original art and photos to depict great baseball moments like Roger Maris' 61st homer in 1961. Another contains turnstiles, lockers, grandstand seats and cornerstones from Ebbets Field, the Polo Grounds and other historic ballparks.

There are exhibits on the general history of the game, how equipment has changed and is manufactured, the Negro and minor leagues, the All-Star Game, the league playoffs and the World Series. There are recordings, ticket stubs, newspaper clippings, stamps and board games, not to mention a high-tech multimedia show in the museum's 200-seat theater.

You can see what is probably the world's best collection of baseball cards, including the rare Honus Wagner T-206 tobacco card, or catch a video presentation of Abbott and Costello's classic "Who's on First?" comedy routine. The uniforms exhibit boasts everything from a shiny satin getup the Boston Braves designed for night games to a special green version of the Cincinnati Reds' uniform — for St. Patrick's Day, of course.

Hall of Fame officials know that no sport reveres statistics as much as baseball. In front of the museum, a small scoreboard carries the results of the previous day's major league games. In the Records Room, wall displays list the game's principal record-holders, as well as the current season's major league leaders. And in the National Baseball Library, historians and writers can use the world's largest collection of baseball reference materials.

For the Hall of Fame, the biggest event of the year occurs in late July or early August. That's when new members are inducted in ceremonies outside the library, then two major league teams play a game at nearby Doubleday Field, a 10,000-seat ballpark built on the same field where Abner Doubleday supposedly created the game. It's a festive weekend, when Hall of Famers like Ted Williams and Robin Roberts and Ralph Kiner are common sights in the lobby of Cooperstown's Otesaga Hotel.

Baseball officials may have made an historical error in picking Cooperstown as the site of the National Baseball Hall of Fame and Museum, but the result is a solid hit.

For more information:

National Baseball Hall of Fame and Museum, PO Box 590, Cooperstown, NY 13326, 607-547-9988.

Located at 25 Main St., the Baseball Hall of Fame and Museum is open 9-5 daily. Admission charge: $6 adult, $2.50 ages 7-15 and free under 7.

Bibliography

BOOKS

Adomites, Paul. *October's Game*. Redefinition, Inc., Alexandria, Va., 1990.

Alvarez, Mark. *The Old Ball Game*. Redefinition, Inc., Alexandria, Va., 1990.

Alexander, Charles C. *John McGraw*. Viking Penguin Inc., New York, 1988.

——————. *Ty Cobb*. Oxford University Press, New York, 1984.

Asinof, Eliot. *Eight Men Out*. Holt, Rhinehart and Winston, New York, 1963.

Bouton, Jim. *Ball Four*. World Publishing Co., New York, 1970.

Cobb, Ty with Stump, Al. *My Life in Baseball, The True Record*. Doubleday & Co. Inc., New York, 1961

Cox, James A. *The Lively Ball*. Redefinition, Inc., Alexandria, Va., 1989.

Creamer, Robert W. *Babe: The Legend Comes To Life*. Simon and Schuster, New York, 1974.

Dickey, Glenn. *The History of American League Baseball*. Stein and Day, New York, 1980.

Dickson, Paul. *The Dickson Baseball Dictionary*. Facts On File, New York, 1989.

Einstein, Charles, editor. *The Baseball Reader*. Lippincott & Crowell, Publishers, New York, 1980.

——————. *The Fireside Book of Baseball*, Fourth Edition. Simon and Schuster, New York, 1987.

Fifer, Steve. *Speed*. Redefinition, Inc., Alexandria, Va., 1990.

Garrity, John. *The George Brett Story*. Coward, McCann & Geoghegan, New York, 1981.

Green, Lee. *Sportswit*. Harper & Row, New York, 1984.

Holway, John. *The Sluggers*. Redefinition, Inc., Alexandria, Va., 1989.

Honig, Donald. *The American League: An Illustrated History* (Revised Edition). Crown Publishers, Inc., New York, 1987.

——————. *A Donald Honig Reader*. Simon and Schuster, New York, 1988.

——————. *The National League: An Illustrated History* (Revised Edition). Crown Publishers, Inc., New York, 1987.

Hoppel, Joe. *The Series*. The Sporting News, St. Louis, 1988.

James, Bill. *The Bill James Historical Baseball Abstract*. Villard Books, New York, 1985.

Kaplan, Jim. *The Fielders*. Redefinition, Inc., Alexandria, Va., 1989.

Kerrane, Kevin. *The Hurlers*. Redefinition, Inc., Alexandria, Va., 1990.

Libby, Bill. *Charlie O. & the Angry A's*. Doubleday & Co., New York, 1975.

McBride, Joseph. *High & Inside: The Complete Guide to Baseball Slang*. Warner Books Inc., New York, 1980.

Mead, William B. *Low and Outside*. Redefinition, Inc., Alexandria, Va., 1990.

Nadel, Eric and Wright, Craig R. *The Man Who Stole First Base*. Taylor Publishing Co., Dallas, 1989.

Nash, Bruce and Zullo, Allan. *The Baseball Hall of Shame*, Vols. 1-4. Pocket Books, New York, 1985, 1986, 1987, 1990.

Nelson, Kevin. *Baseball's Greatest Quotes*. Simon and Schuster, New York, 1982.

Nemec, David. *Great Baseball Feats, Facts & Firsts*. New American Library, New York, 1987.

Okrent, Daniel and Wulf, Steve. *Baseball Anecdotes*. Oxford University Press, New York, 1989.

Reichler, Joseph E., editor. *The Baseball Encyclopedia*. MacMillan Publishing Co., New York, 1988.

Reidenbaugh, Lowell. *Take Me Out to the Ball Park*. The Sporting News, St. Louis, 1988.

Rieland, Randy. *The New Professionals*. Redefinition, Inc., Alexandria, Va., 1990.

Ritter, Lawrence. *The Glory of Their Times*. MacMillan and Co. Inc., New York, 1966.

Ritter, Lawrence and Honig, Donald. *The Im-

age of Their Greatness. Crown Publishers Inc., New York, 1979.

Schlossberg, Dan. *The Baseball Catalog*. Jonathan David Publishers Inc., Middle Village, N.Y., 1980.

Thorn, John, editor. *The Armchair Book of Baseball II*. Charles Scribner's Sons, New York, 1987.

Thorn, John and Palmer, Pete, editors. *Total Baseball*. Warner Books, New York, 1989.

Updike, John. *Assorted Prose*. Alfred A. Knopf Inc. 1960.

Williams, Ted and Underwood, John. *My Turn At Bat*. Simon and Schuster, New York, 1969.

Wood, Bob. *Dodger Dogs to Fenway Franks*. McGraw-Hill Book Co., New York, 1988.

PERIODICALS

Beirig, Joel. "Comiskey: It's Time to Say Soil Long." *The Sporting News*, Oct. 1, 1990.

Blass, Steve. "A Teammate Remembers Roberto Clemente." *Sport*, April 1973.

Brown, Bill. "Nobody Did It Better." *The Sporting News*, Jan. 29, 1990.

Burnes, Brian. "Play Ball." *The Kansas City Star*. July 23, 1989.

Cushman, Tom. "Tony G. Reaches for the Stars." *The Sporting News 1985 Baseball Yearbook*.

Deane, Bill. "Robin Yount Comes of Age." *Street and Smith's Baseball Yearbook*, 1986.

Farber, Michael. "Whoa, Canada." *Sports Illustrated*, March 5, 1990.

Furlong, Bill. "Harmon Killebrew: Anatomy of a Hot Streak." *Sport*, November 1964.

Garrity, John. "Can George Brett Hit .500?" *Sports Illustrated*, May 2, 1983.

Gordon, Alison. "The Jays Fly High." *The Sporting News 1984 Baseball Yearbook*.

Hoppel, Joe. "The First Visit to Cooperstown." *The Sporting News 1989 Hall of Fame Program*.

Killebrew, Harmon, as told to George Vass. "The Game I'll Never Forget." *Baseball Digest*. February 1972.

Kreidler, Mark. "He's More than Just a .326 Hitter." *The Sporting News*, June 1, 1987.

Maisel, Ivan. "At Last, a Man to Shout About." *Sports Illustrated*, June 11, 1984.

Matsumoto, Rick. "Barfield and Bell: Toronto's Killer B's." *Street and Smith's Baseball*, 1987

Mazeroski, Bill. "My 16 Years with Roberto Clemente." *Sport*, November 1971.

McCarl, Neil. "The Numbers Toll for Jays' Bell." *The Sporting News*, Dec. 14, 1987.

Murphy, Austin. "Rising to the Top of the Game." *Sports Illustrated*, April 16, 1990.

Musburger, Brent. "Harmon Killebrew in a Crucial Series." *Sport*, October 1967.

Nightingale, Dave. " 'On-Time' Reds Punch Out A's." *The Sporting News*, Oct. 29, 1990.

_____. "Three Different Routes to Cooperstown." *The Sporting News 1984 Baseball Yearbook*.

Prato, Lou. "Why the Pirates Love the New Roberto Clemente." *Sport*, August 1967.

Rogers, Phil. "Just Call Texas Trio the 3-4-5 Amigos." *The Sporting News*, July 31, 1989.

_____. "The Next Clemente?" *The Sporting News 1990 Baseball Yearbook*.

Schaap, Dick. "George Brett Is a Magnificent Misfit." *Sport*, June 1977.

Shattuck, Harry. "King Richard a Real Highness in Houston." *The Sporting News*, May 26, 1979.

Street, Jim. "M's Davis Fights 'Emotional Violation.' " *The Sporting News*, April 8, 1990.

Woolsey, Garth. "Flying High in Toronto." *The Sporting News 1987 Baseball Yearbook*.

Wulf, Steve. "By George, He Almost Did It." *Sports Illustrated*, Feb. 2, 1981.

_____. "The Stuff of Legend." *Sports Illustrated*, June 12, 1989.

York, Marty. "Raisin' Hell with George Bell." *The Sporting News 1988 Baseball Yearbook*.

Zanger, Jack. "Killebrew & Powell — Why There's Still a Place for the Old-Fashioned Slugger." *Sport*, November 1969.

Photograph and Illustration Credits

Cover, Front: Courtesy Texas Rangers. Back (top): Courtesy Houston Astros. Back (center): Permission granted by the Kansas City Royals. Back (bottom): Courtesy Yankees Magazine.

10, Top: NATIONAL BASEBALL LIBRARY, COOPERSTOWN, N.Y. Bottom: NATIONAL BASEBALL LIBRARY, COOPERSTOWN, N.Y.

12, Courtesy Baltimore Orioles.

16, © 1989 Tadder/Baltimore.

18, © 1967/1989 Tadder/Baltimore.

20, Courtesy Baltimore Orioles.

22, 27, 28, 30, Courtesy Boston Red Sox.

32, Courtesy Cleveland Indians.

37, 39, Courtesy Cleveland Indians.

40, Courtesy Detroit Tigers.

43, Daniel P. George.

45, 47, Courtesy Detroit Tigers.

48, Courtesy Milwaukee Brewers.

52-53, Daniel P. George.

54, 56, Courtesy Milwaukee Brewers.

58, Courtesy Yankees Magazine.

63, NATIONAL BASEBALL LIBRARY, COOPERSTOWN, N.Y.

65, Courtesy New York Yankees.

66, © 1989 Wayne G. Stuber/Aerial Perspective.

71, NATIONAL BASEBALL LIBRARY, COOPERSTOWN, N.Y.

73, Courtesy Toronto Blue Jays.

74, Top: Courtesy California Angels. Bottom: NATIONAL BASEBALL LIBRARY, COOPERSTOWN, N.Y.

76, Top: Courtesy California Angels. Bottom: Joe Zanatta/Bon A Tirer.

81, UPI/The Bettmann Archive.

83, Courtesy California Angels.

84, Courtesy Hellmuth, Obata & Kassabaum, Inc., Sports Facilities Group.

87, Daniel P. George.

89, NATIONAL BASEBALL LIBRARY, COOPERSTOWN, N.Y.

91, Courtesy Chicago White Sox.

92, 96, 98, 100, Permission granted by the Kansas City Royals.

102, 105, 107, 109, Courtesy Minnesota Twins.

110, Courtesy Oakland Athletics.

115, UPI/The Bettmann Archive.

117, Courtesy Oakland Athletics.

118, 121, 123, 125, Courtesy Seattle Mariners.

126, 129, 131, 133, Courtesy Texas Rangers.

134, Top: Courtesy Pittsburgh Pirates. Bottom: Daniel P. George.

136, © Stephen Green, courtesy Chicago Cubs.

141, UPI/The Bettmann Archive.

143, Courtesy Chicago Cubs.

144, 147, 149, 151, Courtesy Montreal Expos.

152, 156, © Marc S. Levine, courtesy New York Mets.

157, 159, Courtesy New York Mets.

162, Courtesy Philadelphia Phillies.

166, Al Tielemans, © 1990 Philadelphia Phillies.

168, 170, Courtesy Philadelphia Phillies.

172, 177, 179, Courtesy Pittsburgh Pirates.

180, Courtesy St. Louis Cardinals.

184, Joe Zanatta/Bon A Tirer.

186, NATIONAL BASEBALL LIBRARY, COOPERSTOWN, N.Y.

188, Courtesy St. Louis Cardinals.

190, Top: Courtesy Cincinnati Reds. Bottom: © 1989 Los Angeles Dodgers, Inc.

192, 195, J. Sebo, courtesy Atlanta Braves.

197, 199, Courtesy Atlanta Braves.

200, 205, 207, Courtesy Cincinnati Reds.

208, Courtesy Houston Astros.

211, © Hall Puckett, courtesy Houston Astros.

213, 215, Courtesy Houston Astros.

Photograph and Illustration Credits

216, © 1985 Los Angeles Dodgers, Inc.
221, UPI/The Bettmann Archive.
223, Courtesy Los Angeles Dodgers.
224, Courtesy San Diego Padres.
226, Joe Zanatta/Bon A Tirer.
229, 231, Courtesy San Diego Padres.

232, NATIONAL BASEBALL LIBRARY,
COOPERSTOWN, N.Y..
237, San Francisco Giants/Dennis Desprois,
© San Francisco Giants.
240, Top: NATIONAL BASEBALL
LIBRARY, COOPERSTOWN, N.Y.
Bottom: Daniel P. George.

Book and Magazine Credits

Excerpts from the following sources have been included in *Baseball Vacations*. Additional background sources are listed in the Bibliography.

SPORT

"Harmon Killebrew: Anatomy of a Hot Streak" by Bill Furlong. Reprinted from November, 1964 *Sport*, ©1964, Peterson Publishing Company.

"Why the Pirates Love the New Roberto Clemente" by Lou Prato. Reprinted from August, 1967 *Sport*, ©1967, Peterson Publishing Company.

"Harmon Killebrew In A Crucial Series" by Brent Musburger. Reprinted from October, 1967 *Sport*, ©1967, Peterson Publishing Company.

"Killebrew & Powell - Why There's Still a Place for the Old-Fashioned Slugger" by Jack Zanger. Reprinted from November, 1969 *Sport*, ©1969, Peterson Publishing Company.

"My 16 Years with Roberto Clemente" by Bill Mazeroski. Reprinted from November, 1971 *Sport*, ©1971, Peterson Publishing Company.

"A Teammate Remebers Roberto Clemente" by Steve Blass. Reprinted from April, 1973 *Sport*, ©1973, Peterson Publishing Company.

"George Brett Is a Magnificent Misfit" by Dick Schapp. Reprinted from June, 1977 *Sport*, ©1977, Peterson Publishing Company.

THE SPORTING NEWS

May 26, 1979. "King Richard a Real Highness in Houston" by Harry Shattuck. Reprinted by permission of *The Sporting News*.

June 1, 1987. "He's More than Just a .326 Hitter" by Mark Kreidler. Reprinted by permission of *The Sporting News*.

December 14, 1987. "The Numbers Toll for Jays' Bell" by Neil McCarl. Reprinted by permission of *The Sporting News*.

July 31, 1989. "Just Call Texas Trio The 3-4-5- Amigos" by Phil Rogers. Reprinted by permission of *The Sporting News*.
January 29, 1990. "Nobody Did It Better" by Bill Brown. Reprinted by permission of *The Sporting News*.

April 8, 1990. "M's Davis Fights 'Emotional Violation'" by Jim Street. Reprinted by permission of *The Sporting News*.

October 1, 1990. "Comiskey: It's Time to Say Soil Long" by Joel Beirig. Reprinted by permission of *The Sporting News*.

October 29, 1990. "'On-Time' Reds Punch Out A's" by Dave Nightingale. Reprinted by permission of *The Sporting News*.

THE SPORTING NEWS 1984 BASEBALL YEARBOOK. "Three Different Routes to Cooperstown" by Dave Nightingale. "The Jays Fly High" by Alison Gordon. Reprinted by permission of *The Sporting News*.

THE SPORTING NEWS 1985 BASEBALL YEARBOOK. "Tony G. Reaches for the Stars" by Tom Cushman. Reprinted by permission of *The Sporting News*.

THE SPORTING NEWS 1987 BASEBALL YEARBOOK. "Flying High in Toronto" by Garth Woolsey. Reprinted by permission of *The Sporting News*.

Index

Index